T5-CQA-833

Collaborating with Parents for Early School Success

The Guilford Practical Intervention in the Schools Series

Kenneth W. Merrell, Series Editor

Books in this series address the complex academic, behavioral, and social–emotional needs of children and youth at risk. School-based practitioners are provided with practical, research-based, and readily applicable tools to support students and team successfully with teachers, families, and administrators. Each volume is designed to be used directly and frequently in planning and delivering educational and mental health services. Features include lay-flat binding to facilitate photocopying, step-by-step instructions for assessment and intervention, and helpful, timesaving reproducibles.

Recent Volumes

Helping Schoolchildren with Chronic Health Conditions: A Practical Guide
Daniel L. Clay

Interventions for Reading Problems: Designing and Evaluating Effective Strategies
Edward J. Daly III, Sandra Chafouleas, and Christopher H. Skinner

Safe and Healthy Schools: Practical Prevention Strategies
Jeffrey R. Sprague and Hill M. Walker

School-Based Crisis Intervention: Preparing All Personnel to Assist
Melissa Allen Heath and Dawn Sheen

Assessing Culturally and Linguistically Diverse Students: A Practical Guide
Robert L. Rhodes, Salvador Hector Ochoa, and Samuel O. Ortiz

Mental Health Medications for Children: A Primer
Ronald T. Brown, Laura Arnstein Carpenter, and Emily Simerly

Clinical Interviews for Children and Adolescents: Assessment to Intervention
Stephanie H. McConaughy

Response to Intervention: Principles and Strategies for Effective Practice
Rachel Brown-Chidsey and Mark W. Steege

The ABCs of CBM: A Practical Guide to Curriculum-Based Measurement
Michelle K. Hosp, John L. Hosp, and Kenneth W. Howell

Fostering Independent Learning: Practical Strategies to Promote Student Success
Virginia Smith Harvey and Louise A. Chickie-Wolfe

Helping Students Overcome Substance Abuse: Effective Practices for Prevention and Intervention
Jason J. Burrow-Sanchez and Leanne S. Hawken

School-Based Behavioral Assessment: Informing Intervention and Instruction
Sandra Chafouleas, T. Chris Riley-Tillman, and George Sugai

Collaborating with Parents for Early School Success: The Achieving–Behaving–Caring Program
Stephanie H. McConaughy, Pam Kay, Julie A. Welkowitz, Kim Hewitt, and Martha D. Fitzgerald

Collaborating with Parents for Early School Success

The Achieving–Behaving–Caring Program

STEPHANIE H. McCONAUGHY
PAM KAY
JULIE A. WELKOWITZ
KIM HEWITT
MARTHA D. FITZGERALD

THE GUILFORD PRESS
New York   London

© 2008 The Guilford Press
A Division of Guilford Publications, Inc.
72 Spring Street, New York, NY 10012
www.guilford.com

All rights reserved

Except as indicated, no part of this book may be reproduced, translated, stored in a retrieval system, or transmitted, in any form or by any means, electronic, mechanical, photocopying, microfilming, recording, or otherwise, without written permission from the Publisher.

Printed in Canada

This book is printed on acid-free paper.

Last digit is print number: 9   8   7   6   5   4   3   2   1

LIMITED PHOTOCOPY LICENSE

These materials are intended for use only by qualified professionals.

The Publisher grants to individual purchasers of this book nonassignable permission to reproduce all materials for which photocopying permission is specifically granted in a footnote. This license is limited to you, the individual purchaser only, for use with your own clients or students. Purchase by an institution does not constitute a site license. This license does not grant the right to reproduce these materials for resale, redistribution, or any other purposes (including but not limited to books and handouts or slides for lectures or workshops). Permission to reproduce these materials for these and any other purposes must be obtained in writing from The Guilford Press.

Library of Congress Cataloging-in-Publication Data

Collaborating with parents for early school success : the achieving–behaving–caring program / by Stephanie H. McConaughy . . . [et al.].
     p. cm. — (The Guilford practical intervention in the schools series)
  Includes bibliographical references and index.
  ISBN-13: 978-1-59385-593-2 (pbk. : alk. paper)
  ISBN-10: 1-59385-593-1 (pbk. : alk. paper)
  1. Problem children—Education (Elementary)   2. Education, Elementary—Parent participation.   3. Behavior disorders in children—Prevention.   I. McConaughy, Stephanie H.
  LC4801.C583 2007
  371.93—dc22
                                                              2007029315

About the Authors

Stephanie H. McConaughy, PhD, is Research Professor of Psychiatry and Psychology at the University of Vermont and a Vermont-licensed practicing psychologist and nationally certified school psychologist. She collaborated on the research design and outcome evaluation of the Achieving–Behaving–Caring (ABC) research project and was Co-Investigator of the ABC outreach project. She is the author of numerous journal articles, chapters, books, and published instruments on assessment of children's behavioral, emotional, and learning problems. Dr. McConaughy's research has been funded by the U.S. Department of Education, National Institute on Disability and Rehabilitation Research, National Institute of Child Health and Human Development, National Institute of Mental Health, Spencer Foundation, W. T. Grant Foundation, and the University of Vermont Research Center for Children, Youth, and Families.

Pam Kay, MEd, who passed away in December 2006, was Research Associate in the University of Vermont College of Education and Social Services. Her research, funded by the U.S. Department of Education, Office of Special Education and Rehabilitation Services (OSERS), focused on prevention programs for children at risk for behavioral and emotional problems and collaborative relationships between parents and teachers. She served as Project Director on the original ABC research project and Principal Investigator of the ABC outreach project. With Bob Algozzine, Ms. Kay was coeditor of *Preventing Problem Behaviors: A Handbook of Successful Prevention Strategies*, published in 2002. She was also an elementary school teacher and an executive in several community agencies. Ms. Kay passed away suddenly from pancreatic cancer as this book reached completion. As a single parent, she adopted two sons who had significant emotional and behavioral issues arising from their preadoption histories. They are now independent and productive adults.

Julie A. Welkowitz, PhD, is Associate Professor at Southern New Hampshire University (SNHU) and a licensed clinical psychologist. She currently serves as the Assistant Academic Coordinator of the Graduate Program in Community Mental Health at SNHU. Dr. Welkowitz was previously a Research Assistant Professor in the College of Education and Social Services at the University of

Vermont, where she was a Co-Investigator on the ABC outreach project. Her research, primarily funded by OSERS, has focused on school- and community-based initiatives to support students with emotional and behavioral disorders.

Kim Hewitt, MEd, joined the ABC research team as a Parent Liaison for children and families who participated in the original ABC research project, and then served as Parent Liaison Consultant/Educator in the ABC outreach project. She is the mother of three children, including one with special needs. She was Chairperson of the Advisory Board of the grassroots organization Vermont Parent-to-Parent in the mid-1980s, and has been an active advocate for children and families since that time. Ms. Hewitt received her master's degree in education from the University of Vermont with a specialization in students experiencing emotional disturbance. She is now pursuing a teaching career emphasizing strength-based and family-centered practices.

Martha D. Fitzgerald, EdD, is Professor Emerita of Education at the University of Vermont. She was Principal Investigator of the original research grant to develop and test the ABC Program model and the grant for ABC outreach efforts funded by OSERS. Her three decades of research have focused on prevention programs for children at risk for learning, behavioral, and emotional problems; early education services for preschool children with disabilities; and school-based approaches to special education mediated by consulting teachers. In addition to her research and teaching, Dr. Fitzgerald served as Department Chair, Interim Dean of the College of Education and Social Services, and Associate Dean of the Graduate College of the University of Vermont. Dr. Fitzgerald and her husband, Edward Knight, are parents of five adult children and grandparents of seven children.

Acknowledgments

In the Achieving–Behaving–Caring (ABC) Program, parents and teachers work together as *equal partners* for the benefit of children who are at risk for emotional and behavioral problems. Respectful collaboration forms the foundation of the ABC Program. In the same spirit, we five authors worked together as equal partners to design and carry out the ABC Program and to create this book.

The U.S. Department of Education Office of Special Education Programs (OSEP) in the Office of Special Education and Rehabilitation Services (OSERS) supported our research to develop and test the efficacy of the ABC Program. Martha Fitzgerald served as Principal Investigator of the original ABC research grant (Grant No. H237F50036) and the ABC outreach grant (Grant No. H324R000094). Pam Kay was Project Director of both grants. When Martha Fitzgerald accepted Emerita status at the University of Vermont (UVM), Pam Kay became Principal Investigator of the ABC outreach project, with Stephanie McConaughy and Julie Welkowitz as Co-Investigators. Kim Hewitt joined the original ABC research project as a Parent Liaison and then served as Parent Liaison Consultant/Educator in the ABC outreach project. Martha Fitzgerald, Pam Kay, Julie Welkowitz, and Kim Hewitt carried out the fieldwork in multiple sites to develop and test the ABC Program. Stephanie McConaughy collaborated on research design and outcome evaluation of the ABC Program and wrote the manuals for Parent Liaisons and administrators that formed the basis for this book.

First and foremost, we would like to thank the families and teachers who were involved in the ABC Program. It is from their experiences that we have learned the most about effective, meaningful, and respectful practices. In this book, we have included several vignettes or "stories" of individual children to illustrate the collaborative process in the ABC Program. The vignettes are composites based on our research experience involving many children, parents, and teachers. All of the names for the vignettes are pseudonyms, and details of actual case material have been altered to protect confidentiality.

We are grateful to the following Vermont schools, school districts, and supervisory unions who committed to participating in the ABC Program in support of children and families: Alburg Community Education Center, Barre Supervisory Union (SU), Chittenden South SU, Colchester

School District, Franklin Central SU, Franklin Northeast SU, Franklin Northwest SU, and Windham Southeast SU. In the ABC outreach project, we were joined by community partners: the Champlain Islands Parent Child Center, the Family Center of Northwestern Vermont, the Parent Child Center of Windham County, and the Vermont Department of Education. In addition, we thank our Parent Liaisons, whose creative, caring efforts and vigilance kindled the flames of parent and teacher collaboration and kept those fires burning: Carol Benway, Heidi Brouillette, Marie Burns, Cindy Coble, Colleen Coffey, Kate Conway-Biles, Brian Frederich, Joy Hammond, Brenda Kennedy, Lizabeth Sewell McCann, Sandra Paquette, Mary Rivard, and Gail Sullivan. Much of this book represents what we have learned from these Parent Liaisons and the families and teachers with whom they worked.

In our research and the creation of this book, we have benefited from the help and advice of many colleagues. We are particularly grateful to Cyndi Snyder for her creativity, loyalty, and tireless efforts as Administrative Assistant to the research team and through several versions of this book. We have appreciated the advice of Helen Thornton and Renee Bradley, Project Officers at OSEP. Their vision and encouragement kept us moving forward through years of collaborative research and writing for this book and related publications. We thank Craig Thomas, Editor at The Guilford Press, and Ken Merrell, Series Editor for The Guilford Practical Intervention in the Schools Series, for their advice, guidance, and patience in producing this book. We also thank Jill Tarule, former Dean of the UVM College of Education and Social Services, for her support and encouragement throughout this work, and Fran Carr, UVM Vice President for Research, for her faith in the success of this book. Many other people at UVM have worked with us over the past decade, and we appreciate their contributions: Penny Bishop, Debra Bouffard, Marge Coahran, Margo Rabon, Gail Rose, Jane Ross-Allen, and Amy Ryan. Finally, we thank our graphic artist, Holly Gault, for her creative renditions of our Parent–Teacher Action Research Cycle and the reproducible brochure for the ABC Program.

Opinions expressed in this book are those of the authors and do not necessarily represent opinions of the U.S. Department of Education or offices within it.

Contents

List of Figures, Tables, and Appendices

FIGURES

TABLES

APPENDICES

Introduction

Parents are human beings, just like teachers. Each has to appreciate that about the other. The best way to do it is to have them working side by side to benefit the children.
—COMER, as cited by FRAZIER (1999, p. 57)

NEW ABCs: ACHIEVING–BEHAVING–CARING

Achieving, behaving, and caring are as basic to education in the 21st century as was learning the alphabet in the early 20th century. From the wording of the No Child Left Behind Act (NCLB) of 2002, to the language in the Individuals with Disabilities Education Improvement Act (IDEA) of 2004, the messages are clear. In order to teach our children so that they achieve academically, we must teach them how to behave, and how to care about others. To do this, we must start early in their lives, we must engage their parents or other caretakers in their education, and we must work with the communities around our schools and homes.

The students for whom academic achievement, appropriate behavior, and positive relationships in their communities are the most difficult are the children who are identified as having emotional or behavioral disorders. These are the students who are (1) least likely to graduate from high school (U.S. Department of Education, 2002), (2) least likely to be employed following graduation (National Center on Secondary Education and Transition, 2004), and (3) most likely to be incarcerated (Quinn, Rutherford, & Leone, 2001). Some of the problems facing these children are due to biochemical or genetic malfunctions that will be with them for life, some are the product of social or environmental conditions, and many are a combination of the two. Regardless of cause, our schools have the responsibility of educating all children, including those with emotional or behavioral issues. Proactive, preventive programs need to start early, and an early parent–teacher-mediated intervention can even serve to improve student outcomes without the need for special education.

THE ABC PROGRAM

The Achieving–Behaving–Caring (ABC) Program is an empirically sound prevention strategy, which addresses the needs of students in the early grades who have emotional or behavioral

1

issues that place them at risk of school failure. The purpose of the ABC Program is to prevent these students from losing ground academically, and to begin addressing their psychosocial issues in the general education setting. The three components of ABC, however, are designed to reach more than just the students who are at risk of school failure. ABC also has an impact on classmates, parents or other primary caretakers, and classroom teachers.

ABC begins with a primary or universal prevention component, a research-based *social skills curriculum* for all students in the general education classrooms. For those children who lack skills, the social skills curriculum develops new skills. For those children who have social skills, the lessons provide an opportunity for practice, and give them a common language to use with classmates who need help with skills. At the very least, the social skills curriculum should span the grades in which the ABC Program is active. Ideally, the same social skills curriculum would be used throughout an entire school, and in the preschool settings that feed into the school.

The next component is the most unusual element of ABC, *collaborative action research* by the parents and classroom teachers of selected individual children. Over the past 50 years, action research in education has improved both individual teacher practices and faculty collegiality (Cochran-Smith & Lytle, 1993). Action research involves a continuous cycle of problem definition, observation and data collection, theory building, and action planning. Teachers use action research in their classrooms to make changes in their individual professional practices. When action research is applied to school improvement, teachers can implement change collaboratively, create ties with colleagues, adopt and adapt techniques from each other, learn to manage group process with adults, and build trust among the faculty. Parent–Teacher Action Research (PTAR) provides a basis for a similar process of trust-building and collaborative action between parents and teachers (Cheney, 1998; Ho, 2002; Kay & Fitzgerald, 1997; McConaughy, Kay, & Fitzgerald, 1998, 1999, 2000; Thompson, 1996).

PTAR is at the heart of the ABC model, providing a secondary prevention component for selected students. For each child, the parents and the classroom teacher form a team to agree on mutual goals and engage in action research to accomplish those goals. Over a 2-year span, parents and teachers meet monthly, and willingly change their practices to meet the child's needs, creating greater consistency between home and school. As Henderson and Berla (1994) noted, "When parents and teachers collaborate to help children adjust to the world of school, bridging the gap between the culture at home and the mainstream American school, children of all backgrounds tend to do well" (p. 11).

The third component of ABC is a *Parent Liaison,* an experienced and trained community member, who facilitates the action research process. The Parent Liaison arranges regular meetings between parents and teachers, guides parents and teachers through the action research process, and supports parents as they carry out their self-assigned tasks. Although Parent Liaisons are not advocates for either parent or child, they can be powerful role models for the parents and guardian caregivers who participate in ABC. Working with a Parent Liaison for 2 years, parents can learn effective approaches to productive advocacy for their children. They can learn to work with teachers and other school personnel to get their child's needs met, without needing to resort to angry, legalistic tactics that often alienate school personnel.

Many children in the early grades encounter cultural differences between home and school. Although most children handle this transition easily, those who have a hard time will show it in their behavior. We believe that children are reassured by knowing that their parents and teachers often speak with each other, work together to keep them safe, and speak positively about each other. If meeting children's needs is beyond the present skills of their parents and teachers, the ABC Program finds them resources to call upon. Parent Liaisons are there to provide parents with ways to learn new skills, help parents find community resources, and encourage parents as they learn how to meet the children's needs. The classroom teacher, too, has resources in the school to call upon for information on behavioral strategies, academic interventions, and encouragement to continue working with children and parents. In ABC, neither parents nor classroom teachers step away from their responsibilities for children, nor do they hand children's social and emotional issues over to others to resolve. In this way, the ABC Program keeps the power to make changes in children's lives in the hands of the adults who are closest to them.

CONCEPTS BEHIND THE SOCIAL SKILLS COMPONENT OF THE ABC PROGRAM

Teaching social skills in the general education classroom is an essential feature of the ABC Program. A social skills curriculum builds a foundation of *universal prevention* to support the social and emotional learning of all students. Osher, Dwyer, and Jackson (2004) explain that "Universal interventions prevent risk factors from developing or intensifying and build a foundation that supports the efficiency and effectiveness of early and intensive interventions" (p. 9). A school that offers neither universal nor selected prevention programs may find many more of its students in need of intensive special education programs to address serious emotional and behavioral disorders (Sugai, Sprague, Horner, & Walker, 2000).

What Are Social Skills?

The terms *social skills* and *social competence* cover broad areas of children's development. Educational and psychological literature has many different definitions of these terms. Gresham, Sugai, and Horner (2001) use the term *social skills* to describe specific behaviors that can be taught, learned, and performed. *Social competence* indicates that the behaviors are appropriate in the judgment of significant other people. *Social validity* refers to the relevance or importance of a social skill for success in a specific setting or situation. We define social skills as "behaviors that significant others judge to be appropriate for the setting and situation" (Kamps & Kay, 2002, p. 59). This definition combines the concepts of social skills, social competence, and social validity discussed by Gresham and colleagues.

Starting a conversation, giving a compliment, entering into an existing group, and settling a disagreement are all examples of good social skills for many settings. However, some social skills that are successful in one setting may be unsuccessful in another setting. For example, among many African American girls, loud, competitive conversations containing many put-downs, or *snaps*, are considered an indicator of social success. Yet the same girls will usually get into trouble if they hold those kinds of conversations in the halls at school or on the school bus. As another example, fighting back is not an acceptable response to aggression in school. Regardless of who started it, students are expected to walk away from a fight, and either solve the problem another way, or tell an adult about the problem. In the neighborhood, however, a boy who does *not* fight back to defend himself may be marking himself as a potential victim. Worse yet, asking an adult to help can invite even more assaults in the future (Canada, 1995).

Significant other people who judge the appropriateness of children's social behaviors will vary across settings. At school, significant others include teachers, administrators, other school staff, and a student's peers. At home, significant others include parents, siblings, other family members, and sometimes family friends. Significant others in the community can include store owners, police, and members of a family's religious group and other social organizations.

As they develop, children must learn social skills appropriate for many different settings. They must also learn how to adapt their social behavior to match the expectations of significant other people. Agreement and consistency among significant others' expectations across settings will help in this learning process. In the early grades, and during transitions from one school to another, consistency between classroom teachers and parents or guardian caregivers is especially important.

Why Teach Social Skills in School?

Success in life depends not only on a person's accomplishments and talents, but also on the ability to get along with others in society. Children do not enter the world with built-in social skills. Instead, we must teach them how to behave in socially appropriate ways. Some may argue that teaching social skills is the responsibility of the family, not the school. However, the demands of modern life and changes in family structure are making it more difficult for families to meet this responsibility by themselves. The need to work limits the time that parents can spend with their children. In many families, both parents work outside the home to meet their economic needs. Economic pressures are even more of a burden for single-parent families. Other social and environmental factors, such as increased violence in television and movies, and real violence in some children's neighborhoods, have additional negative impacts on children's social learning.

In the 1990s, developing children's social behavior became an important concern in public schools. For example, a 1993 survey of state competency standards by the National Center for Educational Outcomes found that the number of states with standards for children's personal and social adjustment was almost equal to the number of states with standards for academic and functional literacy (Spande & Thurlow, 1994). Tragic outbreaks of violence in schools also brought children's social development into the forefront.

Poor social skills are often associated with academic and behavioral or emotional problems. Many research studies documented poorly developed social skills in children with high-incidence disabilities, including specific learning disabilities, emotional disturbance, mental retardation, and attention deficit hyperactivity disorder (Gresham et al., 2001). Outside of special education, many children with emotional problems also have difficulties with social skills. The mental health report of the U.S. Surgeon General estimated that 20% of students experience mental health problems in the course of a year (U.S. Department of Health and Human Services, 1999). Although social skills lessons alone will not alleviate serious mental health problems, teaching social skills creates the foundation for a safe and supportive school environment (Osher et al., 2004).

At the turn of the century, the nation began to focus heavily on academic success, and schools were hard pressed to find time to include programs for social and emotional learning. However, researchers are now finding a strong connection between social, emotional, and academic learning (Zins, Weissberg, Wang, & Walberg, 2004). Children with poorly developed social skills can interfere with the learning and development of other students. They often do not work well with others in a group. They may disrupt classroom routines with arguments, rule-breaking, teasing, clowning, or angry outbursts. Some argue and refuse to follow rules and directions. Some get into fights resulting in injuries to themselves and others. When they get into trouble, they often blame others because they have difficulty understanding reactions to their own behavior. Some children with poorly developed social skills may not disrupt others, but may be equally unavailable for learning. Their withdrawn behaviors can cause other students to ignore or exclude them from groups. Their unwillingness to speak aloud makes it difficult to assess their learning, and frequent illnesses may cause excessive absence.

When children fail to cooperate, participate, and behave appropriately, teachers have to spend more time on classroom management, leaving less time for teaching academic skills. These children can consume administrators' time as well. Including social skills as a routine part of instruction can help to prevent such problems and improve the learning environment for all children.

The research evidence is growing: social and emotional learning are strongly associated with academic learning (Zins et al., 2004). Programs that begin early in the child's schooling have been shown to have a greater effect than those which begin in the middle years (Hawkins, Kosterman, Catalano, Hill, & Abbott, 2005). Schools that are willing to invest time and money in teaching students how to get along in the classroom, the school, and the community will reap the benefits in improved test scores and long-term outcomes.

CONCEPTS BEHIND THE PTAR COMPONENT OF ABC

The essential elements in PTAR are the child's story, mutual goals for the child, observations, reflections on those observations, hypotheses about the child's behavior, an action plan, and the ground rules. A set of strengths-based questions called Making Action Plans (MAPs) guides the process of telling the child's story (Forest & Pearpoint, 1992). Telling the child's story begins to weave new connections between parents and teacher, and prepares them to find shared goals for the child.

The PTAR cycle (see Figure I.1) sets the agenda for the meetings between parent and teacher, and creates a meeting of equals (Cheney & Osher, 1997). Its structure keeps them focused on the child's needs, and reduces or eliminates blaming behaviors. PTAR keeps parents and teachers "working side by side to benefit the children," to use James Comer's words (as cited by Frazier, 1999, p. 57). As they work, parents and teachers can begin to appreciate the other as human beings, and can see and hear the real concern that the other has for the child. Their growing relationship impacts the child, and increases the child's sense of security (Henderson & Mapp, 2002).

Because PTAR does not resemble "business as usual" in school systems, it frees all participants to build relationships different from those traditionally held by parents and teachers. Numerous researchers and authors have called for the creation of new ways for parents and teachers to work together. For example, Harry (1992) charged professionals "to provide communication structures that will make dialogue possible and mutual understanding likely" (p. 239). As Christenson and Sheridan (2001) noted, Harry recommended that these communication structures be used not just in special education, but "wherever an alteration in the balance of power is needed" (p. 47). In Lawrence-Lightfoot's (2003) characterization of parent–teacher dialogue as *"the essential conversation,"* she outlines a process almost identical to PTAR:

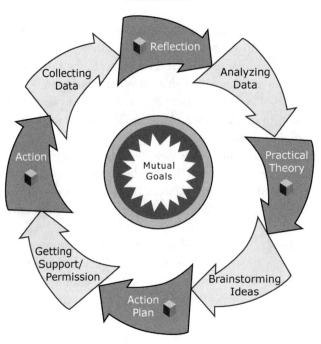

FIGURE I.1. The Parent–Teacher Action Research cycle.

Parents and teachers . . . must observe with a keen and sympathetic (not sentimental) eye that allows them to see who the child is and what he or she needs. This caring attentiveness and careful documentation of the child's life—his or her strengths and challenges, his or her capacities and gifts—will help teachers and parents know how they can best support the child's learning and growth, and in so doing give substance and authenticity to the ritual conversations between them (p. 79).

When parents and teachers begin PTAR, the ground rules give notice that the meetings will not be typical parent–teacher conferences. (See Chapter 8 for a complete list of the ground rules.) The rule that "Parents talk first" lays the foundation for equality by erasing the parents' impression that the teacher will be in charge of the meeting. The rule that "All ideas will be recorded in the team member's own words" gives credence to the knowledge about the child that both parents and teachers possess. The rule that "All ideas are to be expressed as positively as possible" focuses on the child's strengths and discourages negative labeling. As PTAR team members recognize their equality, they can develop a new level of trust that builds upon the initial ground rules.

Parent–teacher teams follow the PTAR cycle with a series of observations of the child, reflections on the factors contributing to the child's behavior, and hypothesis-building. They use this new knowledge of the child to build action plans, where parents and teachers deliberately make changes in their own practices. Often those changes in practice have already been occurring at different points in the cycle, unmentioned, and perhaps even unnoticed. For example, the teacher who went out on the playground specifically to observe Chipper's behavior came back in with the new knowledge that other boys were setting up Chipper to get into trouble. In the classroom, the teacher rearranged desks to minimize eye contact between Chipper and the other boys, and began to praise Chipper each time she saw him acting appropriately. When she met with his mother to make an action plan, the teacher decided to assign recess buddies three times a week to ensure that Chipper made new friends. She did not think to mention the other changes that she had made in her classroom, although she was already noticing an improvement in Chipper's behavior.

Chipper's mother had also been collecting data about him by asking him specific questions about school when she came home from work. She wrote his answers on a worksheet, and thanked him for helping with her homework. In making the action plan, Chipper's mother said that his father would have Chipper invite one new friend to go with them when they went fishing or bowling on Saturdays. However, once the action plan was in place, Chipper's mother stopped asking her son questions about school. At the end of the week, Chipper sadly asked his mother if she didn't care what happened to him at school anymore. She realized that her data collection had made an important change in her daily interactions with her son, something that was not included in the action plan. This is a good example of how subtle changes in practice, by parents at home and teachers at school, can have an impact on the child's behavior, along with the more obvious aspects of the PTAR action plan. When Chipper's mother and his teacher compared notes at their next meeting, they realized how important it was to continue their data collection and to keep moving around the PTAR cycle.

PTAR fosters parents' *engagement* with children's education, a term that implies that parents are involved with their children's learning at home. Several studies have highlighted the value of home-based parent involvement, an often neglected element in school-centered family involvement literature (Christenson & Sheridan, 2001). Ho (2002) also examined specific activities that parents do with their children at home, and noted that those activities were significant predictors of school achievement over and above the level of parent education or socioeconomic status of the family. Similar findings have been reported by Delgado-Gaitan (1991), Fantuzzo, McWayne, Perry, and Childs (2004), and Henderson and Berla (1994), who reviewed 66 studies of family involvement. Henderson and Berla concluded:

> If children know that their parents and teachers understand and respect each other, that they share similar expectations and stay in touch, children feel comfortable with who they are and can more easily reconcile their experiences at home and school (p. 11).

Finally, PTAR empowers both parents and classroom teachers to be more effective in responding to children's emotional and behavioral needs. The term *empowerment* is often misunderstood, as when a rankled teacher might say wryly, "Who wants empowered parents?" In ABC, we define *parent empowerment* as having the knowledge and the confidence to ensure that one's child gets the best possible education. This is not having power *over* teachers and administrators, but power *with* them. Teachers, too, value their own empowerment, and the chance to sharpen their skills in working with the whole child. When students' emotional and behavioral concerns are assigned to experts outside of the classroom, teachers can feel *deskilled* or *disempowered* and their ability to respond to the affective needs of all of their students can be diminished.

The principles of empowerment for parents and teachers have been expressed in many diverse ways, but they all include Maeroff's (1988) three elements: *status*, being seen as a person of value; *knowledge*, having fresh information and new insights; and *access*, the power to act on new knowledge (Irwin, 1996; Perrone, 1991). Dunst, Trivette, and Deal (1988) also lay out conditions for fostering empowerment, which include a belief that individuals are capable of competence and growth, creating opportunities for individuals to display and use that competence, and ensuring that individuals can attribute change to their own actions. Irwin's (1996) definition of *empowered educators* embraces parents, teachers, and administrators as educators. She begins her definition with "Empowered educators are persons who believe in themselves and their capacity to act" (p. 13). The PTAR process encourages educators, both parents and teachers, to study children deeply, in the context of home and school, and to learn more about effective responses to their behavior. With that new knowledge, parents and teachers increase their capacity to act to meet the children's needs, and therefore increase their own empowerment.

CONCEPTS BEHIND THE PARENT LIAISON COMPONENT OF ABC

The Parent Liaison is a *culture broker*, a person who can interpret the school culture for parents and the community culture for teachers. Parents can view the Parent Liaison as a peer who is experienced in working with the school. Teachers can appreciate the ability of the Parent Liaison to reach out to those who may not be accessible through the usual invitations that schools extend to parents. Both parents and teachers benefit from having a third person arrange their meetings, keep them focused on their goals for the child, and maintain the structure of the PTAR cycle to guide their conversations. The Parent Liaison helps to build a two-way street between home and school, and shows parents how to become effective advocates for their children.

Perhaps the best-known group of culture brokers or *boundary spanners* (Bond & Keys, 1993) in education comes from Head Start, where parents are employed to reach out to other parents to draw them into classes and meetings (Lodge, 1998). A similar group is the R.A.I.N.makers in Miami, Florida, a parent-based organization which reaches out to a large immigrant population to connect parents with needed community services (Alameda, 1996). Like Head Start, the R.A.I.N.makers offer day care and preschool classes for children, while providing leadership options and an *occupational ladder* for parents (Lawson & Briar-Lawson, 1997).

In Portland, Oregon, parent associates have been effective at increasing the consistency of low-income families bringing their children to mental health centers for counseling (Koroloff, Elliott, Koren, & Friesen, 1994). Two major national advocacy groups for students with disabilities, Parent-to-Parent and the Federation of Families for Children's Mental Health, operate on a similar principle of families reaching out to other families to help them access the services that their children need.

Although many schools are now employing parent coordinators or home–school coordinators, their functions are not identical to those of ABC's Parent Liaison position. Often, home–school coordinators are trained professionals from social work or other human services professions, hired specifically to intervene with families when students exhibit needs beyond those that the classroom teacher can meet. Even when parents are hired at a school to serve in an intermediary position with families, they often are there to help fulfill the school-identified and school-centered needs of children. In contrast, the ABC Parent Liaison is a member of the community who is there to help the parents work with the classroom teacher to identify and fulfill individual child-centered needs in the contexts of home, school, and the larger community. By reaching out to parents of children who are at risk and drawing them in as experts on their own children, the ABC Parent Liaisons strengthen the abilities of families to continue to work with schools and community agencies as their children grow.

OUR RESEARCH FINDINGS FOR THE ABC PROGRAM

The ABC Program includes the following features considered essential for prevention programs focused on children at risk for emotional and behavioral problems:

- ABC is an early intervention, targeted at children in the elementary grades.
- ABC involves parents, guardian caregivers, or other family members as key players.
- ABC involves classroom teachers as key players.
- ABC does not give any of the key players sole responsibility for improving learning or behavior.
- ABC involves collaboration among the key players.
- ABC leads to consistency across settings, especially home and school.
- ABC focuses on enhancing children's strengths and positive behaviors, along with reducing problem behaviors.
- ABC promotes academic achievement by removing barriers to learning.

Under two grants funded by the U.S. Office of Special Education Programs (OSEP), our research team tested the efficacy of the ABC model and its viability as a school and community program. The research project employed randomly assigned intervention and control groups of children in first and second grades. Kindergarten teachers used a standardized screening measure, the *Systematic Screening for Behavior Disorders* (SSBD; Walker & Severson, 1990), to develop prioritized lists of their students who had exhibited behaviors of concern during their kindergarten school year. With parental consent and teacher cooperation, additional baseline measures were collected, using the *Child Behavior Checklist* (CBCL; Achenbach, 1991a; Achenbach & Rescorla, 2001), the *Teacher's Report Form* (TRF; Achenbach, 1991b; Achenbach & Rescorla, 2001), and the *Social Skills Rating System* (SSRS; Gresham & Elliott, 1990). Pairs of students were matched on gender, age, first-grade classroom, and their problem scores on the parent and teacher rating scales. One of each pair was randomly assigned to an intervention group and the other to a control group.

To provide the classroom social skills component, the teachers in the first and second grade at each school chose a curriculum to implement. Our research team felt that teacher choice was crucial to the successful implementation of the social skills curriculum. The criteria were that social skills lessons were given by or with the classroom teacher, at least twice a week for the entire school year, with materials sent home to parents.

Parent Liaisons were recruited from each school district, and employed as members of the university research team. School staff were asked to name parents who were good communicators, and had strong connections to local communities. We wanted parents who did not participate visibly in their children's education to see the Parent Liaison as "one of us." The research team also placed ads for the Parent Liaison position in the local newspapers. Most of our Parent Liaisons were parents who had raised or were raising "a challenging child." Other Parent Liaisons included a volunteer *guardian ad litem* in the courts, a single father, a young woman awaiting her first child, and a grandmother. Parent Liaisons had varying levels of formal education, including high school diplomas, associates degrees, and college degrees.

After their initial training, Parent Liaisons sought out the parents of children who had been selected for the ABC Program by the kindergarten teachers. They were successful in recruiting

93% of the targeted parents. With supervision by the university-based researchers, Parent Liaisons led each PTAR team through an Action Research Cycle, supported parents in meeting their goals for children, facilitated parent–teacher relationships, and helped parents complete measures to evaluate the effectiveness of the program. Retention of 40 out of 43 PTAR teams for the 2-year cycle gave testimony to the acceptability of the Parent Liaisons and the PTAR process.

Our research findings showed many positive outcomes from the ABC Program. At the end of 2 years, teachers reported that children with PTAR teams showed significant declines in internalizing problems and rule-breaking behaviors compared to baseline measures and control group children without PTAR teams. PTAR parents reported declines in rule-breaking and other externalizing behaviors, plus improvements in their children's competencies. Independent observers also rated PTAR children significantly lower on internalizing behaviors (e.g., nervousness and unhappiness) at the end of the 2-year period in contrast to higher problem ratings for control children. Both PTAR and control children showed improvements from baseline measures in teacher-rated academic performance, adaptive functioning, and social skills, while showing declines in total problems (McConaughy et al., 1998, 1999, 2000).

By comparing 1-year versus 2-year outcomes, our ABC research team demonstrated that a longer period of prevention (2 years) was much more effective than a shorter period of 1 year (McConaughy et al., 2000). At the end of 2 years as part of a PTAR team, parents of the intervention group children also indicated that they felt more capable of obtaining school-based services that their children needed. By contrast, the data showed that the control group parents felt *less* capable of obtaining needed services than they had 2 years earlier. Many teachers commented that they wished they could carry out PTAR with the parents of all children in their classrooms. Some teachers who had not been teaching social skills in their classrooms prior to the research project declared their intentions to continue with the social skills curriculum after the end of their involvement with the project.

ABOUT THIS BOOK

The material in this book is designed to help schools and communities start and maintain their own ABC Program. The book provides information for administrators in schools and community agencies as well as information for parents, teachers, and Parent Liaisons. It is a product of our ABC outreach grant, which supported the start-up process for the ABC Program in three school districts in Vermont. The program is now in the hands of schools and agencies in those districts, with every sign of its being sustained.

Part I: For Program Administrators

Part I contains guidelines for personnel (including school administrators, school psychologists, guidance counselors, educators, and others) who are setting up and managing an ABC Program in their schools and community. The guidelines suggest two different approaches to administering an ABC Program, a *school-centered* model and a *family–school–community* model. The school-centered model manages the program by adding Parent Liaisons to the school staff, with their supervision and program administration provided by student support staff. The family–school–community model suggests that the school contract with a local human service agency to employ, supervise, and support the Parent Liaisons. We discuss the advantages and drawbacks of each model.

We gave initial versions of both parts of the book to administrators in the schools where the ABC outreach grant took place. Administrators provided written comments and suggestions for revision of Part I. Then we met with administrators and Parent Liaisons in two focus groups to discuss the book and their efforts to institutionalize the ABC Program in their schools. Our revisions of Part I were guided by their thoughtful suggestions.

Part II: For Parent Liaisons

Part II is written for Parent Liaisons, and covers their work with parents throughout the 2 years of the program. It provides step-by-step guidelines for Parent Liaisons for recruiting parents into the program and conducting the PTAR team meetings. The emphasis is on using the PTAR framework to enable parents and teachers to work as equal partners in addressing children's needs. In addition to guidelines for facilitating the PTAR team meetings, Part II shows Parent Liaisons how to offer additional support to the parents as they move through the Action Research Cycle, how to teach parents to advocate for their children's needs without alienating teachers, and how to find additional resources for parents when they need them.

Parent Liaisons in the ABC outreach grant used a draft of Part II of the book for training and working with parents and teachers. We asked Parent Liaisons to make notes on each chapter as they used it, then brought them together in focus groups to hear their suggestions. Their shared wisdom guided our revisions for the final version of Part II.

We offer the chapters in Part II as guidelines for Parent Liaisons in facilitating the PTAR process, not as a set of rigid directives. Parent Liaisons should use their own judgment in working with each parent–teacher team, and make thoughtful adaptations as their teams work to address the needs of individual children. They might also use action research to improve their own practices as Parent Liaisons.

FREQUENTLY ASKED QUESTIONS

- *Can the role of the Parent Liaison be assumed by a home–school coordinator or other member of the student support services staff?* Much depends on the relationship that the home–school coordinator already has with parents and guardian caregivers who are considered "hard to reach." (We prefer to think of them as "easy to miss.") If that person has a good rapport with most families, and is usually seen as a neutral party in home–school conflicts, then he/she may be a very effective Parent Liaison. However, you should be careful not to assume that all parents feel comfortable coming into your school and talking with your teachers. Anyone who serves as a Parent Liaison should be willing to meet with some parents and teachers outside of the school on neutral territory.

- *How many PTAR teams should a classroom teacher have?* In the first year of participation in ABC, we recommend that teachers take on no more than two PTAR teams. Even though each monthly meeting with parents usually takes little more than an hour, action research involves making observations or collecting other data on the child and may require additional time to seek out new information on strategies that would help the child. School administrators may also want teachers and parents to complete questionnaires on each child's progress in order to evaluate the ABC Program's effectiveness. Completing those measures twice a year will require at least another 2 hours of the teacher's time per child. After the first year, when teachers know what the PTAR process requires, they can decide how many teams they can handle.

• *Shouldn't a special educator, guidance counselor, or school psychologist attend PTAR meetings?* The purpose of the PTAR meeting is for parents and teachers to do action research together. This can be done without involving specialists. However, if *both* the parent and the teacher on a PTAR team agree to have someone else attend one or more of their meetings to give advice, then the outside expert is invited. Other school personnel should never assume that their expertise is required in order for the parents and teacher to succeed, and thereby invite themselves into a PTAR meeting. Occasionally an outside expert or other person may become a regular member of a team, but this decision is always made by mutual agreement of parents and teachers on the PTAR team.

• *Why does ABC not focus on parent education or teacher training?* The adults participating in ABC are learning new skills and increasing their depth of knowledge about each other's way of meeting the child's needs. However, their learning is self-directed and pragmatic, providing two of the strongest motivators in adult education (Cross, 1981). The ABC Program keeps the focus on the child, and encourages parents and teachers to learn how to deliver what that individual child needs. In that way, PTAR is a very efficient use of parent and teacher time.

• *Is ABC a prereferral intervention?* From the perspective of special education personnel, ABC might be considered as a prereferral intervention. At any point in the PTAR process, if the parents and classroom teacher believe that the child should be tested for special education eligibility, then they would bring the data that they had collected to the school referral team. To us, the term *prereferral* makes ultimate referral seem inevitable. By contrast, ABC is a *prevention* program, not a program for evaluating children's need for more intensive help.

• *Can we use the ABC Program without teaching social skills in the classrooms?* We have not tested the effectiveness of ABC without the social skills component. Moreover, in our research, we did not have a control group of children who did not receive social skills instruction. Our research findings showed that both the PTAR children and the control children improved in social skills. Without further research, we have no evidence to say whether children would show the same types of gains that we saw without the social skills instruction. Other researchers have argued that whole-class social skills instruction, like that which we used in ABC, is one of the most effective ways to help children generalize their skills to many different settings (Kamps & Kay, 2002; Gresham et al., 2001).

• *Where can schools and community agencies find the money to support an ABC Program?* The ABC Program meets criteria for using Title I funds (Moles, 1996) and money for Safe and Drug Free Schools, among other sources. The Individuals with Disabilities Education Improvement Act of 2004 also encourages school districts to implement " . . . effective strategies for addressing inappropriate behavior of students with disabilities in schools, including strategies *to prevent children with emotional and behavioral problems from developing emotional disturbances that require the provision of special education and related services* [italics added]." A district may use up to 15% of its special education funding to address student needs prior to the intensive and expensive testing that a referral for special education can initiate. As a primary and secondary prevention program, ABC may qualify for this use of special education monies.

I

FOR PROGRAM ADMINISTRATORS

IMPLEMENTING THE ABC PROGRAM

Welcome to the group of creative administrators who are willing to implement a prevention program in general education classrooms to help students succeed in school! Part I of our book is written primarily for administrators of the ABC Program in elementary schools, such as principals and assistant principals, deans, pupil personnel administrators, guidance counselors, and school psychologists. We think this book is also useful to administrators of preschools and community human service agencies that may be launching the ABC Program. You may find it helpful to read or skim Part II of the book before you plunge into Part I.

There are three elements in the ABC Program; your staff may already be familiar with one or two of them. The heart of ABC is Parent–Teacher Action Research, or PTAR. PTAR is a unique approach to parent–teacher engagement, and is effective in reducing some of the social and emotional problems that keep children from learning. It is considered a *secondary prevention* tool that aims to prevent problems or improve the environment of particular children considered to be at risk for more severe problems. PTAR is supported by a *primary* (or *universal*) *prevention* tool, social skills lessons for all students in the general education classroom, and by the work of a Parent Liaison, a member of the community who is trained to facilitate PTAR and support the parents of children at risk. (For more information on the research behind ABC, see the Introduction.)

There are at least two different approaches to implementing ABC in the early years of schooling: one is *school-centered* and the other is a *family–school–community partnership*. In the school-centered model, Parent Liaisons are part of the school staff. Student support staff provide Parent Liaison supervision and ABC Program administration. The advantages of this approach are that ABC can be closely tied to the school's existing student referral system and that the Parent Liaisons know the teachers as colleagues. The disadvantages are that families who may already feel disenfranchised and alienated from the school will see the Parent Liaisons as school personnel, and may lack trust in them for that reason alone. Often these are the families whose children are most in need of the ABC Program. Also, a Parent Liaison who is tied to a particular school cannot

13

move with students who may transfer to other schools, and thereby may have to withdraw support at a time when parents and students sorely need it.

In the family–school–community model, the school system contracts with a local human service agency to employ, supervise, and support the Parent Liaisons. Usually this agency is one that works with families in other ways, and is known to have a good rapport with parents. Examples are Parent Information and Resource Centers, or PIRCs, local offices of economic opportunity that run day care and preschool programs, or community mental health centers. With the ABC Program centered in the community, parents may be more inclined to view the Parent Liaison as "one of us." In this model, Parent Liaisons can also be mobile, and can move with students within the area to implement ABC in their new schools. In addition, human service agencies usually have a strong system of referral to other services in the community that are focused on the whole family, not only on a particular child. The disadvantage of this model is that it takes time to establish a partnership between a school and a community agency, if one does not exist already. There is also an extra layer of bureaucracy involved in this model. As an administrator, you need to weigh the advantages and disadvantages of each model as you build a foundation for the ABC Program in your schools.

Chapter 1 addresses some initial questions about implementing the ABC Program in your school or community. What will the program do for our children? How should ABC be managed? What will it cost, and where will we find the money? Who would be the best partners in our community?

Although Part II of the book will provide detailed guidance for your Parent Liaisons, Chapter 2 provides administrators with guidelines on recruiting, training, and supervising them. The guidelines apply whether you are adopting ABC as a school-centered model or a family–school–community partnership.

In Chapter 3, we discuss the primary prevention element of the ABC Program, a social skills curriculum provided for all students in general education classrooms. Even if you already have a social skills curriculum in your classrooms, you will find information on making that program more effective. If you are choosing a new program, Chapter 3 provides tools for involving teachers in making that choice.

Chapter 4 focuses on the selection of students who will benefit most from the ABC Program. This chapter will help you set up a screening and referral system for your ABC Program. Remember that ABC is a *prevention* program and is not designed for students with emotional or behavioral issues who are already in need of intensive special education services, counseling, or one-on-one support to succeed in the general education setting.

As an administrator who makes data-based decisions, you will find Chapter 5 important. To sustain the ABC Program, you'll need scientific measurement and evaluation of its effectiveness. Chapter 5 will help you choose your evaluation design and instruments, and then establish a timeline for data collection. We found that parents and teachers were willing to complete questionnaires about their experiences with ABC once they understood the importance of evaluating and sustaining the program. Figure PI.1 provides a comprehensive checklist of important considerations and steps that you might take as you start to implement the ABC Program.

Building a Foundation for the ABC Program (Chapter 1)

☐ Choose either a school-centered model or a family–school–community partnership.

☐ Create and find funding for a 2-year budget.

☐ Present ABC to board members and other administrators.

☐ Enlist teacher participation.

☐ Establish a relationship between the school and a community agency:
  - Choose partners.
  - Establish guidelines for evaluation (see Chapter 5).
  - Come to an agreement on roles and budgeting.
  - Formalize the relationship.

☐ Let parents and the public know about the ABC Program.

Recruiting and Training Parent Liaisons (Chapter 2)

☐ School and community partners decide on the qualities of a Parent Liaison.

☐ School and community partners decide on the roles and responsibilities of a Parent Liaison.

☐ Recruit Parent Liaison candidates.

☐ Interview and hire Parent Liaisons.

☐ Provide Parent Liaisons with training and supervision.

Selecting and Implementing a Social Skills Curriculum (Chapter 3)

☐ Identify social skills that are important in your classrooms.

☐ Identify and prioritize your students' social skills needs or deficits.

☐ Review available social skills programs for their fit in your school.

☐ Choose a social skills curriculum.

☐ Prepare to implement your selected social skills curriculum.

☐ Let parents and the public know about the social skills curriculum.

Selecting Child and Family Participants for ABC's PTAR Teams (Chapter 4)

☐ Use a standardized screening instrument or other indicators of child growth and behavior:
  - Consider all children in the participating classrooms.
  - Look for both internalizing and externalizing problem behaviors.
  - Exclude children who are already receiving intensive services.

☐ Invite parents to participate.

☐ Take baseline evaluations of children's behavior.

☐ Establish and publicize other methods for referral.

Evaluating the Effectiveness of the ABC Program (Chapter 5)

☐ Choose your evaluation design:
  - Single-case design.
  - Experimental group design.
  - Group design without control group.
  - Qualitative approaches.

☐ Select evaluation instruments.

☐ Set timeline for data collection.

☐ Analyze and report your results.

FIGURE PI.1. Checklist for starting an ABC Program.

1

Building a Foundation
for the ABC Program

┌───┐
│ **Questions to Be Addressed in This Chapter**   │
│   │
│ • What will ABC do for our school?   │
│ • What will ABC cost?   │
│ • Whose support do we need to get started?   │
└───┘

The recommendations in this chapter are drawn from the experiences of the school systems that participated in developing and testing ABC. Our first recommendation for instituting and sustaining the ABC Program is "Don't go it alone." While you might start with one school as a pilot program, there is strength in numbers. The strongest ABC Program will involve several schools within a school district. Teachers appreciate knowing that their colleagues in other schools are participating in ABC's PTAR and may benefit from exchanging ideas. If teachers incorporate action research into their *individual personal development plans (IPDPs)*, a staff development coordinator could work with several ABC teachers to help them assess their learning.

There are two models of ABC discussed in this chapter. One model, the *school-centered* approach, keeps ABC entirely "in house," with Parent Liaisons as school system employees, supervised by pupil-personnel staff. In the second model, the *family–school–community* approach, the school contracts with a community agency to deliver ABC.

We found several advantages to having Parent Liaisons employed within the community and outside of the school system. When Parent Liaisons are not school employees, they are often more able to reach out to parents who did not have a good school experience themselves, or to parents who view the school as part of an oppressive social services system. Parents can look on the Parent Liaisons as "one of us," and learn from them how to work *with* teachers rather than *against* them. Although Parent Liaisons may still be assigned to work with specific schools, in this model they can follow children who may move within the district and help maintain continuity for the child

17

and family. In a multilingual community, one Parent Liaison per school is not sufficient. Different schools may need the services of Parent Liaisons who speak the native language of families in that school. When a community agency is the employer, there is more flexibility within the ABC Program to meet parents and children wherever they are located. In addition, the program can draw support and funding from the community in ways other than school taxes.

WHAT WILL ABC DO FOR OUR SCHOOL?

Benefits for Children from Social Skills Lessons

Our research indicates that there are benefits for all of the children when the classroom teachers choose and use a common social skills program. Appendix 1.1 lists those advantages, and Chapter 3 will provide more information about a social skills curriculum.

Benefits for Children from PTAR

Children whose parents and teachers form PTAR teams and work toward mutual goals benefit to a greater degree than those who receive only social skills lessons. The first section of Appendix 1.2 summarizes the measurable improvements found in students from our research project whose parents and teachers worked together in PTAR teams. The second section lists the themes found in the program evaluations done by parents and teachers.

Benefits for Teachers

While the benefits for students were measured with quantitative data, the benefits for teachers emerged from conversations in interviews and evaluation meetings (see Appendix 1.3). Not every teacher perceived every benefit, of course, but teachers generally found ABC to be a positive learning experience.

Benefits for Parents

Parents who had been part of PTAR teams spoke enthusiastically about their experiences in the evaluation meetings at the end of our 2-year research period. Many took the time to write letters and to complete written evaluations. In addition, parents completed the *Family Empowerment Scale—School Version* (McConaughy et al., 1999; see Chapter 5). Appendix 1.4 summarizes the benefits identified by parents who participated in PTAR teams over a 2-year span.

WHAT WILL ABC COST?

Creating and Funding a Budget

Even when Parent Liaisons are employed outside a school system, the funding and impetus for such collaboration usually has to come from or through the school. Title I or Title IV funds, monies to prevent drug and alcohol abuse, and other school-based funding mechanisms can all cover the costs of the ABC Program. For the family–school–community model, the United Way is another resource, as are community foundations and corporate contributions. Although grants from foundations and corporations can often provide seed money to start ABC, administrators will want to lay the foundation for sustaining the program from the outset.

Funds are needed for the following aspects of ABC:

- The employment and supervision of Parent Liaisons. At 20 hours per week, new Parent Liaisons generally start with eight families, increasing in their second year of experience to between 12 and 16 families, depending on the needs of the children and families assigned to them.
- The initial purchase of copies of this book for administrators and Parent Liaisons.
- Time for teacher training and materials to support the social skills curriculum.
- Evaluation tools and data analysis.

You may also want to consider:

- Technical assistance to begin both ABC and the social skills curriculum.
- Staff development stipends for participating teachers.
- An outside evaluator to supervise the collection and analysis of outcome data.

Figure 1.1 gives an example of a budget planning worksheet for the first year in one school, where there are four first grades and four second grades. (There is a blank copy of this worksheet for your use in Appendix 1.5.)

In the school in this example, all of the first- and second-grade teachers have agreed on a common social skills program. Each of four first-grade teachers has agreed to participate in two ABC teams, so eight children will have PTAR teams this year. The administrator estimates the total cost at $21,176 for the first year. The hourly rate of $11.50 for the position of Parent Liaison has been set at the rate of the highest-paid paraprofessional in the district, since there are no existing positions similar to that of a Parent Liaison. Several items are one-time costs, such as the purchase of two copies of this book ($60), social skills starter kits for four teachers in first grade, plus an additional four teachers in second grade ($600), and advertising to recruit a Parent Liaison and Program Coordinator.

There are three other schools in the district that are going to begin the ABC Program this year. Administrators from all four schools have agreed to share in the costs of employing a Program Coordinator and operating the program. They hope to reduce costs in the second year and beyond by inviting other district elementary schools to participate.

In the second year, one Parent Liaison will continue to serve the eight children who will now be in second grade, and add eight new first graders. If there are children whose parents and teacher need to meet more than once a month, or families whose primary language is not represented among the Parent Liaisons, the help of an additional Parent Liaison may be needed. Costs in the second year are estimated at $21,992, only slightly more than the first year, doubling the number of children who have PTAR teams. The cost per targeted child is now $1,375, which does not take into account the benefits for all first- and second-grade children from the social skills curriculum.

In evaluating the budget for ABC, you can compare it with the cost of an alternative, traditional approach without using ABC.

ABC Budget Planning Worksheet—First Year

Item	Cost per Unit	Number of Units	Subtotal	Additional Costs	Est. TOTAL
1 Parent Liaison	$11.50/hr	20/hr × 40 wk = 800 hrs	$9,200	FICA@8% = $736	$9,936
Personnel and Fringe $9,936					
ABC books	$30	2 copies	$60		$60
Social skills materials: Starter Kits	$75	8 copies (4 1st-grade and 4 2nd-grade teachers)	$600		$600
Travel for Parent Liaison	$0.32/mi	200/mi/mo × 10	$640		$640
Teacher stipends	$150/child	4 teachers in 2 teams; 2 children/teacher	$1,200		$1,200
Screening & evaluation materials	$5/child	8 children	$40		$40
School Operating Costs $2,540					
Program Coordinator 75% time	$25,000 or $2,500/mo	10 mo	$25,000 divided by 4 = $6,250	Fringe@30% = $1,875	$8,125
Postage & shipping	$50/mo	10 mo	$500 divided by 4		$125
Printing & photocopying	$30/mo	10 mo	$300 divided by 4		$75
Advertising/recruitment	$200	one-time cost	$200 divided by 4		$50
Administrative costs	total $26,000	5% of joint costs	$1,300 divided by 4		$325
School Share of Joint Operating and Administrative Costs $8,700					
Total Cost to School $21,176					

(continued)

FIGURE 1.1. Example of a completed ABC budget planning worksheet.

ABC Budget Planning Worksheet—Second Year (and Beyond)

Item	Cost per Unit	Number of Units	Subtotal	Additional Costs	Est. TOTAL
1 Parent Liaison at 2% increase	$11.73/hr	20/hr × 40 wks = 800 hrs	$9,384	FICA@8% = $751	$10,135
Personnel and Fringe $10,135					
Travel for Parent Liaison	$0.32/mi	200/mi/mo × 10	$640		$640
Teacher stipends	$150/child	8 teachers, 2 children/ teacher	$2,400		$2,400
School Operating Costs $3,040					
Program Coordinator 75% time	$25,500 or $2,550/mo	10 mo	$25,500 divided by 4 = $6,375	Fringe@30% = $1,913	$8,288
Postage & shipping	$50/mo	10 mo	$500 divided by 4		$125
Printing & photocopying	$30/mo	10 mo	$300 divided by 4		$75
Administrative costs	total $26,300	5% of joint costs	$1,315 divided by 4		$329
School Share of Joint Operating and Administrative Costs $8,817					
Total Cost to School $21,992					

FIGURE 1.1. *(continued)*

- Scenario 1: The child requires a weekly meeting between the teacher and a consulting school psychologist throughout the year: $100 per hour times 30 weeks of the school year = $3,000.
- Scenario 2: The child is tested for emotional or behavioral disorders ($750), found eligible for special education services, and is bused to another school: $32,000 + $750 = $32,750.
- Scenario 3: The child is tested ($750) and is given a Section 504 plan which requires a one-on-one paraeducator for half of each school day: (180 days × 3 hours × $15 per hour) + $750 = $8,850.

If only half (8) of the 16 children to be served by ABC required these traditional services, the least expensive service would cost $3,000 × 8 = $24,000, and the most expensive would total

$32,750 \times 8 = \$262,000$ for 1 year. This does not take into consideration the traditionally poor long-term outcomes of students who receive special education services for emotional or behavioral disorders.

WHOSE SUPPORT DO WE NEED TO GET STARTED?

The materials available in this book can help administrators in making presentations to boards of education, superintendents, and other colleagues. With the principals of several schools and the superintendent joining you in your support of ABC, the more likely it is that you will get the cooperation of community agencies and potential funding sources.

If you choose to organize your ABC Program completely within the school, you will need to build the task of Parent Liaison supervision and ABC coordination into the job description of another administrator, a counselor, or the home–school coordinator. In some settings, the home–school coordinator has a close enough relationship with those easy-to-miss parents whose children might be selected for ABC to serve as the Parent Liaison. Your counselor will certainly want to be involved in the choice of a social skills curriculum, but be careful not to let the counselor make the decision without real give and take with the classroom teachers. In our experience, teachers who have a social skills curriculum imposed on them are less likely to play an active role in teaching the lessons. They may abandon their responsibility to reinforce the lessons throughout the day, or find reasons to leave the classroom while the counselor delivers the lessons. Students are quick to pick up on teacher apathy or antipathy toward affective education, which seriously diminishes its impact.

Enlisting Teacher Participation

No matter which model you choose to deliver ABC, your classroom teachers are the group you must convince. Many teachers find children with behavioral or emotional issues challenging to teach. Some enjoy the challenge, and others feel overwhelmed. Research has also shown that *acting-out children* are the ones teachers are most likely to refer for special education services. Often the referral does not occur until the children's behavior begins to affect them or their peers academically (Abidin & Robinson, 2002). On the other hand, the children whose emotional issues are turned inwardly may not be referred at all. As a program that includes both primary and secondary prevention, ABC is designed to catch children at risk for behavioral and emotional problems before their problems become serious enough to warrant special education.

Tell teachers that ABC is a prevention program that involves three elements:

- Social skills lessons for all children in the general education classroom.
- Monthly PTAR teams for targeted children.
- Parent Liaisons who connect with the parents of selected children, arrange the meetings between parents and teachers, and guide the action research process.

Teachers are responsible for delivering both primary and secondary prevention components of ABC. That is, teachers teach social skills to their entire class *and* participate in PTAR teams for one or more identified children in their classes. If your school does not already have a social skills curriculum in place, teachers will have many questions about fitting it into their crowded school day. Chapter 3 discusses social skills instruction in detail and suggests ways to go about choosing a curriculum that meets your students' needs.

School personnel who have adopted *character education* programs ask if those meet the criteria for social skills programs. Some do, and some do not. For example, a character education program that uses direct instruction of the skills a student needs to show *respect* to others, with modeling and role playing, might be sufficient to teach those social skills. If the character education program is based on class discussion of concepts with no direct instruction, then that program is not sufficient to teach social skills. We have found that a social skills curriculum is more likely to teach character education than vice versa.

Some of your best allies in adopting ABC will be teachers who have already done *action research* alone or with colleagues. Before scheduling a teachers' meeting to introduce the ABC Program, you might want to explain ABC to teachers who are familiar with action research. At the meeting, your staff development personnel can join in the discussion. A key aspect of ABC's PTAR is teachers coming to think of parents as colleagues who have wisdom to share about their child. Expect some healthy skepticism on this point! We found that ABC created a very different relationship between teachers and parents from what teachers had experienced in the past. The Parent Liaison supports the teacher in arranging the meeting and providing the agenda, and supports the parent in carrying out plans. Several teachers in the original ABC research commented "I wish I could do this with every child in my classroom!"

Establishing a Partnership between the School and a Community Agency

Once you have teacher support, your next step in the family–school–community model is to establish or strengthen the relationship between the school and a community agency. Some administrators may be as doubtful about this partnership as teachers may be in thinking of parents as colleagues. Others may see it as an opportunity to increase community involvement with the school. Whichever your viewpoint, there are good reasons why we recommend such a partnership.

Many parents of children with emotional and behavioral issues may not have any desire to get directly involved with school personnel. Some of this stems from their own childhood school experiences, and some from fear that school personnel will blame their child's problems on them. Others may be too overwhelmed with the tasks of daily living to think about arranging time to talk with school personnel. Some may have language and cultural barriers that make connections difficult. Even schools that have excellent parent involvement programs may not be reaching these parents. Rather than labeling these parents as *hard to reach,* encourage your staff to think of them as *easy to miss.* A school that is working to *leave no child behind* is usually a school that wants to make a connection with all families. ABC can help to create and strengthen that connection.

Choosing Partners

To implement the family–school–community model successfully, you will want to choose an agency that is already doing a good job at reaching the parents of your students. Nongovernmental agencies are often less threatening to parents than schools, especially those agencies that offer early childhood services. We chose Parent Information Resource Centers, or PIRCs, as the partners for our implementation phase of ABC. Congress established PIRCs in 1994 to help parents become more actively involved in the education of their children. While services are targeted locally, PIRC programs are generally open to all parents of children from birth through high school. PIRCs are found throughout all fifty states and in seven U.S. territories. More information on PIRCs can be found at *www.ed.gov/programs/pirc.* See Appendix 1.6 for information on finding other potential community agency partners.

If you decide to work with a community agency, that agency should be willing to employ and supervise the Parent Liaisons, work closely with your appointed school-based ABC coordinator, and be accountable for the results of ABC by using appropriate measures. Once you have a prospective partner, you will want to agree on the roles played by agency and school, create and fund a 2-year budget, establish guidelines and procedures for evaluation, and formalize the relationship with a written agreement. If you will not be working with a community agency, you will want to assign these responsibilities within your school or district.

Agreeing on Roles

As a rule, the school is responsible for student selection, teacher participation, teacher support, delivering a social skills program, and the collection and analysis of data for evaluation. The school and agency may share the responsibility for funding Parent Liaisons and, possibly, their supervisor, through a contract. The community agency is responsible for the work of Parent Liaisons and the care and maintenance of an advisory committee. The school system and the community agency share the responsibility for results and need to establish mutual guidelines for evaluation.

Formalizing the Relationship

Issues regarding supervision, mileage and expense reimbursements, and agreements on confidentiality also need to be addressed in any cooperative agreements between school systems and outside community agencies. Appendix 1.7 is a sample agreement between a school and the community agency with which it partners to provide ABC services. It describes the general roles for participants in ABC.

An *advisory committee* can provide important expertise to your ABC Program, and strengthen the connections between the school and the community. At a minimum, you will want to include at least one principal, the school psychologist, social worker or guidance counselor, the school's ABC Program coordinator, and a representative of the community agency. Other helpful members to consider are a school nurse, a home–school coordinator, a participating teacher, a parent, members of the school and agency boards, and representatives of various faith-based communities.

Letting Parents and the Public Know about ABC

Appendix 1.8 is a copy of a brochure that provides an overview of the ABC Program. We are sure that you will improve the brochure as you tailor it for your school. There are many audiences you will want to reach as you discuss the possibility of opening doors to the ABC Program in your community. One brochure may not be the answer to reaching school board members, teachers, and parents. You may also want to create a PowerPoint presentation about ABC, and tailor the slides to match your local situation. You might use the PowerPoint at a teacher's meeting, a PTA meeting, with members of the new ABC Advisory Committee, and at a local service organization's regular meeting. For audiences of other administrators or potential funding organizations, you can obtain reprints of the articles written on ABC research by contacting the first author of this book.

Benefits of Using a Social Skills Curriculum
in the Classroom

RESULTS IN BRIEF FROM QUANTITATIVE RESEARCH ON ABC

Using standardized rating scales, teachers and parents reported increases in total social skills, cooperation, assertiveness, self-control, adaptive functioning, and academic performance across both the target and the control groups. Over a 2-year period, parent and teacher measures also showed reductions in problems among both groups of children (McConaughy et al., 1998, 1999, 2000).

THEMES FROM EVALUATIONS BY PARENTS AND TEACHERS

- Children with social skill deficits learn new social skills or improve skills.

- Children are more likely to generalize those skills to new situations when they are taught in the classroom rather than in a pull-out setting.

- Children with behavior problems are not singled out.

- Children without deficits have opportunities to model good social skills with their peers, and coach others in informal settings.

- Children learn positive behaviors to replace undesirable or inappropriate behaviors.

- Teachers, children, and parents learn a common language to communicate expectations about social behavior.

- Classroom members develop a sense of caring, community, and social responsibility.

From Stephanie H. McConaughy, Pam Kay, Julie A. Welkowitz, Kim Hewitt, and Martha D. Fitzgerald (2008). Copyright by The Guilford Press. Permission to photocopy this appendix is granted to purchasers of this book for personal use only (see copyright page for details).

How PTAR Teams Benefit Children

RESULTS IN BRIEF FROM QUANTITATIVE RESEARCH ON ABC

The effectiveness of the ABC Program was demonstrated by decreases in problem behavior and increases in adaptive behavior during the 2-year period. Compared with their matched controls, children with PTAR teams showed significantly greater decreases in teacher-reported internalizing problems and rule-breaking behavior, and parent-reported total problems, externalizing, and rule-breaking behavior. Independent observers also noted improvements in internalizing behaviors (McConaughy et al., 1998, 1999, 2000).

THEMES FROM EVALUATIONS BY PARENTS AND TEACHERS

- Each PTAR team pays special attention to an individual child.

- PTAR teams emphasize children's strengths over their shortcomings.

- Children see their parents and teachers working together in a positive relationship.

- Children hear consistent messages from parents and teachers about their expectations for behavior.

- When parents and teachers collaborate, children are not caught in the middle of conflicting goals and consequences for their behavior.

- When parents and teachers collaborate, children can have more positive and productive experiences in school.

- When children attend PTAR meetings, they can express their feelings, explain their own views of their actions, and feel that parents and teachers are listening to them.

From Stephanie H. McConaughy, Pam Kay, Julie A. Welkowitz, Kim Hewitt, and Martha D. Fitzgerald (2008). Copyright by The Guilford Press. Permission to photocopy this appendix is granted to purchasers of this book for personal use only (see copyright page for details).

How PTAR Teams Benefit Teachers

- PTAR teams provide a method for observing and monitoring children's behavioral and educational growth.

- Teachers have a structure for communicating with parents about educational and behavioral goals for children.

- Teachers can develop trusting and meaningful relationships with parents.

- Teachers come to understand parents' perspectives on children's strengths and challenging behaviors.

- Teachers expand their repertoire for managing children's behavior.

- Parents and teachers set common goals, and Parent Liaisons help parents carry them out.

- Consistency in behavioral expectations increases between school and home.

From Stephanie H. McConaughy, Pam Kay, Julie A. Welkowitz, Kim Hewitt, and Martha D. Fitzgerald (2008). Copyright by The Guilford Press. Permission to photocopy this appendix is granted to purchasers of this book for personal use only (see copyright page for details).

How PTAR Teams Benefit Parents

RESULTS FROM QUANTITATIVE RESEARCH ON ABC

PTAR parents scored higher than control parents on the Family Empowerment Scale—School Version (FES-S), indicating that they felt a greater sense of empowerment in obtaining school services for their children by the end of the 2-year period. In particular, PTAR parents rated themselves significantly higher than control parents for their knowledge base, feelings of competence, and systems advocacy by the end of the 2-year period (McConaughy et al., 1999, 2000).

THEMES FROM EVALUATIONS BY PARENTS AND TEACHERS

- Parents meet regularly with their child's teacher in a neutral setting.

- Parents have a structure for communicating with teachers about educational and behavioral goals for their children.

- Parents can share their perspectives on their children's strengths and challenging behaviors.

- Parents come to understand teachers' perspectives on their children's learning and behavior.

- Parents are empowered as equal partners with teachers in reaching common goals for their children.

- Parents get support from Parent Liaisons in communicating with teachers and seeking additional community services when needed.

- Parents learn collaboration skills and ways to advocate for their children in school.

- Parents ensure that their children get effective behavioral guidance from teachers that meshes with guidance at home.

From Stephanie H. McConaughy, Pam Kay, Julie A. Welkowitz, Kim Hewitt, and Martha D. Fitzgerald (2008). Copyright by The Guilford Press. Permission to photocopy this appendix is granted to purchasers of this book for personal use only (see copyright page for details).

ABC Budget Planning Worksheet—First Year

Item	Cost per Unit	Number of Units	Subtotal	Additional Costs	Est. TOTAL
___ Parent Liaison					
Personnel and Fringe					
ABC books					
Social skills materials: Starter Kits					
Travel for Parent Liaison					
Teacher stipends					
Screening & evaluation materials					
School Operating Costs					
Program Coordinator 75% time					
Postage & shipping					
Printing & photocopying					
Advertising/recruitment					
Administrative costs					
School Share of Joint Operating and Administrative Costs					
Total Cost to School					

(continued)

From Stephanie H. McConaughy, Pam Kay, Julie A. Welkowitz, Kim Hewitt, and Martha D. Fitzgerald (2008). Copyright by The Guilford Press. Permission to photocopy this appendix is granted to purchasers of this book for personal use only (see copyright page for details).

ABC Budget Planning Worksheet— Second Year (and Beyond)

Item	Cost per Unit	Number of Units	Subtotal	Additional Costs	Est. TOTAL
___ Parent Liaison at 2% increase					
Personnel and Fringe					
Travel for Parent Liaison					
Teacher stipends					
School Operating Costs					
Program Coordinator 75% time					
Postage & shipping					
Printing & photocopying					
Administrative costs					
School Share of Joint Operating and Administrative Costs					
Total Cost to School					

How to Find Potential Community Agency Partners

- Contact your local United Way, and ask for the names of parent- and family-oriented not-for-profit organizations in your area.

- If you have a local Education Foundation, share your information on ABC with the director or a board member. To find one in your area, go to the website of the Public Education Network, a national association of 89 local education funds working to improve public school quality in low-income communities nationwide: *www.publiceducation.org*

- The National Dissemination Center for Children with Disabilities (NICHCY) has national and statewide lists of parent support organizations that are open to serving all children, not only those with an identified disability: (800) 695-0285; *www.nichcy.org*

- The National Center for Family & Community Connections with Schools at the Southwest Educational Development Laboratory (SEDL) has information on engaging community organizations in the development of excellent schools: (800) 476-6861; *www.sedl.org/ connections*

- The Federation of Families for Children's Mental Health is a national, family-run organization dedicated exclusively to helping children with mental health needs and their families achieve a better quality of life: (240) 403-1901; *www.ffcmh.org*

- Contact a local coalition of faith-based organizations, or find the nearest coalition at the Interfaith Alliance: (800) 510-0969; *www.interfaithalliance.org*

From Stephanie H. McConaughy, Pam Kay, Julie A. Welkowitz, Kim Hewitt, and Martha D. Fitzgerald (2008). Copyright by The Guilford Press. Permission to photocopy this appendix is granted to purchasers of this book for personal use only (see copyright page for details).

Sample Agreement to Implement the ABC Program between Boxwood Public Schools (BPS) and the Boxwood Family Center

In order to provide the ABC Program to students in Boxwood Public Schools (BPS), the Boxwood Family Center and BPS agree on the following:

Scope of Work: Under contract with BPS, the Boxwood Family Center will deliver the ABC Program in all BPS elementary schools. The BPS Superintendent of Schools and the Executive Director of the Family Center share the responsibility for the success of ABC.

- The Family Center will employ an ABC Program Coordinator who will provide Parent Liaison training and supervision, organize the collection of measures for program evaluation, and work closely with the BPS School Psychologist to ensure the smooth progress of the program in each school.
- The Family Center will employ, train, and supervise Parent Liaisons to facilitate the Parent–Teacher Action Research (PTAR) process, provide support to participating parents, and assist parents in completing measures of progress.
- The Guidance Counselor, as the BPS administrator of the ABC Program, will oversee the selection of students for ABC, meet with participating teachers as needed, assist them in completing measures of student progress, and analyze and interpret the results of program evaluation.

Confidentiality: Each party to this agreement will maintain only those records required for effective management of the program, and store those records in locked hard-copy files or password-protected computer files. All ABC staff and supervisors will receive training in the confidentiality protocol observed by BPS staff. Questions of confidentiality will be resolved between the Program Coordinator and the School Psychologist.

Advisory Committee: An advisory committee will include, at a minimum, representatives of the schools, the Family Center, and the community at large. The advisory committee will receive regular reports of progress from the Program Coordinator and will meet quarterly with the Program Coordinator and the BPS School Psychologist to discuss evaluation results and plan constant improvement. The Advisory Committee will also increase public awareness of the program and help obtain the necessary funding.

Funding: In addition to funding the salaries, wages, benefits, and travel costs of ABC staff, BPS will pay indirect costs of 8% to the Family Center to cover its expenses in administering the program.

From Stephanie H. McConaughy, Pam Kay, Julie A. Welkowitz, Kim Hewitt, and Martha D. Fitzgerald (2008). Copyright by The Guilford Press. Permission to photocopy this appendix is granted to purchasers of this book for personal use only (see copyright page for details).

ABC Brochure

The ABC Program

**Teamwork
for
Success in School**

Achieving

Caring

ABC

Behaving

Contact
your school principal
for more information

( ) -

The ABC Program

Achieving

Caring

ABC

Behaving

The ABC Program

**ACHIEVING
BEHAVING
CARING**

A gift we give
our children

Design by holly geel

From Stephanie H. McConaughy, Pam Kay, Julie A. Welkowitz, Kim Hewitt, and Martha D. Fitzgerald (2008). Copyright by The Guilford Press. Permission to photocopy this appendix is granted to purchasers of this book for personal use only (see copyright page for details).

The ABC Program

Children learn social skills for getting along with each other in their classrooms.

Some children who are very shy and some who are very bold get extra support from their parents and teachers.

The ABC Program helps every child to be successful in school.

ALL children can be achieving, behaving, and caring!

CHILDREN

Teachers meet monthly with parents to do Parent-Teacher Action Research. The Parent Liaison arranges and attends the meetings. Teachers appreciate the chance to learn more about children from their parents.

TEACHERS

Design by holly geel

PARENTS

Parents meet once a month with their child's classroom teacher and their Parent Liaison from the community. Together, the parent-teacher team helps the child to succeed.

Achieving · Caring · Behaving
ABC

2

Recruiting and Training
Parent Liaisons

Questions to Be Addressed in This Chapter
• What is the role of Parent Liaisons?
• How are Parent Liaisons supervised?
• How will we recruit and hire Parent Liaisons?
• What training do Parent Liaisons need?

WHAT IS THE ROLE OF PARENT LIAISONS?

Parent Liaisons play a key role in the ABC Program. Parent Liaisons are community members, usually parents themselves, who are trained to support parents as they work with teachers to meet their children's needs. It is the Parent Liaisons who arrange meetings and guide parents and teachers through the PTAR process. Between meetings, Parent Liaisons talk with parents, and can refer them to other resources in the community, when the parents themselves identify the need for extra support or information.

Ideally, Parent Liaisons are current members of the local community who are good communicators. As indicated in Chapter 1, Parent Liaisons may be employed by a community agency, such as a Parent Information and Resource Center (PIRC), or by a school district. Parent Liaisons who are employed by agencies outside of the school may find it easier to build trust with parents because parents may more easily view them as "one of us." This can be especially effective with parents who may have unpleasant childhood memories of school. When a school district employs Parent Liaisons directly, they should have enough autonomy to act flexibly and effectively with all parents. They should never be used as agents of the school, nor should they be asked to deliver negative news to parents about their children.

Qualities of a Parent Liaison

Good Parent Liaisons are individuals who understand the local community and can bridge the cultures of home and school. They enjoy collaboration and can communicate ideas in clear language that parents and teachers easily understand. They have a special interest in helping parents become more involved in their children's education. They keep an open mind about the many different forms of family structure, patterns of childrearing, and alternative lifestyles. Often, as parents themselves, Parent Liaisons have experienced challenges with their own children's learning and behavior. From their own experiences, Parent Liaisons can model strategies they have learned and can act as supportive peers for other parents. Although Parent Liaisons are *not* advocates, they can help parents learn to advocate effectively for their children.

An essential quality for Parent Liaisons is the ability to listen to and talk with both parents and teachers. Parent Liaisons are open to parents' and teachers' perspectives on children's learning and behavior. They are familiar with the requirements and routines of schools and the expectations teachers have for children. They are also aware of the challenges parents face in raising children. When disagreements or conflicts arise between teachers and parents, Parent Liaisons remain open to different points of view and different ways to solve problems. They keep in mind the many demands on both parents' and teachers' time and energy. Parent Liaisons maintain a positive attitude and persist in trying to find mutually agreeable solutions to promote children's learning and school adjustment.

There are also practical qualities to consider for Parent Liaisons. First, Parent Liaisons need to be well organized and able to manage their time efficiently. They must be able to organize the activities and materials needed to carry out the ABC Program. They must arrive on time and meet deadlines. Many aspects of the position require good management. Parent Liaisons arrange meetings among parents, teachers, and others as needed, collect any necessary forms from parents and teachers, and keep written records of transactions during the program.

Second, Parent Liaisons must have a reasonably flexible schedule that can accommodate the agendas of parents and teachers. Teachers often need to schedule meetings early or late in the school day so as not to miss required instructional time. Parents also have limited times when they can attend meetings due to child care demands, work schedules, or other family requirements.

Third, Parent Liaisons should have access to their own transportation. If they do not own a car or other vehicle, then they will need easy access to other transportation, such as a bus or subway system. Parent Liaisons must be able to travel to meetings, and make home visits to families when necessary.

Appendix 2.1 suggests some qualities to look for in a Parent Liaison. Along with all of the attributes listed, a pleasant and friendly style with people, coupled with a good sense of humor, will go a long way toward making Parent Liaisons' efforts successful.

Roles and Responsibilities of a Parent Liaison

Parent Liaisons have two major roles. One is to support parents in collaborating with teachers about their child's learning and development. Another is to act as an unbiased link between homes, schools, and community agencies. To fulfill these roles, Parent Liaisons have the specific responsibilities outlined in Appendix 2.2.

The first task of a Parent Liaison is to contact parents of children whom the school has identified as possible participants in the ABC Program. (See Chapters 1, 4, and 6 for discussion of the procedures for informing parents about ABC.) The Parent Liaison calls parents, sends invitational letters, and meets with parents to inform them about the program. Once a parent has agreed to participate, the Parent Liaison usually works with that family throughout the duration of the program. The Parent Liaison then organizes and facilitates PTAR team meetings, including arranging dates, times, and places to meet. The Parent Liaison develops a structured agenda for each PTAR meeting that focuses on the team's mutual goals for the child. Between meetings, the Parent Liaison links families with support systems in the community and refers families to other agencies and resources, as needed.

If you plan to ask parents and teachers to complete assessment instruments for your ABC Program evaluation process, Parent Liaisons can be very helpful in ensuring parent participation. (For more information on methods of assessment, see Chapter 5.) Parent Liaisons can distribute questionnaires and help parents to complete them, as needed. The agency or school may expect Parent Liaisons to keep field notes about their work, and to write reports.

HOW ARE PARENT LIAISONS SUPERVISED?

Parent Liaisons should have a supervisor in their employing agency or school system who thoroughly understands all of the roles that they play: organizer and facilitator of PTAR team meetings, expert on the PTAR process, role model and support person for parents, and data collector. Ideally, the supervisor will confer weekly with each Parent Liaison to keep informed on his/her activities, inquire about the progress of PTAR teams, and discuss sensitive issues that may arise. In addition, monthly meetings of all local Parent Liaisons can provide continued training, mutual problem solving, and sharing of ideas. Occasional gatherings with those in similar positions in the wider area can reduce the Parent Liaison's sense of isolation, and lead to new knowledge and skills. Some examples of persons in similar positions are home visitors for early childhood programs, lead parents in Head Start classes, or liaison positions in Title I programs.

The supervisor should inform Parent Liaisons about the limits of confidentiality as established by state and federal laws. Parent Liaisons have the responsibility of maintaining confidentiality about their work with families and teachers, according to policies of the school district and cooperating agencies. They should be sufficiently knowledgeable about the limits of confidentiality when communicating information to families. Teachers should be assured that Parent Liaisons have been trained in confidentiality and that they will not engage in conversations about the child and family outside of PTAR meetings. The supervisor can also explain mandated reporting in cases of possible child abuse and give Parent Liaisons a protocol to follow if they have reasons to suspect that a child may be being abused.

Parent Liaisons may continue to work with certain families during the children's transitions from grade to grade, changes in schools, or moves to a new community. For example, a Parent Liaison might help to set up a PTAR team with a willing teacher in a new school. A Parent Liaison might also work with parents and school staff to suggest the best type of new classroom for a child. If a family moves to a place far from the child's former school, the Parent Liaison might still stay in touch with the family through phone calls and letters during a transitional period. The degree to which Parent Liaisons can work with families during transitions from school to school will be a local decision, largely dependent on funding. The supervisor's role during transitions may be to pave the way through telephone calls or personal contact with the principal in the new school, and to help the Parent Liaisons understand how and when to reduce and remove their support.

HOW WILL WE RECRUIT AND HIRE PARENT LIAISONS?

Administrators can recruit Parent Liaisons in a variety of ways. One approach is to ask school staff for names of individuals who might make effective Parent Liaisons. School principals, special education coordinators, teachers, and special educators can all suggest qualified parents who might be interested in applying for the position. Pupil personnel staff, such as guidance counselors, school psychologists, behavioral specialists, and home–school coordinators may also have good suggestions for Parent Liaisons, based on their frequent contact with families. While a parent–teacher organization might be a good place to look for Parent Liaisons, you want to be sure that the parents in the organization typify the communities and cultures of the parents you are trying to reach. The list below suggests some ways to recruit Parent Liaisons.

WAYS TO RECRUIT PARENT LIAISONS

Ask school administrators, teachers, and special educators for names.

Ask school guidance counselors, school psychologists, behavioral specialists, and other pupil personnel staff for names.

Ask staff at the local Parent–Child Center, Head Start, or other cooperating agency for names.

Ask other Parent Liaisons for names.

Place notices on bulletin boards or send notices to e-mail lists in the school district and cooperating agencies.

Place a notice in school newsletters or newsletters from local family agencies.

Run an advertisement in the local newspaper.

Send ads or notices to the local chapter of Parent-to-Parent, the Federation of Families for Children's Mental Health, and other parent support groups.

School administrators can ask staff at the local PIRC, Head Start program, and other family agencies to suggest candidates for Parent Liaisons. If a local agency, such as the PIRC, is to be the primary employer of the Parent Liaison, administrators at that agency can ask staff for suggestions. If the agency or school district already employs people in positions similar to that of Parent Liaison, administrators can ask them to suggest names of other candidates for the position. In addition to asking people directly for suggestions, you can place notices on bulletin boards in schools or agency buildings, send e-mail notices to staff, and place notices in school or agency newsletters.

Another option for recruiting Parent Liaisons is to run an advertisement in the local newspaper. Appendix 2.3 shows an example of what you might include in an ad. Sending notices to local chapters of family support organizations is yet another way to recruit Parent Liaisons. Parent-to-Parent and the Federation of Families for Children's Mental Health are two well-known national family support organizations. To find such organizations in your area, you can contact The

National Dissemination Center for Children and Youth with Disabilities at *www.nichcy.org*. Their toll-free number is (800) 695-0285. You can also call local parent support groups to ask directly for suggestions of people who might be interested in becoming Parent Liaisons.

The ABC Program brochure from Appendix 1.8 will be helpful when recruiting Parent Liaisons. You might also use the reproducible forms in Appendices 2.1 and 2.2, Suggested Attributes of Parent Liaisons and Roles and Responsibilities of Parent Liaisons. You can adapt these descriptive materials to fit your particular school district or agency.

When you have a list of potential Parent Liaisons, you can send each person a letter inviting him/her to apply for the position, and follow up with a phone call. Appendix 2.4 shows a sample letter that you can adapt for your use.

A sample application form for the Parent Liaison position is shown in Appendix 2.5. You can use this reproducible version and adapt it for your use. When mailing the application form to Parent Liaison candidates, include copies of Suggested Attributes of Parent Liaisons and Roles and Responsibilities of Parent Liaisons, along with a brochure about your ABC Program.

Interviewing and Hiring Parent Liaisons

As in most employment situations, the hiring process begins with an interview. We suggest that representatives of the school and any cooperating agency be present. Those who will be supervising the Parent Liaisons should lead or participate in the interviews. Interviewing Parent Liaisons could be a task for an ABC advisory group, if you have formed one. However, be mindful that a group interview can be intimidating, especially for those who have not been employed recently. One way to alleviate anxiety is to suggest that a Parent Liaison candidate bring a friend to the interview. At the interview, you will want to have extra copies of the ABC brochure and the Parent Liaison job description, including salary and the number of hours to be worked. Make information on professional development and training available. Some of the questions you might ask candidates are given in Appendix 2.6.

In addition to the questions asked during the interview, you might use some scenarios to learn more about the Parent Liaison candidates. Appendix 2.7 includes a few scenarios that are designed to elicit the candidate's views on behavior, parenting, teachers, and the school in general. Pose the situation and then ask the candidate how she/he would react to the situation. Be sure to mention that there are no right or wrong answers.

When the interviews are complete, interviewers should review their notes. Reread the Suggested Attributes of Parent Liaisons and the Roles and Responsibilities of Parent Liaisons. You might ask interviewers to rank each candidate from one to five, with one being the least appropriate and five being most appropriate. Another approach is to ask each interviewer to order the candidates from top to bottom; go around the group and ask each person to argue for their top choice, then next choice, and on through the stack of applications. Consider whether you have enough good candidates to fill your positions, whether they are representative of the cultures, ethnicities, and first languages of the parents you want to reach, and whether you have some work to do to find additional candidates. Make your decisions, and send letters to all candidates.

Once you have selected and hired your Parent Liaisons, introduce them to teachers with a letter that describes the strengths that each Parent Liaison will bring to your school community. Teachers also need to see that the school principal trusts and values the Parent Liaison. This helps build teachers' trust in the Parent Liaisons with whom they will be working. Your letter should give teachers a way to reach their Parent Liaison and his/her supervisor, by telephone or e-mail, and let teachers know that the Parent Liaisons will be contacting them to start the ABC process with parents.

WHAT TRAINING DO PARENT LIAISONS NEED?

After hiring your Parent Liaisons, arrange initial training sessions and send them welcome letters. The welcome letter should include the date, time, and place for their training sessions, and enclose materials to read before the first meeting. Appendix 2.8 shows a sample welcome letter.

In Appendix 2.9 (Kay & Benway, 1998) you will find a case study, written by an ABC Parent Liaison, which new Parent Liaisons have said they enjoyed reading. The case study gives an overview of the job over a 2-year period, and shows what can be accomplished. You can decide whether to send this book to Parent Liaisons before the training begins, or wait to distribute it at the first meeting. Sending the book ahead of time will help Parent Liaisons to become familiar with the structure of the program, particularly the process for PTAR meetings.

Training Sessions

Training for Parent Liaisons follows the chapters in Part II of this book, giving Parent Liaisons time to practice each new skill and discuss the reasoning behind each step. Expect to provide approximately 20 hours of orientation and training before Parent Liaisons begin contacting parents. We found that the initial, day-long training sessions worked well when given 1 week apart, with time between for Parent Liaisons to read their books and talk with others about their new positions. Appendix 2.10 contains outlines for two initial training workshops.

Parent Liaisons as a group should meet with their supervisor monthly; this meeting provides an opportunity to share successes and concerns, and to learn the skills needed for the next step that they will be taking with their teams. In this meeting Parent Liaisons should be given the same opportunities to grow as they are offering to parents in the PTAR meetings. The supervisor should be skilled in listening, quick at capturing ideas on a chart pad in the words of the speakers, and able to recognize leadership as it emerges from the group. Responsibility for leading this meeting can shift gradually from the supervisor to each of the Parent Liaisons in turn.

Besides the group meeting, the supervisor will want to be in touch with each Parent Liaison weekly, and more frequently at first. The supervisor should stay abreast of the progress in all PTAR teams, and can be called upon for problem solving if necessary. From these contacts come the agenda items for the monthly Parent Liaison meetings.

Suggested Attributes of Parent Liaisons

- Interested in promoting good communication and collaboration among families, schools, and community resources.

- Interested in helping parents become involved with their children's education.

- Open-minded and nonjudgmental about various forms of family structure, patterns of child rearing, and alternative lifestyles.

- Experienced in raising a challenging child, or experienced in supporting parents of challenging children.

- Good at listening to and talking with parents and teachers.

- Open to both parents' and teachers' perspectives on children's learning and behavior.

- Knowledgeable about resources and support systems in the community.

- Able to maintain a positive attitude, even when faced with conflict.

- Well organized and able to manage time efficiently.

- A reasonably flexible time schedule.

- Access to own transportation or public transportation systems.

From Stephanie H. McConaughy, Pam Kay, Julie A. Welkowitz, Kim Hewitt, and Martha D. Fitzgerald (2008). Copyright by The Guilford Press. Permission to photocopy this appendix is granted to purchasers of this book for personal use only (see copyright page for details).

Roles and Responsibilities of Parent Liaisons

ROLES OF A PARENT LIAISON

- To act as an unbiased link between homes, schools, and agencies.

- To support parents in collaborating with teachers around their child's social and emotional development and learning.

RESPONSIBILITIES OF A PARENT LIAISON

- To provide information about ABC to families of selected children so that parents can make a fully informed decision about their participation.

- To support and encourage parents in their roles as members of the child's team.

- To organize and facilitate meetings of the Parent–Teacher Action Research (PTAR) teams, and arrange dates, times, and places for the meetings.

- To link families with support systems in the community.

- To know the resources in the community and the process to follow in referring families to these resources if they need them.

- To help parents complete questionnaires as needed.

- To complete reports as required.

- To meet regularly with their supervisors and other Parent Liaisons for continued training, solving problems, and sharing ideas.

- To participate in evaluations of the ABC Program.

- To maintain confidentiality and to understand its limits as established by law.

From Stephanie H. McConaughy, Pam Kay, Julie A. Welkowitz, Kim Hewitt, and Martha D. Fitzgerald (2008). Copyright by The Guilford Press. Permission to photocopy this appendix is granted to purchasers of this book for personal use only (see copyright page for details).

Sample Advertisement for Parent Liaisons

WANTED: PARENT LIAISONS

The Achieving–Behaving–Caring (ABC) Program, a joint venture between [agency] and [school] will be hiring several parents to serve as Parent Liaisons in [area; school district]. The Parent Liaison's role is to support parents and teachers in reaching common goals for children, so that all children will be successful in school. Parent Liaisons must have good organizational, communication, and listening skills, flexible schedules, and their own transportation or access to public transportation systems.

It's as easy as ABC . . .
Call [phone number] to ask for a job description and application.
Visit our website at [website address].
Or send a letter of interest to: [address].

We are an Equal Opportunity/Affirmative Action Employer. Applicants of diverse backgrounds and those with disabilities are encouraged to apply.

From Stephanie H. McConaughy, Pam Kay, Julie A. Welkowitz, Kim Hewitt, and Martha D. Fitzgerald (2008). Copyright by The Guilford Press. Permission to photocopy this appendix is granted to purchasers of this book for personal use only (see copyright page for details).

Sample Letter to Potential Parent Liaisons

[Date]

[Address]

Dear Mr./Mrs./Ms. _____:

Your name was suggested to us as someone who might be an excellent Parent Liaison for the ABC Program in [name of school/school district]. The ABC Program is a cooperative effort between [name of school/school district] and [name of community agency]. The goal of the ABC Program is to ensure that all children will be successful in learning and social and emotional development. The Parent Liaison's role is to support parents and teachers in reaching mutual goals for a particular child. You would play a key role in facilitating partnerships between parents and teachers in team meetings.

Enclosed are two pages describing the suggested qualities and roles and responsibilities of Parent Liaisons, and a brief description of the ABC Program.

If you are interested in applying for the Parent Liaison position, please complete and return the enclosed application form. I will call you next week to check on your interest and to answer any questions you might have about the position. If you would like to talk with me sooner, call [phone number]. Please leave a message on my voicemail if I am not available. You can also contact me at [e-mail address].

I hope you will consider being a Parent Liaison. I look forward to speaking with you soon.

Sincerely,

[Name]

[Title]

Enclosures

[Note: Be sure that the letterhead includes your address and phone number]

From Stephanie H. McConaughy, Pam Kay, Julie A. Welkowitz, Kim Hewitt, and Martha D. Fitzgerald (2008). Copyright by The Guilford Press. Permission to photocopy this appendix is granted to purchasers of this book for personal use only (see copyright page for details).

Parent Liaison Application

Name _____ Social Security Number _____

Mailing address _____
(P.O. Box, House or Apt. Number, Street)

_____
(City/Town, State, ZIP Code)

Street address (if different from above)

_____

Telephone: (daytime) _____ (evening) _____ Best time to call: _____

Are you a veteran of the U.S. Military?
　　[ ] YES: Give date of discharge　_____　[ ] NO

Are you a U.S. citizen or resident alien?
　　[ ] YES
　　[ ] NO →　Can you submit verification of your legal right to work in the United States?
　　　　　　　[ ] YES　　　　[ ] NO

If you have a résumé, please attach it to this application. If not, please answer the question below and provide your employment record on the back of this page.

EDUCATION:
Please circle the highest grade completed:
　　8　9　10　11　12　College:　1　2　3　4　Graduate degree:

I agree to allow [agency or school district] to conduct a criminal record check of my background.

Signed:

PLEASE TURN TO THE OTHER SIDE

From Stephanie H. McConaughy, Pam Kay, Julie A. Welkowitz, Kim Hewitt, and Martha D. Fitzgerald (2008). Copyright by The Guilford Press. Permission to photocopy this appendix is granted to purchasers of this book for personal use only (see copyright page for details).

45

Please write one or two sentences in answer to the questions below:

1) Why are you interested in this position?

2) In your opinion, what leads to strong partnerships between parents and teachers?

3) In your opinion, what are the most important "social skills" for children to learn in the first and second grades?

[You do not have to complete this section if you attach a résumé.]

EMPLOYMENT RECORD: (Please list most recent employment first.)

Employer	Dates of Employment	Address	Telephone

Reference Contact Name and Phone Number

[Please use an extra sheet of paper if needed.]

Questions for a Parent Liaison Interview

- What interested you in the position of Parent Liaison?

- What background do you have that suggests that you would be good for the position?

- What are your strengths? Your weaknesses?

- How flexible is your schedule? (Parent Liaisons must be available to meet the needs of both parents and teachers.)

- When would you be able to start? (If your training days are already scheduled, ask if those days will work for the candidate.)

From Stephanie H. McConaughy, Pam Kay, Julie A. Welkowitz, Kim Hewitt, and Martha D. Fitzgerald (2008). Copyright by The Guilford Press. Permission to photocopy this appendix is granted to purchasers of this book for personal use only (see copyright page for details).

APPENDIX 2.7

Scenarios for a Parent Liaison Interview

1) You are in a crowded grocery store and find a mother and child blocking your path. The child is on the floor, crying, writhing around, and yelling "No!" You look up, and the mother's eyes meet yours. What are you thinking, and what might you say?

2) Your neighbor gets her mail from the mailbox, and stops to talk with you on her way in the door. "Another letter from the school!" she exclaims. "What could my son have done wrong this time? I wish . . . just once . . . that they would tell me that he has done something right!" What are you thinking, and what might you say?

3) A friend has just become a substitute teacher in the local elementary school. When she comes home from her first day on the job, she calls you to vent her feelings. "These children need help," she says. "They could not sit and read quietly to themselves for 10 minutes! One or two tried, but the others were constantly out of their seats. They could not choose books from the reading table by themselves. One boy just put his head down on the desk and fell asleep." What are you thinking, and what might you say?

From Stephanie H. McConaughy, Pam Kay, Julie A. Welkowitz, Kim Hewitt, and Martha D. Fitzgerald (2008). Copyright by The Guilford Press. Permission to photocopy this appendix is granted to purchasers of this book for personal use only (see copyright page for details).

Welcome Letter to Newly Hired Parent Liaisons

[Date]

[Address]

Dear Ms./Mrs./Mr. _____ :

Congratulations on your new position as Parent Liaison, and welcome to the ABC Program!

I look forward to our first meeting on [date]. The meeting will be at [place] and directions are enclosed. The meeting will run from [A.M.] to [P.M.] Lunch will be provided.

At this first meeting, you will learn more about the ABC Program and your role and responsibilities as Parent Liaison. You will also meet other Parent Liaisons. We will be doing hands-on activities that will help with learning some of the skills you will need as Parent Liaisons. A special focus will be on how to introduce the ABC Program to parents. We will also share some of the common joys and challenges of the children, parents, and teachers who have participated in the program.

The Essential Role of Parent Liaisons is a case study that was written by an ABC Parent Liaison, Carol Benway, to describe what Parent Liaisons do in their work with families and school staff. The book, *Collaborating with Parents for Early School Success: The Achieving–Behaving–Caring Program,* describes the ABC Program. Part II of the book is a how-to guide that you will use throughout the program. Please look over the book before our meeting. We will talk more about all of these materials during the meeting.

If you have any concerns about the first meeting, including travel or weather conditions, please call [contact person's name] at the [agency name] at [phone number]. You can also call me if you have any questions or concerns you would like to discuss before our meeting at [phone number]. I look forward to meeting and working with you.

Sincerely,

Supervisor
ABC Program
[Agency School]

From Stephanie H. McConaughy, Pam Kay, Julie A. Welkowitz, Kim Hewitt, and Martha D. Fitzgerald (2008). Copyright by The Guilford Press. Permission to photocopy this appendix is granted to purchasers of this book for personal use only (see copyright page for details).

The Essential Role of Parent Liaisons

Carol Benway

TOM AND KIMBERLY

Tom lives with his mom, Kimberly. She is a single parent. They live on a back road in a very rural New England town. Kimberly works full time as a file maintenance clerk, in a town 40 miles away. This means that she and Tom have to wake up very early in the morning. Tom is dropped off at daycare, 10 miles from home, at approximately 5:30 A.M., so that Kimberly can arrive to work before 7:00 A.M. Tom then rides the bus from daycare to school. After school, he rides a different bus to his home, where Kimberly meets him every day. Kimberly has a second, evening job, selling cosmetics. She brings Tom along with her.

Kimberly is very proud of the fact that she has independently raised Tom since his birth. She acknowledges that he needs to become more independent. Tom loves and gets along well with other people. Being an only child, Tom is used to having all of his mom's attention, and he does whatever he can to get it. He interrupts her, and when this doesn't work, he has temper tantrums, sometimes banging his head on the floor.

Kimberly and Tom do not have any close friends or relatives, and there really isn't a lot of spare time for her and Tom to socialize with others. One thing that they do enjoy is taking Tae Kwon Do classes together, two evenings a week.

PARENT LIAISON ROLE

After recruiting a parent and before the initial Parent–Teacher Action Research (PTAR) meeting, Parent Liaisons set up a home visit with the parents of families in the target group, at their convenience. The visit with Tom and Kimberly had a few different purposes. First, it bonds the Parent Liaison with the family. I tried to find as many ways as I could, during the course of the visit, to identify with the family and get them comfortable. I did this by sharing a little bit about myself that might be pertinent, but being sure not to overdo it. I needed to always remember that I was there to learn about the family. One important way to make them feel comfortable was to not overdress. I needed to remember that this was a rural community, so casual dress was best. I personally did my home visits wearing jeans and a sweater or T-shirt.

The second reason for my visit was to ask some questions about the family background and strengths of the family. This was meant to help me better understand the family. Of course, I was sure to let parents know they were always free to skip any questions they were not comfortable answering.

In Tom's case, this initial meeting with Kimberly was slightly difficult. Kimberly is a very quiet, soft-spoken person. She only answered me when I asked questions. She really wasn't comfortable enough to carry on very much of a conversation. She very briefly answered the family background questions and told me only exactly what she felt I should know—not much more. I was able to find out that Kimberly was a single parent, but I wasn't too sure about Tom's dad. Kimberly did not offer to elaborate. She told me that Tom has only seen him a few times in his life. Apparently, there is no real communication with the dad at all, and Kimberly seems to accept this.

(continued)

From a presentation made by Pam Kay and Carol Benway at *Building on Family Strengths*, the conference of the Research and Training Center on Family Support and Children's Mental Health, Portland, Oregon, April 1998. Reprinted with permission in Stephanie H. McConaughy, Pam Kay, Julie A. Welkowitz, Kim Hewitt, and Martha D. Fitzgerald (2008). Copyright by The Guilford Press. Permission to photocopy this appendix is granted to purchasers of this book for personal use only (see copyright page for details).

The third reason for the visit was to answer any questions the parent may have about the project and to explain what we would be doing in our PTAR meetings. I brought along a copy of the Making Action Plans (MAPs) process and the questions we would use at our first meeting. I left these materials with Kimberly and asked her to think about the questions, if she had time, before our meeting. I also needed to find out from her the best time to meet, and to assure her that we would be meeting in a neutral place, outside of the school, so everyone would feel comfortable.

At the same time that I was doing my initial family visit, I was also trying to connect with the first-grade teacher who would be involved. Of course, this could be more difficult to arrange because I did not have home phone numbers for teachers. This meant calling the teacher at school and most likely leaving a message to call me back. Since this was early fall, and school was just under way, teachers were really busy. It often took several messages before reaching the teacher. Some teachers were just as nervous as the parents about the PTAR meetings and avoided returning phone calls. For some, it meant my showing up in the classroom. Tom's teacher, Susan, was one of the more difficult teachers to contact. I did end up knocking on her classroom door. But this turned out to be fine. She was very cooperative once I caught up with her, and we found a mutual time and date when we could meet.

The first- and second-grade teachers were also beginning a social skills curriculum as part of the requirement of the ABC project. At this particular school, Susan and the second-grade teacher, Donna, chose to do Skillstreaming, which they team-taught with the first- and second-grade together. Since the two teachers were already friends, they did a really good job role playing, which is what this curriculum entails. Although it was really difficult at the beginning, they soon became quite comfortable with it. And now, as a matter of fact, they are going to continue teaching Skillstreaming after the project ends, and they are expanding it to include the third grade.

Once the meeting time and date had been coordinated, the Parent Liaison's next task was to find a neutral meeting place—a place where everyone would be comfortable, hopefully empowering the parent and reducing some of the "phobias" related to school. This neutral place could be hard to find, especially in a rural area. The town that Kimberly and Tom lived in, for example, has no real meeting place, except the town school. There is no public library, recreational buildings, or banks. The town doesn't even have its own post office. All major activities, including town meetings, take place at the school. So this meant looking to two neighboring towns, both of which also had limited meeting spaces. We were lucky to find a comfortable meeting room at the local bank, which we used for nearly all of our meetings. We also used the local library.

PARENT–TEACHER ACTION RESEARCH (PTAR) MEETINGS

So, with the home visit done, connecting with the teacher done, meeting place found, we were then ready to begin our PTAR meetings. As a Parent Liaison, I facilitated these meetings, following the MAPs process. Even though we had explained ahead of time that we would be following this process, some teachers, being familiar with their usual parent–teacher conferences, came to the PTAR meetings with their own agenda. And, again, some teachers came to the meetings as nervous as the parents. This first meeting was important in that it would surely set the tone for the meetings that would follow. Susan tended to be a very hard-shelled teacher, with quite a "tough-guy" image. I was anxious about this, especially with Kimberly being a quiet, reserved person. I thought I was going to have to emphasize the rules of "parents speak first" and "saying things as positively as possible."

(continued)

The first meeting went really well. Following the MAPs process, Kimberly and Susan described Tom as being very lovable, liking people, and able to express himself well. They both described him as being impatient and not liking to share or being told what to do. His friends were mainly those he played with at school and daycare. Both had dreams that Tom would learn how to read better by the end of the first grade and both saw him as going on to college, after completing high school. When we talked about fears, Kimberly brought up that she was afraid that Tom might be sexually molested because he is such a nice-looking child. She also worried that something might happen to her and Tom would end up alone. These fears seemed to really concern Kimberly. She expressed these same fears several times during the school year.

After going through the MAPs process, Kimberly and Susan set two goals for working with Tom. These two goals were (1) to develop his listening skills and patience, and (2) to provide socialization opportunities outside of school. We also decided, at the end of the meeting, that Kimberly and Susan would take notes, and keep track of the progress made. Both thought they should keep journals until our second meeting.

In the second meeting, Kimberly felt that the journal idea wasn't working well for her, so we came up with a list of questions for her to ask Tom that would help her to learn more about his school day.

MAKING PROGRESS

As the meetings progressed through the school year, Kimberly admitted that she really didn't know a lot about parenting and had no real role models. She started to realize that a lot of Tom's impatience came from the fact that she catered to him maybe a little too much. She admitted, during one of our PTAR meetings, that she had done almost everything for him, when he wanted her to, always at a second's notice. Maybe it was time to let him grow up a little; he could pour his own drinks at home, get his own snack, put away his own boots and shoes. Maybe she should enforce a more regular bedtime. Instead of stopping whatever it was she was doing and immediately getting whatever Tom wanted, Kimberly began making him wait. She also gave him simple chores to do, like making his bed and setting the table. She made Tom do simple tasks for himself, like getting his coat and his snack. She no longer made herself available to him at an instant's notice.

At this point, I gave Kimberly the book, *Raising Your Spirited Child* (Kurcinka, 1991) to read. As Kimberly started to change her attitude and make Tom do more for himself, Tom began to misbehave more often. He would keep repeating himself over and over, whine, and fuss. Kimberly would send him to his room to calm down. He would sometimes have temper tantrums, banging his head on the floor or wall. It was really hard for Kimberly to follow through when Tom behaved this way. She really disliked seeing him upset, and she had anxiety attacks whenever she herself got upset. At this point, I gave her the 800 phone number of the Parent's Assistance Line, and gave her reading material on how to deal with an angry child and how to deal with temper tantrums. Susan provided her with praise and encouragement. She helped, also, by sharing what worked for her as a parent, much to our surprise. Susan further encouraged Kimberly by suggesting that she follow the Skillstreaming steps for the skill of asking for help at home. She suggested that Kimberly remind Tom to ask himself the question, "Can I do this alone?"

Susan also reinforced independence at school. Tom was constantly asking for help with work. Susan would make him go back to his desk and try the work on his own. Susan also noticed how Tom would act out during classroom activities when he wanted attention. He would make noises, tap his pencil on the table, and shout out. Susan began using time outs when Tom acted out and praise when he behaved appropriately during class time.

(continued)

52

As a result of the combined efforts of Kimberly and Susan, Tom became much more responsible, both in the classroom, as well as at home. At home, he was helping himself with snacks and also learned to tie his own shoes. At school, he was waiting for help more patiently, completing more of his independent work by himself, and was able to share a little more easily with his classmates.

KEEPING IN TOUCH

A key responsibility of Parent Liaisons is to provide follow-up to monthly PTAR meetings. I did this by making phone calls at least once a month to each parent. I also provided my phone number to all my families, in case they wanted to call me at any time. I constantly encouraged the parents to keep in touch with the teacher also, although I don't think Kimberly ever attempted to contact Susan.

Parent Liaisons make two home visits during the school year, one in the fall, and again in the spring, to fill out parent questionnaires, and also to find out how things are going in the home. It was during the fall home visit that I really saw how much Tom "controlled" the household. He had to have my full attention while Kimberly was filling out her questionnaires. He showed me his math papers and how he did the math, got out some holiday decorations to show me, and then he took the questionnaire envelope and tore the stamp off it. Kimberly tried several times to make him sit still, but he just went from one thing to another, not listening to her at all. I could really see the attention-getting tactics, and I could also see how Kimberly was worried that he might get too upset if she intervened.

When I made the second home visit in the spring, I encountered a much different atmosphere. Tom had a friend visiting. They were outside playing when I arrived. After about a half hour, the two of them came inside. Tom took out a Slim Jim, and he shared it with his friend. He then asked to watch television. Kimberly remarked, "No, remember last night." Tom responded, "Oh yeah, I forgot." That was the end of the conversation. Tom did not make a scene or a fuss at all. I was impressed. Tom and his friend then went back outside to play. Kimberly was able to complete the questionnaires almost without interruption.

At the end of the school year, I wrapped up my PTAR meetings with a transition meeting involving the second-grade teacher. This meeting was meant to introduce the new teacher to the child, as well as to acquaint the parent with the new teacher. Since the first and second grades worked very closely together, Donna already knew Tom, so this meeting was more for Donna and Kimberly to meet and get acquainted. At this meeting, we again described Tom, adding anything new we had learned through the school year, and we discussed the progress made with the goals that had been set in our initial PTAR meeting. Both Kimberly and Susan felt that Tom had shown a big improvement with his listening skills and patience. He still had some bad days, but overall, there had been a big change. Tom also had more opportunities to socialize outside of school over the past few months. He was visiting with his friends occasionally, both at his home as well as at theirs, and he had also joined the local baseball team.

THE SECOND YEAR

I was very nervous about working with Donna. I worried that she might bring a negative attitude into our PTAR meetings with Kimberly. But this wasn't the case at all. Donna was very supportive of Kimberly, saying, "We have to remember that he is just a little boy," "Look at all the progress he has made in the past year," and "You should be very proud as a parent."

(continued)

53

Kimberly and Donna's goals for working with Tom were to improve his reading skills and to make good choices in the classroom as well as outside the classroom. To help keep track of the progress, they agreed that Donna would send a note home daily about Tom's day. There would be a sticker on the note if he had a great day, just a note if he had an all right day, and a note telling what went wrong if he had a bad day. The first month, the notes were consistent. Shortly after the second PTAR meeting, Donna decided to stop sending home the notes. At our third PTAR meeting, Kimberly asked Donna why the notes weren't being sent home. Donna responded, "I didn't think they were useful, since I didn't get any feedback from you." Kimberly replied, "I didn't think you wanted feedback, since this was already discussed in our meeting." She went on to say that she really liked the notes. If the note was bad, Tom would lose the privilege of watching cartoons for the night. If it was very bad, he had to spend time in his room. If she did not see notes, she assumed he had a good day. It was a wonderful surprise for me to see Kimberly be assertive and address this issue herself. It was also great to see this communication problem solved through our team meetings.

THE PARENT LIAISON AS A RESEARCHER

In addition to being a facilitator at the PTAR meetings, and being a link for the parents, Parent Liaisons were expected to keep detailed notes on each team meeting and to regularly submit these notes to the university research team. These notes included the PTAR meeting notes, as well as field notes about our own observations and impressions of the team's progress. All phone calls and conversations with teachers and parents were documented.

Parent Liaisons also met with the university research team on a monthly basis. We used this time to share our team's progress with each other, as well as to enlist support and feedback from the research team and other Parent Liaisons if needed.

As you can tell, I was extremely pleased with the success of the PTAR teams involving Kimberly, Susan, and Donna. As the Parent Liaison, I helped to close the gap between home and school. As shy and quiet as Kimberly was, she may have never made the effort to meet with Tom's teachers alone. But she wanted Tom to be successful, and this was of such importance to her that she made that effort. During the team meetings, Kimberly, Susan, and Donna learned what works best for Tom, and how he learns best. As a result of their sharing, caring, and communicating together, Tom made many gains during his first- and second-grade years, both socially and academically. I was sure that this positive experience encouraged Kimberly to continue communicating regularly with Tom's teachers in the future. This ongoing communication would surely have a positive impact on Tom's life, both at school and at home, for years to come.

Outline for Preliminary Workshops for Parent Liaisons

WORKSHOP 1 ON THE ABC PROGRAM

Date:

Time: From _____9:30_____ To _____2:00_____

Place:

Hour:	Content:	ABC Book Chapter:
9:30	Introductions	
9:45	What makes ABC work? • Social Skills Lessons • Parent Liaisons • Parent–Teacher Action Research (PTAR)	Introduction
10:15	Getting started as a Parent Liaison • Role play invitational meeting	Chapters 6 and 7
11:00	MAPs—Making Action Plans • Break into trios for role play with coaching from trainers	Chapter 8
12:00	Lunch	
12:45	Getting from MAPs to mutual goals • Why do the parent and teacher need mutual goals? • What is a good goal? • Suppose the parent and teacher cannot agree? • How do the goals drive the action research process?	Chapter 8
1:30	Homework: Role play the invitational meeting with a friend	
1:35	Questions	
1:50	Evaluation • What was the most useful part of today for you? • What should be done differently the next time this workshop is given? • What is your most pressing question?	

(continued)

From Stephanie H. McConaughy, Pam Kay, Julie A. Welkowitz, Kim Hewitt, and Martha D. Fitzgerald (2008). Copyright by The Guilford Press. Permission to photocopy this appendix is granted to purchasers of this book for personal use only (see copyright page for details).

WORKSHOP 2 ON THE ABC PROGRAM

Date:

Time: From _____9:30_____ To _____2:00_____

Place:

Hour:	Content:	ABC Book Chapter:
9:30	Reflections on homework and pressing questions	
10:00	The importance of the Action Research Cycle	Chapters 9, 10, 11
	• Keeps the focus on the needs of the child	
	• Encourages both teacher and parent to observe and reflect on the child's behavior	
	• Builds mutual commitment to the action plan	
	• Usually results in crucial changes in practice for both the parent and the teacher	
11:00	Moving from goals into data collection: Role play in trios	
11:45	The questions that make the cycle go 'round	Chapter 12
12:00	Lunch	
12:45	Hands-on experience with the cycle	
	• Each Parent Liaison takes a turn role playing one step on the cycle, with trainers as parent and teacher; others observe and ask questions	
1:30	The next steps in training:	
	• Scheduling the next Parent Liaison meeting	
1:35	Questions	
1:50	Evaluation	
	• What was the most useful part of today for you?	
	• What should be done differently the next time this workshop is given?	
	• What is your most pressing question?	

3

Selecting and Implementing
a Social Skills Curriculum

```
Questions to Be Addressed in This Chapter
• What are the essential features of a successful social skills curriculum?
• How will we choose a social skills curriculum?
• How will we prepare to implement a social skills curriculum?
• How will we teach social skills in our classrooms?
```

WHAT ARE THE ESSENTIAL FEATURES
OF A SUCCESSFUL SOCIAL SKILLS CURRICULUM?

Many educators and behavioral specialists feel that teaching social skills in schools can be a powerful educational strategy. What does the research suggest educators do to ensure the success of social skills instruction? Several recommendations are outlined below for administrators and teachers to consider when developing a social skills curriculum.

```
HOW TO MAKE SOCIAL SKILLS INSTRUCTION MORE SUCCESSFUL

Begin social skills instruction early, before children develop hard-core deficits.

Make social skills instruction part of the general education curriculum.

Teach social skills regularly and frequently, throughout the school year.

Send materials home to parents on a regular basis.

Match instruction to types of social skills deficits exhibited by students.

Add small-group instruction and individual contracting for students with
    intensive needs.

Use the same social skills curriculum across settings.
```

Begin Social Skills Instruction Early

Ideally, social skills instruction should be a routine part of the early elementary curriculum. Based on a large body of research, Kazdin (1995) and other behavioral experts have argued that interventions to reduce antisocial behavior must begin before age 8 to produce real changes in children's behavior. After age 8, most interventions merely manage rather than remediate antisocial behavior. Teaching social skills in the early grades as replacement behaviors for learned antisocial behaviors can be an effective way to prevent more severe behavior later (Kamps & Kay, 2002). Although many students may have received social skills instruction in preschool, teachers in kindergarten, first, and second grade know they have a responsibility to help students learn more sophisticated social coping skills that they will need in school.

Make Social Skills Instruction Part of the General Education Curriculum

Teaching social skills to all children in a classroom helps to create a sense of community among students—a sense that they belong in school. Social skills instruction provides a language for students and teachers in communicating about social interactions and social expectations. The general education environment also offers more opportunities for children to practice social skills in natural settings. This promotes generalization of social skills across settings, which is an essential feature of social learning. When we teach social skills only in pull-out programs, students have more difficulty transferring their skills to other important settings (Gresham et al., 2001; DuPaul & Eckert, 1994). Giving social skills instruction to all students in the general education curriculum is preferable to providing pull-out programs for selected students without general education instruction.

Teach Social Skills Regularly and Frequently throughout the School Year

In their review of social skills programs, Alberg, Petry, and Eller (1994) found that the optimal schedule for teaching classroom-based social skills is two 15- to 20-minute lessons a week, continuing throughout the academic year. This assumes, however, that teachers continue with incidental teaching and appropriate reinforcement daily. Many published programs indicate the desired frequency and sequence for their lessons, which should be observed. Research on the success of specific programs is based on a given level of effort, and administrators should not expect similar results with less time or frequency. As Greenberg et al. (2003), noted, "In most cases, short-term preventive interventions produce short-lived results" (p. 470).

Send Materials Home to Parents on a Regular Basis

With an increase in the demands of present-day living, parents may have little time to teach social skills to their children. Many feel guilty that they cannot do more, and are relieved to hear that their children will have social skills lessons in school. Still, parents can contribute to their children's learning by supporting at home the social skills that children learn in school. To do this, parents need information. Before beginning a social skills program, administrators should introduce it to the parents. (If some parents have been involved in choosing the program, you might ask them to speak at a parent orientation meeting.) Explain the goals of the program to parents and show them some of the materials. Reassure parents that the school is there to reinforce the parents' efforts, not to supplant them. If there are parent volunteers in the classroom, you can involve them directly in the social skills lessons. This will help spread the word about the curriculum in the neighborhood. When the program is under way, teachers can assign homework that requires children to interact with parents or other family members. Teachers can inform parents when the class starts to work on a new skill. Several published social skills programs provide teachers with prepared materials to use with parents, such as positive notes when a child has demonstrated a new skill. The more that parents are aware of the social skills being taught at school, the more likely they are to reinforce those skills in the home environment.

Match Instruction to Types of Social Skills Deficits

To be most effective, teachers should gear instruction to students' specific types of social skills deficits. Gresham and colleagues distinguish between three types of social skills deficits (Gresham, 1981, 1998; Gresham et al., 2001). *Acquisition deficits* occur when a student lacks the knowledge to execute a particular social skill or fails to understand which social behaviors are appropriate in particular situations. *Performance deficits* occur when a student knows how to perform a social skill, but fails to do so at acceptable levels in given situations. Gresham calls acquisition deficits *can't do deficits* and performance deficits *won't do deficits. Fluency deficits* occur when a student knows how to perform a social skill, and wants to perform the skill, but is awkward or unpolished in doing so. We call fluency deficits *hard-to-do deficits.* Teachers need to consider the types of deficits their students exhibit when deciding how to teach social skills.

It is also important to consider whether students exhibit competing problem behaviors that interfere with performing a social skill. For example, students who are quick to have temper tantrums may have a hard time learning the social skills of *waiting your turn* or *sharing materials with another student.* Students with competing problem behaviors may need negative reinforcement (removal of a positive outcome for an undesired behavior) or negative consequences (application of a negative outcome for an undesired behavior) to decrease the problem behavior, along with appropriate instruction for the desired social skill.

Add Small-Group Instruction and Individual Contracting for Students with Intensive Needs

Students with severe aggressive or antisocial behavior will probably need more intensive interventions to supplement social skills instruction in the general education classroom. Interventions can include small-group instruction with peers and individual contracting. Usually teachers call on other school staff, such as guidance counselors and school psychologists, to carry out more intensive interventions. Individual contracting can be especially effective with students who exhibit aggressive or antisocial behavior when the students themselves are involved in establishing the goals and reward structure of the contracts. *The Tough Kid Book*, by Rhode, Jenson, and Reavis (1992), is one resource with many good practical suggestions for contracts and other school-based interventions for students with aggressive or antisocial behavior.

We do not recommend grouping students with aggressive or antisocial behavior together for instruction because the group can reinforce undesired behavior. Dishion, McCord, and Poulin (1999) reported that small-group interventions with antisocial adolescents produced *increases* in substance use, delinquency, and violent behavior. They described the phenomenon as *deviancy training*. Small-group instruction can be more effective when positive peer role models are included in the group.

Students who are anxious, depressed, or withdrawn may also need more intensive interventions to supplement whole-class social skills instruction. Sometimes teachers overlook the needs of students with these internalizing problems because they do not disrupt classroom routines. Individual contracting can be effective with students who exhibit internalizing behaviors when the contract includes rewards or incentives for social interactions. Small-group instruction with positive peer role models can also give these students opportunities to rehearse and practice new social skills in a safe environment before trying them out in large-group situations.

Use the Same Social Skills Curriculum across Settings

Whenever you couple intensive interventions with a whole-class social skills curriculum, you will want consistency across the two forms of instruction. This means using the same social skills language and similar lesson structures in the small-group and in the general education setting. For example, a teacher might cover a core set of social skills with an entire class, and the guidance counselor or a school psychologist might teach additional skills to a small group of students at another time. Teachers could form small groups of students to rehearse and practice skills taught to the entire class. When a student needs an individual behavioral contract, that contract should use the same language used in the classroom to describe desired social skills. Consistency across whole-class instruction and more intensive interventions will help students generalize skills across multiple settings.

HOW WILL WE CHOOSE A SOCIAL SKILLS CURRICULUM?

Teachers have always taught social skills informally by using *teachable moments* to remind students of desired social behavior and to praise students for appropriate behavior. However, adopting a formal social skills curriculum school-wide or across several grade levels provides a common structure for teaching specific skills. The structure also makes it easier to ensure that other school staff (e.g., paraeducators, librarians, music, art, and physical education teachers) and nonteaching staff (e.g., custodians, lunchroom personnel, and school bus drivers) have the information and the language that they need to reinforce the skills that students are learning in the classrooms.

Teachers and administrators may choose to create their own social skills curriculum to match the needs of their student body and the social values of their community. This will require much thought, effort, and coordination by school staff. An essential element in any home-grown program should be measuring and assessing the results. See Chapter 5 for more information on evaluating the effectiveness of programs.

Another approach is to choose a curriculum from among the many programs offered by commercial publishers and researchers. Appendix 3.1 lists examples of research-based elementary school social skills programs available from commercial publishers. Teachers and administrators should consult their school psychologists, guidance counselors, and social workers, and review catalogs from publishing companies for descriptions of programs. You will want to verify that the developers have demonstrated that the programs worked with school populations such as yours. Among other sources, the Substance Abuse and Mental Health Services Administration (SAMHSA) maintains a website which describes research-based programs at *www.model-programs.samhsa.gov*. SAMHSA lists programs that social scientists have reviewed and categorized as *promising, effective,* and *model,* meeting stringent requirements for each category. (See Appendix 3.2 for a list of other resources found online.)

Most commercially available social skills programs have a predefined set of social skills and lesson plans for teaching the skills. Some programs have a built-in process for assessing student needs and grouping students for instruction. *Skillstreaming the Elementary School Child* (McGinnis & Goldstein, 1997) is an example of a program that breaks each skill down into manageable segments. To match social skills instruction to student needs, the program provides checklists for teachers, parents, and students themselves to rate students' proficiency on each of 60 skills. *Skillstreaming* organizes skills into five content areas for instruction: classroom-survival skills, friendship-making skills, dealing with feelings, alternatives to aggression, and dealing with stress. Table 3.1 lists *Skillstreaming's* 60 skills and content areas. The *Skillstreaming* programs for preschoolers, elementary students, and adolescents all include lessons, instructional materials, and information to give to parents.

The Tough Kid Social Skills Book (Sheridan, 1995) is another example of a commercial program that has a predefined set of social skills, lesson plans, and built-in assessment procedures. This program outlines lesson plans for 11 social skills, grouped into three areas: social entry (body basics/starting a conversation, joining in, recognizing and expressing feelings), maintaining interactions (having a conversation, playing cooperatively), and problem solving (solving problems, using self-control, solving arguments, dealing with teasing, dealing with being left out, and accepting "no"). The program provides a system for assessing individual students' social skill needs or deficits. The assessment includes a general screening procedure, a teacher checklist for rating a student's proficiency on the 11 social skills, formats for conducting teacher and parent interviews about a student's social skills, and a system for directly observing a student's social behavior in school.

Choosing a social skills curriculum that is well suited to students' needs and teachers' styles can be challenging for several reasons: (1) no one social skills program is best for all students; (2) teachers will need time in the school day for planning and teaching social skills, and time for training; (3) the program may require additional resources and support from other school staff; and (4) school staff will need to communicate effectively with families to maximize the program's benefit.

If administrators and teachers use a commercially available program, they will need to decide which program best fits their particular school environment. To provide a general strategy for such decision making, Figure 3.1 outlines five steps for assessing needs and reviewing social skills programs. The next sections discuss each of the five decision-making steps in detail.

Step 1. Identify Social Skills That Are Important in Your Classrooms

There are many different social skills that could be included in a general education curriculum, and many ways of grouping them. In general, your social skills program should include *communication* skills (e.g., listening, using a quiet voice, apologizing, seeking help), *interpersonal* skills (e.g., making friends, dealing with authority figures, sharing, cooperating), *personal* skills (e.g., dealing with feelings, setting goals, being self-aware), and *response* skills (e.g., following directions, dealing with feedback, resolving conflicts, controlling aggression). As a first step toward

TABLE 3.1. The Skillstreaming Curriculum for Elementary Students

Group I: Classroom Survival Skills

 1. Listening
 2. Asking for Help
 3. Saying Thank You
 4. Bringing Materials to Class
 5. Following Instructions
 6. Completing Assignments
 7. Contributing to Discussions
 8. Offering Help to an Adult
 9. Asking a Question
10. Ignoring Distractions
11. Making Corrections
12. Deciding on Something to Do
13. Setting a Goal

Group II: Friendship-Making Skills

14. Introducing Yourself
15. Beginning a Conversation
16. Ending a Conversation
17. Joining In
18. Playing a Game
19. Asking a Favor
20. Offering Help to a Classmate
21. Giving a Compliment
22. Accepting a Compliment
23. Suggesting an Activity
24. Sharing
25. Apologizing

Group III: Skills for Dealing with Feelings

26. Knowing Your Feelings
27. Expressing Your Feelings
28. Recognizing Another's Feelings
29. Showing Understanding of Another's Feelings
30. Expressing Concern for Another
31. Dealing with Your Anger
32. Dealing with Another's Anger
33. Expressing Affection
34. Dealing with Fear
35. Rewarding Yourself

Group IV: Skill Alternatives to Aggression

36. Using Self-Control
37. Asking Permission
38. Responding to Teasing
39. Avoiding Trouble
40. Staying Out of Fights
41. Problem Solving
42. Accepting Consequences
43. Dealing with an Accusation
44. Negotiating

Group V: Skills for Dealing with Stress

45. Dealing with Boredom
46. Deciding What Caused a Problem
47. Making a Complaint
48. Answering a Complaint
49. Dealing with Losing
50. Being a Good Sport
51. Dealing with Being Left Out
52. Dealing with Embarrassment
53. Reacting to Failure
54. Accepting No
55. Saying No
56. Relaxing
57. Dealing with Group Pressure
58. Dealing with Wanting Something That Isn't Yours
59. Making a Decision
60. Being Honest

Note. From McGinnis and Goldstein (1997). Reprinted with permission from Research Press.

choosing a curriculum, teachers must decide which social skills are most important and which skills are lacking in their particular group of students.

Appendix 3.3 illustrates a Social Skills Needs Checklist, which you can copy for use with your teaching staff. In the first column, teachers rate each skill according to its importance in their own classrooms, with *critical* skills rated 1, *very important* skills rated 2, and those that are some- what *important* rated 3. In the second column, teachers estimate the number of students in their classrooms who have a deficit in critical skills; in the third column, they list the number of stu- dents with deficits in very important skills. At the bottom of the checklist, teachers can indicate other criteria that are important to them when choosing a social skills curriculum.

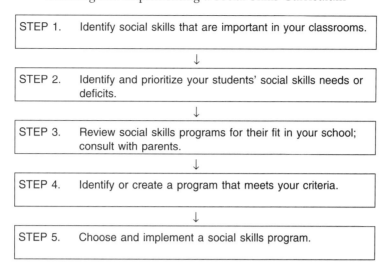

STEP 1.	Identify social skills that are important in your classrooms.
STEP 2.	Identify and prioritize your students' social skills needs or deficits.
STEP 3.	Review social skills programs for their fit in your school; consult with parents.
STEP 4.	Identify or create a program that meets your criteria.
STEP 5.	Choose and implement a social skills program.

FIGURE 3.1. Steps in choosing a social skills curriculum.

Step 2. Identify and Prioritize Your Students' Needs or Deficits

As a final step in using the Social Skills Needs Checklist, administrators can ask teachers if they want to reprioritize their lists of skills according to the numbers of students who need training in that skill. At this point, you may want to engage teachers in a discussion of their priorities, or simply collect the ratings sheets and have them tabulated prior to a discussion. You will need to use those results in Step 3. As an alternative to using the checklist, administrators can ask teachers to develop and prioritize their own list of social skills.

Step 3. Review Social Skills Programs for Their Fit in Your School

After identifying students' social skills needs, the next step is to review program criteria that are essential for your school. In addition to the skills deficits that you have already identified, consider such issues as cost, quality of instructional materials, availability of materials to send home to families, provision of program materials in the requisite languages of your students and their parents, your needs for technical assistance, length of training time available to teachers, and assessment procedures.

Teachers and administrators must consider how much time, money, materials, equipment, and additional staff may be required to implement a social skills program. For example, some programs may require that students view videotapes or use the computer to supplement instruction. Others provide consumable materials that must be replaced every year. The fit between the program and the different cultural values of families in your school is also very important.

Parents and teachers may not agree perfectly on which social skills represent needs or deficits in children. Parents and teachers may also be thinking of different types of behaviors and different situations that represent particular social skills. For example, in one study, Ruffalo and Elliott (1997) reported only low to moderate agreement between parents and teachers in their ratings of children's social skills on the *Social Skills Rating System* (SSRS; Gresham & Elliott, 1990). The researchers also found low agreement between parents and teachers on the importance of particular social skills. The results from the Ruffalo and Elliott study highlight the need to consider the different perspectives that parents and teachers may have about children's social skills.

Whenever possible, administrators will want to involve families in the choice of a social skills curriculum. If your parent–teacher organization is strong, and if its members are truly representative of your school community, you can engage them in a discussion about the social skill needs among children at your school. When there is no organized group of parents available, administrators can ask teachers to speak with responsive parents and ask their opinions. Another option is to put a brief survey in the school newsletter or to provide a place on the school website where families can prioritize a potential list of social skills.

Step 4. Identify or Create a Program That Meets Your Criteria

List the criteria identified in Steps 2 and 3, and choose from three to five programs for closer consideration. You may find the form in Appendix 3.4 helpful for this step. Teachers can use this form to note the features of each program and how well it fits the criteria for use in their classrooms. You can also ask the developers or publishers for examination copies of their materials. Ask for contact information from people who have purchased the program for use in school settings similar to yours. Get your most important questions answered. Determine the fit of each program in your situation.

You may find that your priorities change as you go through this process. For example, if the cost of consumable materials is a deterrent to a program that is an excellent fit otherwise, you can ask the developer or other users about sources of financial support in the community or elsewhere. Does a local service organization take a special interest in this program? Is there an interested foundation from which others have received funding?

Step 5. Choose and Implement a Social Skills Program

The five decision-making steps and the relevant forms in Appendices 3.3 and 3.4 should help administrators and teachers choose a social skills curriculum that covers the skills they consider important and needed by their students. It is unlikely that any one program will be ideal. Typically, programs will be strong in some areas, but lacking in other areas. Teachers and administrators must then decide whether to use one program or to create their curriculum by selecting different parts of various programs. We recommend enlisting the support of other school staff, such as the guidance counselor or school psychologist, in choosing and carrying out certain aspects of the program.

HOW WILL WE PREPARE TO IMPLEMENT A SOCIAL SKILLS CURRICULUM?

Commercially available programs usually have specific instructions or lesson plans for teaching their social skills units. Before the actual teaching begins, however, administrators and teachers need to consider a number of issues in implementing a social skills curriculum. These include (1) determining when and for how long the program will run; (2) setting goals and objectives for intended student outcomes; (3) training teachers and other school staff in the program; (4) planning schedules to allow for coteaching when appropriate; (5) developing plans to help students generalize skills to settings outside of the classroom; and (6) communicating with families about the curriculum.

Once the social skills program has been launched, it is important to check periodically on how the program is progressing. You can ask teachers, staff, students, and families for their opinions about the program. Evaluating the success of the program at the end of the school year is also important in determining whether school resources and efforts were wisely spent. The program evaluation should include assessing student outcomes as well as assessing whether the program was actually carried out in the manner that was intended. Chapter 5 in this book discusses methods for evaluating both student outcomes and the fidelity of implementation of the ABC Program components, including the social skills curriculum.

HOW WILL WE TEACH SOCIAL SKILLS IN OUR CLASSROOMS?

Teaching social skills involves many of the same principles as teaching academic skills. Most commercially available social skills programs have instructions for teaching. Some have scripted lesson plans. Table 3.2 gives guidelines for teaching social skills, adapted from lessons in several published curricula. Each of these is described in detail in the next sections.

Define the Skill for Students

The first step for teaching a social skill is to define the skill in terms of specific behaviors. This will ensure that all students know exactly what is meant by a skill and what is required to do the skill

---

TABLE 3.2. How to Teach Social Skills

- Define the skill for students.
- Model the skill.
    ~ Use this sequence: example/nonexample/example.
    ~ Include students in the modeling.
- Use role plays to rehearse the skill.
- Practice the skill.
    ~ Have students practice in small groups during a natural social activity (academic game, free-time activities).
    ~ Monitor and supervise during the social activity, giving feedback to individuals on their perfomance.
- Summarize the group's performance.
- Assign homework.
    ~ Include suggestions for using the skill in natural settings.
    ~ Provide visual prompt cards with steps in using the skill.
    ~ Provide a process for families to report success.
- Continue incidental teaching and reinforcing skills throughout the school day.
- Use group contingencies to maximize attainment and maintenance of skills.
- Use small-group instruction and/or individual contracting for students with severe problems.
- Communicate with families.

Note. From lessons in published curricula (Jackson, Jackson, & Monroe, 1983; McGinnis & Goldstein, 1997; Sheridan, 1995; Walker, Stiller, Golly, Kavanagh, & Feil, 1998). Reprinted with permission from Corwin Press.

correctly. To begin, teachers can ask students what they think a particular social skill, such as listening, involves. Teachers can pick up on students' correct responses to define the skill according to the lesson plan in the curriculum.

Model the Skill

Modeling is a critical component of social skills instruction. This means demonstrating the skill to students. Modeling can be done through role plays between two adults or a teacher and student, by showing videotapes, or by reading vignettes from stories. McGinnis and Goldstein (1997) suggest using at least two examples for each skill demonstration. The demonstration can include an example of the skill, and then an example of what is *not* the skill, followed by repeating the example of the skill. After teachers demonstrate the skill, they can model the skill with a student who can perform the skill well. McGinnis and Goldstein also suggest using situations similar to students' real-life circumstances, showing only one skill at a time, showing all of the behavioral steps involved in the skill, and showing the skill as having a positive outcome. Research shows that using positive peer role models, older students, or high-status peers (e.g., school athletes or well-liked students) often encourages other students to imitate the desired social behavior.

Use Role Plays to Rehearse the Skill

After modeling the skill, students can rehearse the skill through role plays. Teachers can select students who perform the skill well to role-play in front of the whole class. Then students can pair off with one another to rehearse the skill. Teachers need to be sensitive about not creating embarrassing situations for shy students or for students who do not have the skill or are awkward at performing the skill. Pairing students with deficits with more accomplished peers can help to avoid embarrassment and provide positive peer role modeling.

Practice the Skill

"Practice makes perfect" is an important rule for learning social skills. In order to perfect a new social skill, students need many opportunities to try out the skill in natural settings. Teachers can set up situations for students to practice a new skill in small groups during activities in and outside the classroom. While students practice, teachers can comment on students' performance as opportunities arise. Positive comments about successful performance are most effective because they encourage desired behavior. When a student fails to perform successfully, teachers can rehearse the skill with the student and provide other opportunities to practice. These last two points underline the need for *all* school staff, including recess supervisors, to know the skills being taught.

Summarize the Group's Performance

At the end of each social skill lesson, a teacher can summarize the performance of the whole class, and then select student partners to demonstrate successful examples of using the skill. Teachers can reinforce students' use of a specific social skill throughout the day, and summarize their observations for the whole class at the end of the school day.

Assign Homework

Homework assignments add more opportunities for students to practice a new skill outside of the classroom. Homework underscores the importance of social skills lessons, as it does for academic lessons. When assigning homework, teachers should include suggestions for using a specific social skill in natural settings. Sometimes visual prompt cards are helpful, especially for young students. Providing families with a process for reporting successes will help students generalize social skills to the home setting. If parents are to be involved in homework assignments, teachers should make sure that the assignment fits the home situation and is not too labor intensive. They should alert families to the homework ahead of time, for example, in social skills newsletters or other family communication materials. Encouraging family involvement will give students the message that the same social skills valued at school are also valued at home.

Continue Incidental Teaching and Reinforcing Skills

Incidental teaching means taking advantage of teachable moments throughout the school day to help students rehearse and practice social skills in natural settings. Through incidental teaching, teachers can weave social skills lessons into other parts of the curriculum. For example, if a conflict or disruption occurs during a mathematics class, the teacher can spend some time having students practice an appropriate social skill, such as solving arguments or using self-control. This will help students maintain and generalize social skills to other settings.

Reinforcing skills means taking action to strengthen students' motivation to perform desired behavior. Verbal praise is one of the easiest and best ways to reinforce social skills. To be most effective, teachers should praise a student immediately after he/she has performed a skill, be genuinely enthusiastic, and make eye contact with the student. Teachers can reinforce social skills through reward systems and positive notes home to families. Rewards might include material objects, such as stickers, as well as free time for special activities, time added to recess, and special time with another adult in the school.

Other school staff (e.g., the principal, librarian, secretary, guidance counselor, school nurse, etc.) should support teachers' efforts in reinforcing students' social skills. To do this, school staff need to know what specific social skills are being taught in the classroom during a particular week or month. Staff can then use the same language as teachers to praise students who demonstrate good social skills and intervene with students who fail to use appropriate social skills. *The Tough Kid Principal's Briefcase* (Jenson, Rhode, Evans, & Morgan, 2004) also provides many good suggestions for using group contingencies in school-wide systems for promoting social skills.

Use Group Contingencies to Maximize Social Skills

Group contingencies are rewards given to a group or an entire class when individual students demonstrate desired social skills. Research has shown that group contingencies can be very effective in improving students' social behavior. As one example, school staff could give *good social skill cards* to individual students when they see them performing a social skill in a natural setting. Students could turn in their cards to their teacher or the principal to earn points for the entire class or for a team of students. When students earn a designated number of points, the entire class or team would receive a reward. Sheridan's (1995) *Tough Kid Social Skills Book* provides many good examples of the use of group contingencies.

Communicate with Families

Communication with families is another powerful tool to reinforce students' progress in learning social skills. *Skillstreaming* (McGinnis & Goldstein, 1997) and many other published programs make the teacher's job easier by including materials to copy and send home to families. Homework that asks parents to observe, praise, and note when their children use a new skill can be very effective, if teachers let parents know in advance that homework will be forthcoming. Remind parents that children should not forget about using a learned skill once the class has moved on to a new skill. Finally, social skills often play a big role in the goals that parents and teachers set together in their PTAR teams. Teachers can be flexible in scheduling a lesson for the whole class that only one child needs. Then they can use their extra communication time with that child's parents for additional feedback and suggestions for practice.

APPENDIX 3.1

Examples of Research-Based Elementary School
Social Skills Programs from Commercial Publishers

Bully-Proofing Your School, Third Edition
Garrity, Jens, Porter, Sager, & Short-Camilli (2004); Publisher: Sopris West, 4093 Specialty Place, Longmont, CO 80504-5400; *www.sopriswest.com*

First Step to Success: Helping Young Children Overcome Antisocial Behavior
Walker, Stiller, Golly, Kavanagh, & Feile (1998); Publisher: Sopris West, 4093 Specialty Place, Longmont, CO 80504-5400; *www.sopriswest.com*

Getting Along with Others: Teaching Social Effectiveness to Children
Jackson, Jackson, & Monroe (1983); Publisher: Research Press, Dept. 27, P.O. Box 9177, Champaign, IL 61826; *www.researchpress.com*

Second Step: A Violence Prevention Curriculum
Committee for Children (1997); 172 20th Avenue, Seattle, WA 98122-5862; (800) 634-4449; *www.cfchildren.org/ssf/ssf/ssindex*

Skillstreaming the Elementary School Child
McGinnis & Goldstein (1997); Publisher: Research Press, Dept. 27, P.O. Box 9177, Champaign, IL 61826; *www.researchpress.com*

Taking Part: Introducing Social Skills to Children
Cartledge & Kleefield (1991); Publisher: American Guidance Service, 4201 Woodland Road, P.O. Box 99, Circle Pines, MN 55014-1796; *www.agsnet.com*

The Tough Kid Social Skills Book
Sheridan (1997); Publisher: Sopris West, 4093 Specialty Place, Longmont, CO 80504-5400; *www.sopriswest.com*

Responsive Classroom
While not exclusively a social skills program, the *Responsive Classroom* approach provides an ecological model of classroom management that results in positive social behaviors. Northeast Foundation for Children, 85 Avenue A, Suite 204, P.O. Box 718, Turners Falls, MA 01376-0718; (800) 360-6332; *www.responsiveclassroom.org*

From Stephanie H. McConaughy, Pam Kay, Julie A. Welkowitz, Kim Hewitt, and Martha D. Fitzgerald (2008). Copyright by The Guilford Press. Permission to photocopy this appendix is granted to purchasers of this book for personal use only (see copyright page for details).

Annotated Lists of Empirically Supported/Evidence-Based Interventions for School-Age Children and Adolescents

The following tables provide a list of lists, with indications of what each list covers, how it was developed, what it contains, and how to access it.

I. Universal Focus on Promoting Healthy Development

A. *Safe and Sound: An Educational Leader's Guide to Evidence-Based Social and Emotional Learning Programs* (2002). The Collaborative for Academic, Social, and Emotional Learning (CASEL).		
How it was developed:	*What the list contains:*	*How to access:*
Contacts with researchers and literature search yielded 250 programs for screening; 81 programs were identified that met the criteria of being a multi-year program with at least 8 lessons in one program year, designed for regular ed classrooms, and nationally available.	Descriptions (purpose, features, results) of the 81 programs.	CASEL (*www.casel.org*)
B. *Positive Youth Development in the United States: Research Findings on Evaluations of Positive Youth Development Programs* (2002). Social Development Research Group, University of Washington		
How it was developed:	*What the list contains:*	*How to access:*
77 programs that sought to achieve positive youth development objectives were reviewed. Criteria used: research designs employed control or comparison group and measured youth behavior outcomes.	25 programs designated as effective based on available evidence.	Online journal *Prevention and Treatment* (*journals.apa.org/ prevention/volume5/ pre0050015a*)

(continued)

From the Center for Mental Health in Schools at UCLA. Reprinted with permission in Stephanie H. McConaughy, Pam Kay, Julie A. Welkowitz, Kim Hewitt, and Martha D. Fitzgerald (2008). Copyright by The Guilford Press. This appendix is downloadable from *smhp.psych.ucla.edu/pdfdocs/aboutmh/annotatedlist.pdf.*

II. Prevention of Problems: Promotion of Protective Factors

A. *Blueprints for Violence Prevention* (1998).
Center for the Study and Prevention of Violence, Institute of Behavioral Science, University of Colorado, Boulder.

How it was developed:	What the list contains:	How to access:
Review of over 450 delinquency, drug, and violence prevention programs based on a criteria of a strong research design, evidence of significant deterrence effects, multiple site replication, sustained effects.	10 model programs and 15 promising programs.	Center for the Study and Prevention of Violence (*www.colorado.edu/ cspvblueprints/model/ overview*)

B. *Exemplary Substance Abuse and Mental Health Programs*
Substance Abuse and Mental Health Services Administration (SAMHSA).

How it was developed:	What the list contains:	How to access:
These science-based programs underwent an expert consensus review of published and unpublished materials on 18 criteria (e.g., theory, fidelity, evaluation, sampling, attrition, outcome measures, missing data, outcome data, analysis, threats to validity, integrity, utility, replications, dissemination, cultural/age appropriateness). The reviews have grouped programs as "models," "effective," and "promising" programs.	Prevention programs that may be adapted and replicated by communities.	SAMHSA (*www.modelprograms. samhsa.gov*)

C. *Preventing Drug Use among Children and Adolescents: Research-Based Guide* (1997).
National Institute on Drug Abuse (NIDA).

How it was developed:	What the list contains:	How to access:
NIDA and the scientists who conducted the research developed research protocols. Each was tested in a family/ school/community setting for a reasonable period with positive results.	10 programs that are universal, selective, or indicated.	NIDA (*www.nida.nih.gov/ prevention/prevopen*)

D. *Safe, Disciplined, and Drug-Free Schools Expert Panel Exemplary Programs* (2001).
U.S. Department of Education Safe and Drug-Free Schools

How it was developed:	What the list contains:	How to access:
Review of 132 programs submitted to the panel. Each program reviewed in terms of quality, usefulness to others, and educational significance.	9 exemplary and 33 promising programs focusing on violence, alcohol, tobacco, and drug prevention.	U.S. Department of Education (*www.ed.gov/offices/ OERI/ORAD/KAD/ expert_panel/drug- free*)

(continued)

71

III. Early Intervention: Targeted Focus on Specific Problems or At-Risk Groups

A. *The Prevention of Mental Disorders in School-Age Children: Current State of the Field* (2001). Prevention Research Center for the Promotion of Human Development, Pennsylvania State University.		
How it was developed:	*What the list contains:*	*How to access:*
Review of scores of primary prevention programs to identify those with quasi-experimental or randomized trials and been found to reduce symptoms of psychopathology or factors commonly associated with an increased risk for later mental disorders.	34 universal and targeted interventions that have demonstrated positive outcomes under rigorous evaluation and the common characteristics of these programs.	Online journal *Prevention and Treatment* (*journals.apa.org/ prevention/volume4/ pre0040001a*)

IV. Treatment for Problems

A. American Psychological Association's Society for Clinical Child and Adolescent Psychology, Committee on Evidence-Based Practice List		
How it was developed:	*What the list contains:*	*How to access:*
Committee reviewed outcome studies to determine how well a study conforms to the guidelines of the Task Force on Promotion and Dissemination of Psychological Procedures (1996).	Reviews of the following: • *Depression (dysthymia):* Analyses indicate only one practice meets criteria for "well-established treatment" (best supported) and two practices meet criteria for "probably efficacious" (promising) • *Conduct/oppositional problems:* Two meet criteria for well-established treatments: videotape modeling parent-training programs (Webster–Stratton) and parent-training program based on Living with Children (Patterson and Guillion). Ten practices identified as probably efficacious. • *ADHD:* Behavioral parent training, behavioral interventions in the classroom, and stimulant medication meet criteria for well-established treatments. Two others meet criteria for probably efficacious. • *Anxiety disorders*: For phobias, participant modeling and reinforced practice are well established; filmed modeling, live modeling, and cognitive-behavioral interventions that use self-instruction training are probably efficacious. For anxiety disorders, cognitive-behavioral procedures with and without family anxiety management, modeling, in vivo exposure, relaxation training, and reinforced practice are listed as probably efficacious. *Caution:* Reviewers stress the importance of (1) devising developmentally and culturally sensitive interventions targeted to the unique needs of each child; (2) a need for research informed by clinical practice.	(*www.effectivechild-therapy.com*)

(continued)

V. Review/Consensus Statements/Compendia of Evidence-Based Treatments

A. *School-Based Prevention Programs for Children and Adolescents* (1995). J. A. Durlak. Sage: Thousand Oaks, CA.
Reports results from 130 controlled outcome studies that support "a secondary prevention model emphasizing timely intervention for subclinical problems detected early. . . . In general, best results are obtained for cognitive-behavioral and behavioral treatments and interventions targeting externalizing problems."
B. *Mental Health and Mass Violence*
Evidence-based early psychological intervention for victims/survivors of mass violence. A workshop to reach consensus on best practices (U.S. Departments of HHS, Defense, Veterans Affairs, Justice, and American Red Cross). Available at: (*www.nimh.nih.gov/research/massviolence.pdf*)
C. *Society of Pediatric Psychology*, Division 54, American Psychological Association, *Journal of Pediatric Psychology.*
Articles on empirically supported treatments in pediatric psychology related to obesity, feeding problems, headaches, pain, bedtime refusal, enuresis, encopresis, and symptoms of asthma, diabetes, and cancer.
D. *Preventing Crime: What Works, What Doesn't, What's Promising. A Report to the United States Congress* (1997). L. W. Sherman, Denise Gottfredson, et al. Washington, DC: U.S. Department of Justice.
Reviews programs funded by the Office of Justice Programs (OJP) for crime, delinquency, and substance use. (*www.ncjrs.org/pdffiles/171676.pdf*). Also see Denise Gottfredson's book: *Schools and Delinquency* (2001). New York: Cambridge Press.
E. School Violence Prevention Initiative Matrix of Evidence-Based Prevention Interventions *(1999)*. Center for Mental Health Services (SAMHSA).
Provides a synthesis of several lists cited above to highlight examples of programs which meet some criteria for a designation of evidence based for violence prevention and substance abuse prevention (i.e., synthesizes lists from the Center for the Study and Prevention of Violence, Center for Substance Abuse Prevention, Communities that Care, Department of Education, Department of Justice, Health Resources, and Services Administration, National Association of School Psychologists). (*modelprograms.samhsa.gov/matrix_all.cfm*)

BUT THE NEEDS OF SCHOOLS ARE MORE COMPLEX!

Currently, there are about 91,000 public schools in about 15,000 districts in the United States. Over the years, most (but obviously not all) schools have instituted programs designed with a range of behavior, emotional, and learning problems in mind. School-based and school-linked programs have been developed for purposes of early intervention, crisis intervention and prevention, treatment, and promotion of positive social and emotional development. Some programs are provided throughout a district, others are carried out at, or linked to, targeted schools. The interventions may be offered to all students in a school, to those in specified grades, or to those identified as "at risk." The activities may be implemented in regular or special education classrooms or as "pull-out" programs and may be designed for an entire class, groups, or individuals. There also may be a focus on primary prevention and enhancement of healthy development through use of health education, health services, guidance, and so forth—though relatively few resources usually are allocated for such activity. There is a large body of research supporting the promise of specific facets of this activity. However, no one has yet designed a study to evaluate the impact of the type of comprehensive, multifaceted approach needed to deal with the complex range of problems confronting schools.

Social Skills Needs Checklist

Teacher's name _____   Date _____

SOCIAL SKILLS 1 = critical 2 = very important 3 = important	Importance in your classroom: mark 1, 2, or 3	Number of students with deficits in critical skills (marked 1)	Number of students with deficits in very important skills (marked 2)
Communication Skills			
1. Listening			
2. Speaking			
3. Using a quiet voice			
4. Conversing			
5. Apologizing			
6. Giving feedback			
7. Seeking help			
8. Offering help			
Interpersonal Skills			
1. Asserting oneself			
2. Making friends			
3. Negotiating			
4. Understanding others			
5. Dealing with authorities			
6. Initiating interactions			
7. Interacting with strangers			
8. Interacting with adults			
9. Interacting with peers			
10. Showing consideration			
11. Sharing			
12. Cooperating			

(continued)

From Stephanie H. McConaughy, Pam Kay, Julie A. Welkowitz, Kim Hewitt, and Martha D. Fitzgerald (2008). Copyright by The Guilford Press. Permission to photocopy this appendix is granted to purchasers of this book for personal use only (see copyright page for details).

SOCIAL SKILLS 1 = critical 2 = very important 3 = important	Importance in your classroom: mark 1, 2, or 3	Number of students with deficits in critical skills (marked 1)	Number of students with deficits in very important skills (marked 2)
Personal Skills			
1. Being self-aware			
2. Positive self-concept			
3. Responsible for self-care			
4. Dealing with feelings			
5. Using manners			
6. Setting goals			
Response Skills			
1. Receiving feedback			
2. Following directions			
3. Dealing with criticism			
4. Dealing with frustration			
5. Controlling aggression			
6. Accepting consequences			
7. Responding to peer pressure			
8. Resolving conflicts			
9. Solving problems			
10. Dealing with stress			
11. Empathizing			

Other criteria that are important to me (circle all that apply, and add your own):

Sensitivity to local cultures

Teacher's text or manual

Student assessment instrument(s)

Maintenance/generalization procedures

Consumable student materials

Audio/video technology

Other:

Appropriate language(s)

Visual aids

Outcome evaluation component

Materials to send home

Nonconsumable materials

Computer technology

Criteria for Selecting a Social Skills Program

Program Criteria and Instructional Materials (Use the outline below to determine which of your important instructional materials and requirements apply to each program.)	Program Title: Publisher:	Program Title: Publisher:	Program Title: Publisher:
Instructional Materials: (Number according to teachers' top 10 priorities.)			
Sensitivity to local cultures			
Appropriate language(s)			
Teacher's text or manual			
Visual aids			
Student assessment instrument(s)			
Outcome evaluation component			
Maintenance/generalization procedures			
Materials to send home			
Consumable student materials			
Nonconsumable materials			
Audio/video technology			
Computer technology			
Other			
Instructional Requirements (Write in requirements of each program.)			
Length of instruction			
Frequency of instruction			
Total cost of materials			
Training time			
Technical assistance			

From Stephanie H. McConaughy, Pam Kay, Julie A. Welkowitz, Kim Hewitt, and Martha D. Fitzgerald (2008). Copyright by The Guilford Press. Permission to photocopy this appendix is granted to purchasers of this book for personal use only (see copyright page for details).

4

Selecting Child and Family Participants for ABC's PTAR Teams

Questions to Be Addressed in This Chapter

- Who will select the children who will receive PTAR teams?
- How will we select the children?
- How will we invite parents to participate?
- What are the next steps?

Once teachers have agreed to participate in the ABC Program and are prepared to teach a social skills curriculum, your next step is to identify individual children who might benefit from having their parents and teachers collaborate on PTAR teams. As we stated in the introduction, ABC was developed and tested as a school-based prevention program for children at risk for emotional or behavioral problems. The PTAR process could also be used to address other issues that might impede a child's academic progress, such as a chronic illness, but our focus in this chapter will be on selecting children based on concerns about social and emotional problems.

Secondary prevention programs, such as ABC, target children who are *at risk* for problems and are more likely to develop severe problems if they do not receive some form of early attention. A prevention program is different from an intensive intervention, such as special education or mental health services, and may not be suitable for children who have already been identified as having an emotional or behavioral disability. If children with severe problems are not involved in programs that meet their needs, teachers will find it difficult to address the needs of children at risk.

WHO WILL SELECT THE CHILDREN WHO WILL RECEIVE PTAR TEAMS?

One of the principles of the ABC Program is that children's issues are addressed by those closest to them, usually their parents and classroom teachers. For this reason, classroom teachers should be closely involved in selecting the students for ABC. Remember that ABC does not involve a formal diagnosis of a student's problems. Most classroom teachers are not trained in diagnostic decision making, and the students selected for ABC should not be the ones exhibiting severe problems. Students with severe problems should be referred to behavioral specialists, such as the school psychologist or a special educator.

In order for teachers to have a thorough knowledge of the child, student selection should take place at least 1 or 2 months into the school year. An alternative would be for teachers to select students at the end of a school year, with parents and the teacher in the next grade starting PTAR teams at the beginning of the following school year.

In the ABC research project, we asked kindergarten teachers to select students at the end of the year. Parent Liaisons were able to meet with parents to get their consent before the first-grade year began. First-grade teachers, however, were left out of this selection process. Later, we heard from some first-grade teachers that there were other students in their classes who may have needed ABC more than those chosen by the kindergarten teachers.

Because developmental changes happen so quickly in young children, and because many families move over the summer months, we suggest a third choice. That is to have kindergarten teachers make *recommendations* based on their screening at the end of the year, and then have the first-grade teacher make the actual selections several weeks into the new school year. While this means that PTAR teams do not start until 1 or 2 months into the school year, it may be a better way to ensure that the children who need ABC most are given the opportunity to participate. This does not preclude starting PTAR teams at other times during the year, or in other grades.

HOW WILL WE SELECT THE CHILDREN?

In this section we will describe several methods for identifying children who will benefit most from ABC. The ABC research project used a formal screening procedure, to ensure that our sample met certain criteria. We also omitted students with serious cognitive deficits and those with extensive physical disabilities. Although most children with disabilities are schooled in general education classrooms in Vermont, we wanted the PTAR teams to focus on issues that were not complicated by physical or cognitive limitations.

In our ABC outreach project, schools used a variety of approaches. Some used the whole-class screening process we will describe below. Others made a referral to ABC part of their school's student support team process. A few children were referred by the community agency that employed the Parent Liaisons. One elementary school used its newsletter to invite parents to refer their own children. Other possibilities to consider include:

- Children who are in danger of retention, or children who have been retained.
- Suggestions from the guidance counselor, school psychologist, school social worker, or home–school coordinator.
- Referral from an early childhood setting, such as a PIRC or Head Start.

Issues regarding confidentiality and the need to meet the requirements of the Family Education Rights and Privacy Act (FERPA; 1974) should have been addressed when your local management structure for ABC was created (see Chapter 1). However, you will also need to be familiar with your own school system's regulations concerning parental notification when a screening is to take place. The screening process that we describe here does not involve direct contact with the students. It depends on the classroom teacher knowing his/her students well.

Using a Screening Procedure

Selecting children for a PTAR team is a sensitive task. Some classroom teachers may be reluctant to participate in the selection process. Those who have been trained in general education may believe they lack the experience or training to make such choices. Others may regard such identification as premature for young children, believing that having a PTAR team will label the child as "a problem." Still other teachers may fear that parents will have a negative reaction to the selection of their child. However, given the right tools for screening and strong administrative support, teachers can be very accurate in their assessment of children at risk. (For more information, see Walker, Severson, and Todis, 1990.)

We recommend against simply asking classroom teachers to nominate the children whom they think need ABC without giving teachers any guidelines or screening instruments. Often the children who are chosen this way need more immediate and intense help than the ABC Program provides. Sometimes the teachers are eager to reach the *parents* of certain children, with specific parent-education goals in mind. This approach can distort the focus of ABC, which is always on the child, and what she/he needs. It also can destroy the parent–teacher equality, which is essential in building trust and doing action research together. Parent education is more effective when the parents decide what they need to know about rearing their child than when information is imposed on them.

Administrators should choose screening methods that best fit procedures and policies in their particular school districts and cooperating agencies. You can make use of published screening measures or develop your own procedures. In the next two sections, we describe one of the published screening measures and outline the sequence of steps for creating PTAR teams, utilizing procedures from this measure.

Systematic Screening for Behavior Disorders

Systematic Screening for Behavior Disorders (SSBD; Walker & Severson, 1990) is a widely used published screening measure. The SSBD has been shown to be a reliable and valid tool for identifying children in grades K–6 who are at risk for emotional and behavioral problems. Walker and Severson recommend that the SSBD be used at least once a year in every classroom to help identify students' needs for extra support before their problems become severe. The *Early Screening Project* (ESP; Walker, Severson, & Feil, 1994; Feil, Walker, & Severson, 1995) extends the screening process to children ages 3–5.

Several prevention projects have used the SSBD as a screening measure for identifying students at risk for school problems (Algozzine & Kay, 2002). The SSBD is a good screening measure because it focuses on children with internalizing as well as externalizing behavior. Teachers often refer children with externalizing behavior for special services because their behavior is disruptive in the classroom. However, children with internalizing behavior can be overlooked because they are less disruptive.

The SSBD uses a three-step gating process. In the first gate, classroom teachers review their entire class roster, thinking about each child in turn. They select two groups of students who exhibit externalizing or internalizing behaviors, which are a problem for the child or others. *Externalizing* behavior includes disruptive or aggressive behavior considered inappropriate by school personnel. *Internalizing* behavior includes affective or emotional problems, such as withdrawal from others, frequent somatic problems, or fearfulness. The SSBD provides thorough definitions, with examples and nonexamples, for each type of behavior.

In the SSBD second gate, classroom teachers complete two screening measures for each of their three top-ranked children on the Externalizer and Internalizer lists. The first measure is the Critical Events Index (CEI), which lists 33 problems (e.g., stealing, tantrums, sad affect) that teachers have observed over the past year. The next measure is the Combined Frequency Index (CFI), which includes 12 adaptive behaviors and 11 maladaptive behaviors to be rated on a 5-point scale.

The SSBD manual provides standard scores and percentiles for the CEI and CFI based on large samples of typically developing students. Students who exceed specific CEI and CFI cut-off scores for the normative samples should be considered candidates for the ABC Program. In another study, Gresham, MacMillan, and Bocian (1996) concluded that even one critical event on the SSBD-CEI provided a good initial screen for identifying students at risk for behavioral and social problems. The SSBD scoring process is not time-consuming, and can be done by the classroom teacher.

The SSBD then moves on to a third gate, where trained observers conduct two 15-minute observations of the selected student in their classrooms and at recess. You may want to use the third gate to determine whether any of the students on the teachers' lists should be considered as candidates for prereferral interventions, further assessment for special education, or other services, rather than for ABC. Authors of the SSBD recommend that students who exceed the SSBD age and gender-normative criteria on the observation coding system at the third gate be referred for further testing. We chose not to use the SSBD third gate in the ABC prevention research project because we wanted to be more inclusive in screening for students with problems that placed them at risk.

Administrators who purchase the SSBD may choose to use only certain of its procedures or to utilize normative criteria differently, depending on school demographics or the goals of a particular program. For example, in our research project we reduced the number of children that teachers needed to identify at the first gate to accommodate small-class sizes in rural and semi-rural districts.

Steps in Using the SSBD to Select Children for PTAR Teams

Appendix 4.1 outlines seven steps that you might use with teachers at a screening meeting to select children for PTAR teams. The process begins in Step 1 with understanding the difference between internalizing and externalizing behavior. In Step 2, teachers use their class roster to review their own observations of all the children in their class, then make two separate lists of children who have the SSBD characteristics of internalizing and externalizing problem behaviors. *Problem behaviors* are those that present difficulties for the child or other children in the class, making them less available for learning.

Step 3 helps to identify children who have problem behaviors that are both internalizing and externalizing. In Step 4, teachers eliminate students who are already receiving special services at school to address their emotional or behavioral problems. The teachers should now have short lists of students for whom they will complete another level of screening.

In Step 5, the SSBD provides the CEI and the CFI, discussed earlier in this chapter. Other published rating scales could be used at this step, such as those listed in Chapter 5, or you could develop your own set of criteria. Later in this chapter, we describe a set of indicators of child growth and behavior that could be adapted for use at this stage in the screening.

In Step 6, teachers rank order the children on each list, paying special attention to the needs of children whose names they circled in Step 3. Step 7 asks teachers to combine their lists of children with internalizing and externalizing problems, and rank order the children once again. As they do this, teachers should take the needs of children with internalizing problems as seriously as those with externalizing problems. The result of Step 7 should be a (short) list of students who are candidates for an ABC PTAR team.

Other Indicators of Child Growth and Behavior

An alternative way to approach the broad assessment of a group of children is to use a model developed by the National Center on Educational Outcomes (Ysseldyke, Krentz, Elliott, Thurlow, Erickson, & Moore, 1998; *www.education.umn.edu/NCEO*). The model looks at child growth across eight domains:

1. Presence and Participation
2. Family Involvement
3. Physical Health
4. Responsibility and Independence
5. Contribution and Citizenship
6. Academic and Functional Literacy
7. Personal and Social Adjustment
8. Satisfaction with Education

Within each domain, there are specific results of growth which should be visible at given ages. For example, in the domain of academic and functional literacy, a 6-year-old would demonstrate competence in communication, problem solving, academic skills, and using technology.

Figure 4.1 shows an example of a teacher's review of Joshua's growth on all domains. (A blank version of the worksheet is given in Appendix 4.2.) Since ABC begins by looking at a child's strengths, the teacher checked each point where Joshua showed developmentally appropriate growth. After comparing Joshua's checklist with those of other children on her internalizing list, Ms. Allende placed him at the bottom of the list. His strengths were all in areas related to his academic growth, and she felt that his coping skills were strong enough to overcome some of his social deficits. She also knew that the new social skills curriculum would be helpful for Joshua. Other children on the list were in greater need of a PTAR team than Joshua.

This form and its information also can be helpful when a parent and teacher first start to work together. PTAR starts with the MAPs process, which begins with a list of the child's strengths (see Chapter 8). The teacher who completes this exercise will be able to identify both strengths and concerns for the child when doing MAPs in the PTAR meeting. Parents and teachers might also use this format to develop mutual goals for the child.

CHILD __Joshua N.__ AGE __6__ TEACHER __Allende__ DATE __9/29/07__

DOMAIN	DESIRED RESULTS	✓	POSSIBLE INDICATORS
A. Presence/Participation	A1. Attends school	✓	Attendance book. Always there!
	A2. Participates in group activities		
B. Family Involvement	B1. Demonstrates support for child's learning	✓	Signs notes sent home, sends them back
	B2. Has access to resources to support child	?	
	B3. Makes changes if needed to support child	?	
C. Physical Health	C1. Demonstrates normal development		
	C2. Has access to basic health care	✓	Has immunizations, sees school dentist
	C3. Is aware of basic safety and health needs		
	C4. Is physically fit		
D. Responsibility/Independence	D1. Demonstrates age-appropriate independence		
	D2. Gets about in the environment		
	D3. Is responsible for self	✓	Brings permissions, homework regularly

(continued)

FIGURE 4.1. Sample worksheet for indicators of growth.

DOMAIN	DESIRED RESULTS	✓	POSSIBLE INDICATORS
E. Contribution/Citizenship	E1. Complies with rules, limits, and routines	✓	
	E2. Accepts responsibility for age-appropriate tasks at home and school	✓	Never forgets his classroom jobs
F. Academic and Functional Literacy	F1. Demonstrates competence in communication	✓	(With adults, not peers)
	F2. . . . competence in problem solving	✓	
	F3. . . . competence in academic skills	✓	Excels in math
	F4. . . . competence in using technology		
G. Personal and Social Adjustment	G1. Copes effectively with personal challenges, frustrations, stressors		
	G2. Has good self-image		
	G3. Respects cultural and individual differences	✓	Befriended new student from Somalia
	G4. Gets along with peers		
H. Satisfaction	H1. Parent/guardian satisfaction with education child receives	?	
	H2. Child's satisfaction with educational experience	?	

FIGURE 4.1. (continued)

HOW WILL WE INVITE PARENTS TO PARTICIPATE?

To begin with the end in mind, remember that Parent Liaisons' work begins when they receive a list of potential ABC families from their supervisor. Your management plan should be explicit in how that list is given to the Parent Liaison supervisors. Before setting up an invitational meeting with parents, the Parent Liaison needs to know who has already talked with families about ABC and what they already know about the program (see Chapter 6).

Decide Who Will Make the First Contact with the Parents to Explain the ABC Program

There are several options to consider in making this decision. In the ABC research project, Parent Liaisons were the first people to invite parents to participate. More than 90 percent of those approached said "yes." Some teachers were surprised to have parents who previously had avoided contact with the school agree to participate. When Parent Liaisons are employed by the school or through a school-funded contract with a community agency, your school regulations and confidentiality agreement with the agency may allow Parent Liaisons to be given a list of parent names and to make the first contact.

If you decide that the first contact should be made by school personnel, the teacher may be the person parents know best and trust most. Early in the school year, parents may know and trust last year's teacher more than their child's new teacher. If the family has older children in the school, the principal, guidance counselor, or home–school coordinator may know the parents well, and have a positive relationship with them. Much depends on your school culture, and the way that individual parents may interpret a personal call or conversation with the principal or guidance counselor.

Another option for the first contact may be through the community agency with which you have contracted. If that agency has early childhood programs or parent-support groups, staff members there will know the families well, and are usually trusted within the community. Whichever route you choose for inviting parents into ABC, the first person to make contact needs to be able to converse in the parents' native language, and to be able to answer the questions about ABC which arise from the family's own cultural standpoint. Appendix 4.3 describes the essential points to be covered while making the first contact. If teachers are not going to be the first contact people, they should be told who will contact the parents and when this will happen.

Decide Who Answers the Questions from Parents Who Are Not Invited to Join ABC

Only a few families will be able to participate in the ABC Program each year. Others will hear about ABC, and may want to know if they and their children can participate. The Parent Liaison needs to know whether to refer inquiries from other parents to the classroom teacher, the principal, or the community agency supervisor. The classroom teachers also need to know how to respond to parent inquiries.

WHAT ARE THE NEXT STEPS?

When children have been selected by their teachers and the parents have agreed to meet with Parent Liaisons to consider joining ABC, the next steps are in the Parent Liaisons' hands. In Part II of this book, you will find the information in Chapters 6 and 7 helpful in understanding how the Parent Liaisons prepare parents and teachers for their first PTAR meetings.

If you will be evaluating the effectiveness of your ABC Program (see Chapter 5), you will want to obtain baseline measures from both parent and teacher as soon as possible after parents sign their consent forms. It is preferable to collect baseline information prior to the first PTAR meeting because the MAPs process used in that meeting has the potential to change the parents' and teachers' perceptions of the child. Chapter 7 in Part II instructs the Parent Liaisons to collect measures *if required*.

APPENDIX 4.1

Steps for the Teacher in Using the SSBD
to Select Children for PTAR Teams

Step 1. Study the definitions and examples of internalizing and externalizing behavior in the Systematic Screening for Behavior Disorders (SSBD).

Step 2. Review all children on your classroom roster. Make a list of children in the class who have internalizing problem behaviors, then a list of those with externalizing problem behaviors. List as many children as come to mind, but include at least three in each category.

Step 3. If there is a child who exhibits both types of problem behaviors, choose the list that matches the majority of that child's behaviors. Circle the names of any children for whom you needed to make that choice.

Step 4. Cross out the names of children on each list who already receive intensive special education or other services for emotional or behavioral issues. Do not exclude students who receive services only for speech and language issues.

Step 5. Complete the SSBD Critical Events Index (CEI) and Combined Frequency Index (CFI) (or other screening measure) for each of those children who remain on the lists.

Step 6. Examine the results of the CEI and CFI (or other screening measure) to rank order each list of children with internalizing and externalizing behaviors according to how serious you view their problems to be in your classroom. Pay special attention to children whose names were circled as having both types of problems.

Step 7. Complete the process by combining the two lists, and rank order all of the children on your combined list. Invitations to join you in doing Parent–Teacher Action Research will be extended to families in the order that the children's names appear on this final list.

From Stephanie H. McConaughy, Pam Kay, Julie A. Welkowitz, Kim Hewitt, and Martha D. Fitzgerald (2008). Copyright by The Guilford Press. Permission to photocopy this appendix is granted to purchasers of this book for personal use only (see copyright page for details).

Worksheet for Indicators of Growth

CHILD _____ AGE _____ TEACHER _____ DATE _____

DOMAIN	DESIRED RESULTS	✓	POSSIBLE INDICATORS
A. Presence/Participation	A1. Attends school		e.g., Attendance data; bus behavior charts
	A2. Participates in group activities		
B. Family Involvement	B1. Demonstrates support for child's learning		
	B2. Has access to resources to support child		
	B3. Makes changes if needed to support child		
C. Physical Health	C1. Demonstrates normal development		
	C2. Has access to basic health care		
	C3. Is aware of basic safety and health needs		
	C4. Is physically fit		
D. Responsibility/Independence	D1. Demonstrates age-appropriate independence		
	D2. Gets about in the environment		
	D3. Is responsible for self		

From Stephanie H. McConaughy, Pam Kay, Julie A. Welkowitz, Kim Hewitt, and Martha D. Fitzgerald (2008). Copyright by The Guilford Press. Permission to photocopy this appendix is granted to purchasers of this book for personal use only (see copyright page for details).

DOMAIN	DESIRED RESULTS	✓	POSSIBLE INDICATORS
E. Contribution/Citizenship	E1. Complies with rules, limits, and routines		
	E2. Accepts responsibility for age-appropriate tasks at home and school		
F. Academic and Functional Literacy	F1. Demonstrates competence in communication		
	F2. . . . competence in problem solving		
	F3. . . . competence in academic skills		
	F4. . . . competence in using technology		
G. Personal and Social Adjustment	G1. Copes effectively with personal challenges, frustrations, stressors		
	G2. Has good self-image		
	G3. Respects cultural and individual differences		
	G4. Gets along with peers		
H. Satisfaction	H1. Parent/guardian satisfaction with education child receives		
	H2. Child's satisfaction with educational experience		

Important Points to Cover
When Introducing ABC to Parents

- Our school is part of a program called the ABC Program.

- ABC stands for Achieving–Behaving–Caring.

- There is room for your child in the program, at no cost to you.

- Your child's teacher is interested in working with you on behalf of your child.

- In ABC, parents and teachers meet monthly, and focus on what the child needs to be successful in school.

- A Parent Liaison arranges the meetings every month at a convenient time and place for you and the teacher. [He/she] can help you carry out your part of the plan that you make with the teacher, if you choose.

- If you are interested, our Parent Liaison, _____, can tell you more. May I give your name and telephone number to the Parent Liaison? When and where can [he/she] contact you?

From Stephanie H. McConaughy, Pam Kay, Julie A. Welkowitz, Kim Hewitt, and Martha D. Fitzgerald (2008). Copyright by The Guilford Press. Permission to photocopy this appendix is granted to purchasers of this book for personal use only (see copyright page for details).

5

Evaluating the Effectiveness of the ABC Program

Questions to Be Addressed in This Chapter

- How will we measure the success of our ABC Program?
- What tools will we use?
- How will we report our results?

HOW WILL WE MEASURE THE SUCCESS OF OUR ABC PROGRAM?

Evaluation of the ABC Program takes place on several levels. There are *individual* evaluations, *process* evaluations, and *program* evaluations. Through the action research process, parents and teachers evaluate the effects of their action plans on the children's behavior. Parent Liaisons evaluate their own facilitation skills following PTAR team meetings, and discuss their concerns with their supervisors and peers at monthly meetings. Parents and teachers find it helpful at the end of the year to see the results of objective measures that they and the independent observers complete—proof that the children are making progress. These are all *individual* evaluations, and direct the changes needed for the success of each child. *Process* evaluations take place as well. Parent Liaisons help PTAR teams evaluate their work together, and ask for feedback on their performance, usually at midyear and year's end. Parent Liaisons, their supervisors, and consultants discuss their interactions at appropriate intervals. The schools and their agency partners, too, assess their ability to work together.

Family agencies and schools need *program* evaluation tools to help them sustain practical and proven methods for supporting children at risk for emotional and behavioral problems. Prevention programs like the ABC Program address children's problems before they become so severe that they need more intense interventions, like special education or mental health services. Though many people tout the benefits of prevention, the public needs evidence that such programs are worth the necessary investment of scarce resources. Each budget year, administrators and board members must wrestle with competing demands for funding, staffing, and building space. They face political pressures that can influence decisions about how to allocate resources. As a result of such challenges, careful program evaluation is essential to convince decision makers that prevention programs really work and merit their support.

Approaches to Program Evaluation

Administrators can undertake program evaluation from two different perspectives. One approach focuses on evaluating the outcomes or benefits of the program for its participants. This requires choosing appropriate methods for measuring outcomes for individual participants and groups of participants. A good evaluation plan will focus on specific outcomes of the program. If the evaluation plan extends beyond the aims or scope of a program, then it will be much harder to demonstrate that the program was successful.

As a prevention effort, the primary aim of the ABC Program is to improve school adjustment for children at risk for severe emotional and behavioral problems. Changes in children's school adjustment might occur in two directions: (1) reductions in current problem behaviors, and (2) improvements in positive behaviors and social competencies. To evaluate outcomes for children participating in the ABC Program, measuring changes in both directions is important. Two additional aims of the ABC Program are to improve collaboration between parents and teachers of children who are at risk for severe problems and to teach social skills to all the children in the classroom. To encompass all three aims, an evaluation plan for the ABC Program should include measures of relevant outcomes for individual children at risk, outcomes for parents and teachers who participate in PTAR teams, and outcomes for the entire classroom. Some key questions for evaluating outcomes of the ABC Program are:

- Did parent–teacher collaboration help to reduce problem behaviors of individual children who had PTAR teams?
- Did parent–teacher collaboration help to increase positive behaviors of individual children with PTAR teams?
- Did PTAR teams help parents feel more effective in advocating for services for their children?
- Did having a social skills curriculum help to improve the social behaviors of children considered to be at risk for developing emotional or behavioral disabilities?
- Did having a social skills curriculum change other relevant aspects of the classroom, such as general attitudes and interactions between all children and adults in the classroom?

Another approach to evaluation focuses on the process for carrying out a program. This involves determining whether the program reached and served its intended participants and whether the program was carried out as it was designed. This is assessing *program fidelity*. Some key questions for evaluating program fidelity of the ABC Program are:

- Did agencies and schools select appropriate children and families for PTAR teams?
- Were there specific factors that kept some parents or teachers from participating in PTAR teams?
- Did Parent Liaisons follow the general procedures of the Action Research Cycle to facilitate PTAR teams?

- Did parents receive the support they needed to collaborate with teachers?
- Did teachers receive the support they needed to collaborate with parents?
- Did Parent Liaisons have adequate knowledge of resources and supports for families in the community?
- Did classroom teachers follow the curriculum they adopted for social skills instruction?
- Did classroom teachers send materials home to families to keep them aware of the curriculum for social skills instruction?

WHAT TOOLS WILL WE USE?

Parent and Teacher Questionnaires

One good approach to evaluating outcomes of the ABC Program is to ask parents and teachers to complete questionnaires about children's behavior before and after carrying out the program. Because children's behavior often varies from one situation to the next, obtaining information from both parents and teachers is important. Parents and teachers are also key participants in the PTAR teams for the ABC Program.

Psychological and educational publishing companies and researchers have developed many different parent and teacher questionnaires that you might use as outcome measures. Some of these published instruments will be better suited for the aims of the ABC Program than others. Important features that administrators should consider when choosing among published questionnaires are:

- Does the instrument have a reasonably large pool of items to assess different types of children's behaviors?
- Do the items assess the types of behaviors that might change as a result of participation in the ABC Program?
- Are there items for measuring children's positive behaviors and competencies as well as problem behaviors?
- Are items grouped into scales and total scores for easy interpretation?
- Can scores of an individual child be compared to normative samples to determine whether identified problems and/or competencies are unusually high or low?
- Does the instrument have good reliability? (Does it perform consistently across time and across similar types of informants?)
- Does the instrument have good validity for measuring what it is supposed to measure? (Is that form of validity relevant for the specific aims of the ABC Program?)
- Will parents and teachers easily understand the questions and the directions and complete the questionnaire in a reasonable length of time?
- Is the instrument published in the languages of families in your school or district? If not, can you get permission to translate it?

Instruments with a variety of questions, or items, are preferable to those with only a few items. A larger pool of items will enable evaluators to measure many different behaviors that might change during the program. To evaluate the ABC Program, the item pools should include behaviors that are most likely to be affected by the action research undertaken by PTAR teams and the social skills instruction in the classroom.

To evaluate changes in problem behaviors for children in the ABC Program, parent and teacher questionnaires should include both internalizing and externalizing behaviors. *Internalizing behaviors* include emotional reactions, such as anxiety and unhappiness, withdrawal, shyness, and somatic complaints. *Externalizing behaviors* include disruptive or acting-out behavior, aggression, and rule-breaking. Assessing other behaviors is also important, such as inattention, hyperactivity, disorganized thinking, and social problems.

To evaluate changes in positive behaviors, parent and teacher questionnaires should assess children's competencies and social skills. Only a few published instruments measure both positive and problem behaviors. Therefore, administrators will probably need to use more than one instrument to measure all of the behaviors of interest. Instruments that group items into scales allow evaluators to examine changes in different types of behaviors, making it easier to interpret the results. Administrators should also review the manuals for the published instruments to decide whether they have adequate *normative samples, reliability* (consistency across time and similar informants), and *validity* (measuring what they claim to measure). The best instruments are those that provide standard scores and percentiles (norms) for boys and girls at different age and/or grade levels. The norms should be derived from large samples representative of the U.S. population. Normative scores derived from such *standardized instruments* provide a basis for judging whether individual children show more problems or fewer positive behaviors than expected for their gender, age, and grade. Finally, questionnaires should be clear and easy to understand, and not too time-consuming, so that parents and teachers will be willing to invest the effort to complete them.

There are many published parent and teacher questionnaires that you might use to evaluate children's behavior. Appendices 5.1 and 5.2 list examples of published parent and teacher questionnaires that may be particularly appropriate for the ABC Program. These published instruments provide standard scores based on representative normative samples and have adequate reliability and validity.

The Ages and Stages Questionnaire—Social–Emotional (ASQ:SE) and the Devereux Early Childhood Assessment (DECA) assess young children's adaptive behaviors and problems at different age levels. The Achenbach System of Empirically Based Assessment (ASEBA) and the Behavior Assessment System for Children—Second Edition (BASC-2) instruments include items and scales to assess children's competencies, adaptive skills, and problems, as reported by parents and teachers. The Behavioral and Emotional Rating Scale—Second Edition (BERS-2) focuses on children's strengths or positive behaviors. The Social Skills Rating System (SSRS) measures children's social skills and problem behaviors, as reported by parents and teachers. The Home and Community Social Behavior Scales (HCSBS) and the School Social Behavior Scales—Second Edition (SSBS-2) assess social skills and community competencies.

Direct Observations of Children's Behavior

Directly observing children's behavior at school and at home is another good way to evaluate outcomes of the ABC Program. There are many different approaches to observational assessment. Volpe, DiPerna, Hintze, and Shapiro (2005) provide a good review of methods for classroom observations. Leff and Lakin (2005) review methods for playground observations. Kamps (2002) also describes ways to use direct observations for conduct functional behavioral assessments of children. This section offers some general recommendations for using direct observations to evaluate the success of the ABC Program, as well as examples of observational techniques.

Direct observations should focus on specific, discreet behaviors that the observer can easily recognize and that are amenable to change. Problem behaviors and positive behaviors can be the targets of direct observations. Observers can use either narrative or quantitative methods to record observed behaviors. For *narrative recording,* an observer writes a running log or description of specific behaviors that occurred within a given period. For *quantitative recording,* an observer counts the number of times a specific behavior occurred over a given time or the length of time the behavior was observed.

As an example of the quantitative approach, an observer might count the number of times a child was out of seat, talked out inappropriately, raised his/her hand, or shared materials with another student. Observers could record occurrences of the particular behavior over a specific interval, such as a 10-minute period. Alternatively, the observer could record the duration of time in which a specific behavior occurred, such as out of seat for 5 minutes, disrupted group for 2 minutes, or worked cooperatively with another student for 10 minutes.

Because children's behavior often changes from day to day, it is important to obtain more than one observation over different days. Conducting observations of relatively short duration is also better (e.g., 10–20 minutes) than to rely on one lengthy observation. Observing participants in the program and one or two randomly selected *control* children in the same setting allows evaluators to compare the target child with peers in the same environment.

One of the best approaches to observational assessment is to use independent observers who are not participants in the program. This helps to avoid any biases that might arise in observations by people who know the child well or people who are carrying out the program. Researchers often have the luxury of employing staff members who can serve as independent observers. Administrators must decide if they can afford to hire independent observers for their program evaluations. An alternative is to have other school or agency staff members conduct direct observations. Ideally, staff members should be people who are not directly involved in the program and who do not know the children well. It is also important to conduct observations in a manner that does not alert children to the fact that someone is observing them. Children may change their normal behavior when they know they are being observed.

Administrators should inform parents ahead of time about plans to observe their children for program evaluations. Depending on school or agency policy, obtaining parental permission for such observations may also be necessary, especially if the observers are not regular members of the school or agency staff.

As another approach, observers can use a standardized rating scale to record and score their observations of children's behavior. The ASEBA Direct Observation Form (DOF; McConaughy & Achenbach, 2008) is an example of such a standardized measure. The DOF is especially useful for recording and rating observations of children in group settings, such as classrooms. The DOF contains 88 specific problem items, of which 63 overlap with the ASEBA Teacher's Report Form (TRF) and 51 overlap with the ASEBA Child Behavior Checklist for Ages 6–18 (CBCL/6–18). On the DOF protocol, the observer writes a narrative description of the child's behavior as it occurs over a 10-minute interval. Immediately after the 10 minutes, the observer scores the subject on each DOF item, using a 4-point scale: 0 = no occurrence; 1 = very slight or ambiguous occurrence; 2 = mild to moderate intensity and less than 3 minutes' duration; 3 = severe intensity or more than 3 minutes' duration. The observer also scores the child's on-task behavior for 10 one-minute intervals.

Observers can easily complete separate DOF forms for a target child and a control child. The DOF computer scoring program provides scores for On-Task, Total Problems, and six scales measuring specific problem patterns: Sluggish Cognitive Tempo, Immature/Withdrawn, Attention Problems, Intrusive, Oppositional, and Aggressive Behavior. The program averages scores across multiple observation sessions for each scale for the target child and control child. [An earlier version of the DOF (Achenbach, 1986) also included Internalizing and Externalizing scales along with scales for specific problems.]

The DOF is easy to use and does not require extensive training. Administrators can train paraprofessionals in the recording and scoring procedures. The DOF protocol provides rules for choosing among different items for scoring. However, observers should practice before they obtain observations on children in a program. To first learn the DOF scoring procedures in our research on the ABC Program, pairs of observers rated five nonparticipating children in a local school. They then compared and discussed their observations and ratings on each child with a trainer. Observer pairs then used the DOF to rate an additional 20 nonparticipating children to establish good inter-rater reliability. After training to the point of acceptable reliability, observers made two separate 10-minute DOF observations of PTAR and control children in the fall and spring of each school year.

Outcome Evaluation Designs

In *Preventing Problem Behaviors* (Algozzine & Kay, 2002), McConaughy and Leone (2002; Chapter 10) provide an in-depth, but nontechnical, discussion of approaches for measuring the success of prevention programs. They list several descriptive outcome measures and published instruments used to evaluate the success of six school-based prevention programs. They also discuss different ways to design program evaluations for single cases and groups of participants. The next sections address some key points for evaluating the ABC Program.

As indicated earlier, a major focus for evaluating the success of the ABC Program should be measuring changes in children's behavior. The challenge is to use an evaluation design that clearly links changes in behavior to actions or interventions during the program. A good evaluation design will allow administrators to rule out other factors, beside the program itself, which might explain changes in children's behavior. The first step in choosing an evaluation design is to decide whether the focus will be on single cases or groups of participants, or both.

Single-Case Designs

Single-case designs focus on changes over time for individual children; these designs are most appropriate when there are only a few participants or sites and when a control or comparison group is not available. The typical approach is to obtain data on the participant (target) before beginning the program (baseline data), and then to continue to obtain the same type of data (treatment phase data) during the program or over a specified period (e.g., one school year). For comparison, obtain similar baseline and treatment phase data for another individual (control) who did not participate in the program. Then chart the data for both the target and the control over time to see if the targeted behaviors show any notable increases or decreases.

In single-case designs, it is important to define what is measured, when it is measured, and how it is measured. Often the data involve direct observations of clearly defined discreet behaviors over specific intervals. In the ABC Program, parents and teachers on PTAR teams collect data on a target child as part of the Action Research Cycle (for details, see Chapters 9–11). If done systematically, and if the PTAR team agrees to share its data, an evaluator could use some of these behavioral observations as data points in single-case evaluations. Whenever the PTAR team shares data for program evaluation, however, maintaining guarantees of confidentiality for the child, family, and teacher is essential.

As an example, a teacher might count: (1) the number of minutes that a PTAR child was on-task for the first 15 minutes of math class each day; (2) the number of times a child shared an idea during circle time; or (3) how long the PTAR child participated in group activities at recess over a specific time frame each day. Parents of the PTAR child could record similar observations of specific behaviors at home. The behaviors that parents and teacher would record should be specific to the mutual goals that the PTAR team has developed for the child.

Single-case designs require recording multiple observations over time. Baseline data should be collected first, that is, before the PTAR team has its first meeting or during the period of initial meetings. Then, after the team has developed its action plan for the child, parents and teachers could continue to collect similar treatment phase data regularly over an agreed-upon period. Data collection could continue for several weeks, months, or for the entire school year.

For comparison, the teacher could record similar observations of a control child in the same class. The control should be a child who displays similar types of problems as the PTAR child, but who does not have a PTAR team. Chart the data for the PTAR child and control child across the designated time. By comparing data for the PTAR child and the control child, the PTAR team and program evaluators can measure the success of the team's action plans for the PTAR child compared with the matched control child.

A second approach is to have independent observers collect baseline and treatment phase data on PTAR and control children. The observers could use similar data collection procedures as described previously for the PTAR team. Observers should focus on specific behaviors that they can easily tally or record over discreet intervals. They should also directly relate the specific behaviors to the mutual goals for an individual child set by the PTAR team. This means that they might observe different types of behaviors for different children with PTAR teams. For example, an observer might record on-task behavior during independent seatwork for a child whose PTAR team's goal was to improve the child's productivity in school. For another child whose PTAR team's goal was to improve listening skills and sharing, the observer might record instances when the child raised his/her hand to talk, listened attentively to the teacher or another child, and offered materials or toys to another child.

A third approach is to have independent observers use the DOF to record and rate behaviors for a PTAR child and a matched control child in the same classroom. For example, the observer could use the DOF to obtain two 10-minute observations of the PTAR child and two 10-minute observations of the control child over specific intervals (e.g., one day each week) during the school year. The administrator would average the DOF scores for each observation period, and create a graph showing scores across baseline observations and treatment phase intervals when PTAR team meetings are taking place. By comparing the pattern of DOF scores from baseline through the treatment phase, the PTAR team and evaluators can see whether the PTAR child showed greater reductions in relevant problem behaviors than the control child (who did not have a PTAR team). Figure 5.1 shows an example of how Externalizing scores on the 1986 DOF dropped more dramatically from baseline through the treatment phase for a PTAR child compared to his matched control in the same classroom.

A fourth approach for single-case designs is to have a parent and teacher of each PTAR child complete one or more of the published questionnaires described earlier in this chapter. The par-

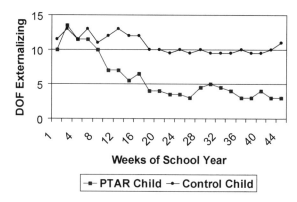

FIGURE 5.1. Observed externalizing problems.

ent's and teacher's questionnaires should be completed before the first meeting of the PTAR team or at least before the team develops its action plan for the child. For example, in the weeks before the first team meeting, a child's parent could complete the CBCL/6–18 and SSRS-P, and his/her teacher could complete the TRF and SSRS-T. Parents and teachers might also complete the BERS-2 to measure additional positive behaviors.

Scale scores from the CBCL/6–18, SSRS-P, TRF, SSRS-T, and BERS-2 could then be used as baseline, or *pretest* measures, of the child's functioning. After a suitable time (e.g., at the end of each school year), parents and teachers can complete the same instruments again as *posttest* measures. By comparing scale scores from time 1 (pretest) and time 2 (posttest), evaluators can determine if the PTAR child's behavior changed over that interval.

For comparison, teachers should also complete a pretest and posttest TRF and SSRS-T for one control child in the class, who has similar problems as the PTAR child, but does not have a PTAR team. Comparing the results for the PTAR child and control child will help determine whether changes in the PTAR child's behavior can be attributed to the PTAR team's efforts. If you take this approach, you must honor guarantees of confidentiality when you report results from parent and teacher questionnaires.

One of the advantages of the parent and teacher questionnaires listed in Appendices 5.1 and 5.2 is that they measure many different types of behaviors. However, PTAR teams' actions would seldom produce changes in all the types of behaviors measured by these instruments. Changes are more likely to occur in behaviors that are the targets of a PTAR team's mutual goals and action plans. Changes may also occur in other types of behaviors, but you will be less clear that the actions of the team affected these changes. For example, if a PTAR team focused its goals on improving a child's self-esteem and happiness, then you could look for reductions in scores on the CBCL/6–18 and TRF Anxious/Depressed and Withdrawn/Depressed scales. The teacher's ratings of the child's happiness on the TRF Adaptive Functioning scale would also be an indicator of progress. Because all children in the classroom also received social skills instruction, the PTAR child might show increases on SSRS-P and SSRS-T Total Social Skills and several social skills subscales. Comparable improvements might also appear on the BERS-2 Intrapersonal Strengths scale. If the same child also showed improvements in TRF and SSRS-T academic performance, this might be related to improved self-esteem or to other factors, such as tutoring or more help with schoolwork at home. By carefully examining the patterns of high and low scale scores on such standardized instruments, administrators can judge which changes reflect improvements that likely are due to participation in the ABC Program.

Experimental Group Designs

Group designs can also use observational data and published parent and teacher questionnaires to measure outcomes before (pretest) and after (posttest) carrying out a prevention program. In contrast to single-case designs, group designs require gathering data for many children and computing averages of scores across groups. Experimental group designs compare the performance of a group participating in a program (treatment group) to a comparable group (control group) that does not participate in the program. When the treatment group shows significantly greater changes in behavior than the control group, evaluators can conclude that the changes were due to the program, and not to other factors that might affect both groups equally, such as developmental maturation.

In our research on the ABC Program, we used an experimental group design to demonstrate the success of PTAR teams for 41 children in 16 different schools. We asked parents to complete the CBCL/6–18 (Achenbach, 1991a) and SSRS-P for each child with a PTAR team and teachers to complete the TRF (Achenbach, 1991b) and SSRS-T. Parents and teachers also completed the same instruments on control children in the same classrooms as PTAR children. We matched the control children to PTAR children on gender, TRF Total Problems, and their pattern of internalizing versus externalizing problems.

After 2 years in the ABC Program, the average scores of PTAR children were significantly lower than scores for control children on several CBCL/6–18 and TRF Problem scales, including scales measuring internalizing and externalizing problems. Scores for PTAR children were also significantly higher on CBCL/6–18 Total Competence and SSRS-P subscales measuring cooperation and self-control (McConaughy et al., 1999, 2000). The comparisons between PTAR and control children clearly showed that the team collaboration between parents and teachers successfully reduced problem behaviors and improved positive behaviors for that group of PTAR children.

Administrators can use a similar experimental group design to evaluate the success of their ABC Programs. This would require aggregating data for students in several different classrooms and perhaps different schools, agencies, or districts. For example, parents and teachers of all children could complete a set of published questionnaires, such as the CBCL/6–18, SSRS-P, TRF, SSRS-T, and BERS-2. Parents and teachers could also complete the same questionnaires on one control child matched to each PTAR child. Ideally, they would match the control children to the PTAR children on gender, age, and pattern of problems (e.g., internalizing, externalizing, or both) as we did in the research on ABC.

The same sets of questionnaires should be completed on PTAR and control children at the beginning of the program (pretest) and after a specified interval (e.g., 6 months or at the end of the school year) (posttest). As in the single-case design, comparisons of pretest and posttest scale scores between the PTAR children and the control children would indicate whether the PTAR teams produced greater changes in the behavior of PTAR children compared to control children.

Independent observers could also gather data for PTAR children and their matched controls for the same pretest and posttest periods. The observational data could focus on specific behaviors like those described for single-case designs. However, for an experimental group design, observers would have to record and chart similar types of observations for each child (e.g., disruptive behavior, antisocial behavior, on-task behavior, raising hand before talking, or sharing materials). Observers would also need accurate operational definitions of the behaviors to ensure that they recorded similar types of observations for each child.

Observers can also use a standardized rating scale, like the DOF, to record and rate behaviors of PTAR and control children at pretest and posttest periods. We recommend that observers conduct two or three 10-minute observations with the DOF for each PTAR child and a control child in the same classroom. Ideally, they should match control children to PTAR children on gender, severity, and pattern of problems, as done for parent and teacher questionnaires. We also recommend that observers be unaware of which children have PTAR teams. Keeping observers unaware of the status of either PTAR or control children will help eliminate any biases. (Parents and teachers who know the children and participate in a PTAR team's collaborative efforts might inadvertently bias the data.)

In our research on the ABC Program, we used the DOF (Achenbach, 1986) to obtain independent observations of children with PTAR teams and matched control children in the same classrooms. Observers obtained two separate 10-minute DOF observations of PTAR and control children in the fall and spring of each school year. DOF scores were then averaged separately across observation periods for the PTAR children and the control children.

Both the PTAR and the control children showed significant improvements in on-task behavior scores over the 2 years of the ABC research. However, the PTAR children showed significant reductions in DOF Internalizing scores at the end of the 2-year program, in contrast to increases in Internalizing scores for the control children. The observed changes in the Internalizing scores for the two groups provided independent evidence of the effectiveness of the PTAR teams. (For details of our research findings for the ABC Program, see McConaughy et al., 1998, 1999, 2000.)

Group Designs without a Control Group

Whenever possible, experimental group designs are preferable to group designs without control groups. When control groups are not feasible, evaluators can compare the performance of a group before the program begins (pretest) with the same group's performance after the program is completed (posttest).

Participating children's scores on standardized instruments can also be compared to the similar scores of the normative sample that was used to develop the instrument. For example, if teachers in the ABC Program complete the TRF, SSRS-T, and BERS-2, then they can compare mean scale scores for children with PTAR teams to mean scores on the same scales for the instrument's normative sample. These comparisons to the normative sample will show whether the PTAR children, as a group, show higher or lower scores on the various scales than would be expected for their gender, age, or grade. Similar normative comparisons can be made for the pretest and posttest scores.

However, administrators must be cautious in their interpretations of the results of group designs without control groups. When control groups share the same characteristics as the group receiving a program, they *control* for other possible explanations of changes in scores. Without comparisons between the group in the program and a control group, there is no way to test whether changes in children's behavior might have been due to other factors unrelated to the program itself.

In our research on the ABC Program, general education teachers taught social skills to all children in their classrooms. Our evaluation results showed that PTAR children and their matched controls all showed improvements in their social skills, as measured on the SSRS-P and SSRS-T. However, we could not test whether these improvements in social skills were actually due to the social skills curriculum, because we did not have a second control group without PTAR teams that did *not* receive social skills instruction. Thus, we had no way of knowing whether children's improved social skills might have been due to maturation or other factors, instead of the specific instruction they received from their teachers.

HOW WILL WE REPORT OUR RESULTS?

The ABC Program is the result of scientifically based research, as defined in the federal government's No Child Left Behind Act of 2001. This means, among other things, that we empirically validated ABC's effectiveness through the use of an experimental design, using valid and reliable measures. We then described the program in sufficient detail for someone to replicate it, and had it accepted for publication in peer-reviewed journals. While this may be reassuring to administrators who try the ABC Program for the first time, it does not answer the question "Is it working here, in our schools?" That is the question asked by those who feel responsible for their local schools, or *key stakeholders.*

Evaluation reports should distribute findings to key stakeholders in an objective and unambiguous manner. Audiences such as school boards, the public, or legislators usually do not need technical details of methods and results. These audiences are usually more interested in summaries of who participated in the program, how well it worked, how it was carried out, and what it cost. Reports for these audiences should present clear and concise descriptions of the major features of the program, evaluation methods, and key findings regarding the program's success. It is also important to discuss the program's limitations and to make recommendations for improvements, if necessary. Use quotes from participants sparingly and anonymously, and only to illustrate specific results. Including too many appreciative, but vague, quotes tends to come across as attempts to "sell" the program. Additional information concerning evaluation instruments, statistical analyses, and background literature can be placed in footnotes or appendices for further examination by interested parties.

An evaluation report that clearly shows the success of a program can bolster arguments for sustaining a prevention program, like the ABC Program, when budget constraints, or other factors, threaten its continuation. If the evaluation report fails to present evidence of success, a program that merely appears promising will be vulnerable to budget cuts. Remember that change takes time, and that our research on ABC found quite different results for children after 2 years of participation than at the end of 1 year (McConaughy et al., 2000). See Chapter 1 for a brief discussion of the recommended duration of ABC.

Examples of Published Parent Questionnaires
for Evaluating Children's Behavior

Achenbach System of Empirically Based Assessment (ASEBA) Child Behavior Checklist for Ages 1½–5 (CBCL/1½–5; Achenbach & Rescorla, 2000)
  www.aseba.org

Achenbach System of Empirically Based Assessment (ASEBA) Child Behavior Checklist for Ages 6–18 (CBCL/6–18; Achenbach & Rescorla, 2001)
  www.aseba.org

Ages & Stages Questionnaires: Social–Emotional (ASQ:SE; Squires, Bricker, & Twombly, 2002) [Ages 6–60 months]
  www.brookespublishing.com

Behavior Assessment System for Children—Second Edition (BASC-2; Reynolds & Kamphaus, 2004) [Ages 2–21 years]
  www.agsnet.com

Behavioral and Emotional Rating Scale—Second Edition (BERS-2; Epstein, 2004) [Ages 5–18 years]
  www.proedinc.com

Devereux Early Childhood Assessment (DECA; LeBuffe & Naglieri, 1999) [Ages 2–5 years]
  www.devereuxearlychildhood.org

Home and Community Social Behavior Scales (HCSBS; Merrell & Caldarella, 2001) [Ages 5–18 years]
  www.assessment_intervention.com

Social Skills Rating System—Parent Version (SSRS-P; Gresham & Elliott, 1990) [Ages 3–18 years]
  www.agsnet.com

From Stephanie H. McConaughy, Pam Kay, Julie A. Welkowitz, Kim Hewitt, and Martha D. Fitzgerald (2008). Copyright by The Guilford Press. Permission to photocopy this appendix is granted to purchasers of this book for personal use only (see copyright page for details).

Examples of Published Teacher Questionnaires
for Evaluating Children's Behavior

Achenbach System of Empirically Based Assessment (ASEBA) Caregiver–Teacher Report Form (C-TRF; Achenbach & Rescorla, 2000) [Ages 1½–5 years]
> *www.aseba.org*

Achenbach System of Empirically Based Assessment (ASEBA) Teacher's Report Form (TRF; Achenbach & Rescorla, 2001) [Ages 6–18 years]
> *www.aseba.org*

Ages & Stages Questionnaires: Social–Emotional (ASQ–SE; Squires, Bricker, & Twombly, 2002) [Ages 6–60 months]
> *www.brookespublishing.com*

Behavior Assessment System for Children—Second Edition (BASC-2; Reynolds & Kamphaus, 2004) [Ages 4–18 years]
> *www.agsnet.com*

Behavioral and Emotional Rating Scale—Second Edition (BERS-2; Epstein, 2004) [Ages 5–18 years]
> *www.proedinc.com*

Devereux Early Childhood Assessment (DECA; LeBuffe & Naglieri, 1999) [Ages 2–5 years]
> *www.devereuxearlychildhood.org*

School Social Behavior Scales, Second Edition (SSBS-2; Merrell, 2002) [Ages 5–18 years]
> *www.assessment_intervention.com*

Social Skills Rating System—Teacher Version (SSRS-T; Gresham & Elliott, 1990) [Ages 3–18 years]
> *www.agsnet.com*

From Stephanie H. McConaughy, Pam Kay, Julie A. Welkowitz, Kim Hewitt, and Martha D. Fitzgerald (2008). Copyright by The Guilford Press. Permission to photocopy this appendix is granted to purchasers of this book for personal use only (see copyright page for details).

II

FOR PARENT LIAISONS

Welcome to the ABC family! You have been chosen as a Parent Liaison for the local Achieving–Behaving–Caring (ABC) Program, and are about to make a difference in the lives of children and families in your community. Since you were chosen very carefully for this role, we know certain things about you.

Parent Liaisons are a special group of people. You are people who understand the heritage of the local community and can bridge the cultures of home and school. You enjoy collaboration and can express ideas in clear language that both parents and teachers can understand. Parent Liaisons have a special interest in helping parents become engaged in their children's education. You can keep an open mind about the many different forms of family structure, patterns of child rearing, and alternative lifestyles.

An essential quality for Parent Liaisons is the ability to listen to and talk with both parents and teachers. You are familiar with the requirements and routines of schools and the expectations that teachers have for children. You are also aware of the challenges in raising children. This is true whether there are two parents or one, custodial or noncustodial parents, foster parents, grandparents, or other kin raising children. When disagreements or conflicts arise among teachers and parents, Parent Liaisons remain open to different points of view and different ways to solve problems. You keep in mind the many demands on both parents' and teachers' time and energy. You maintain a positive attitude and persist in trying to find mutually agreeable solutions to promote children's learning and school adjustment.

Your success as a Parent Liaison is more about you as a human being, and less about your ability to do everything in this book as we have written it. If we don't say it often enough throughout the text, remember that this is *not* a set of directives. The book is quite detailed because Parent Liaisons have told us how much the details matter. Even if we write "Do this . . . ," or "Do that . . . ," you may have a better way of getting the job done. Trust your own best judgment and rely on it!

What is your relationship to parents and teachers? Figure PII.1 describes some characteristics that might help you think through your new role.

Our research team at the University of Vermont knew that young children who were having a hard time adjusting to school in the early grades could develop emotional and behavioral prob-

To parents, you are:		
Friend or colleague	NOT	Social worker
Co-learner	NOT	Teacher
Encourager	NOT	Critic
Supporter	NOT	Advocate
Source of helpful information	NOT	Set of helping hands

To teachers, you are:		
Assistant	NOT	Adversary
Co-learner	NOT	Expert
Encourager	NOT	Critic
Guide on the side	NOT	Sage on the stage

FIGURE PII.1. Characteristics of the Parent Liaison role.

lems in later years. These problems would hinder them, and sometimes their classmates, from learning. Our research team developed and tested a three-part program to give children extra support in adjusting to school. One part ensures that all children learn how to get along together in the classroom, another part brings parents and teachers together in a new way, and the third part is you, the Parent Liaison.

Teachers have told us that all children benefit when classmates learn and practice social skills lessons together. Parents and classroom teachers can work together as equals to address children's issues if they have a specific structure to follow, and someone to bring them together to meet regularly. The structure in the ABC Program is called Parent–Teacher Action Research, or PTAR. (You will want to say each letter—P-T-A-R—in this acronym, rather than pronouncing "ptar" as one word.) Finally, we believe that growth occurs at all ages through relationships. That means that the person who brings parents and teachers together needs to be someone skilled in relationship-building—a Parent Liaison.

The results of our research, which was sponsored by the U.S. Department of Education, were encouraging. Both parents and teachers reported that children improved in cooperation and self-control. They said that children had fewer problems, such as breaking rules. Teachers reported that shy children became more outgoing. Classroom observers noted improvements in children's school behavior. You will find more details about our findings in the introduction to the book. We think that your community can get similar results for its children, and that is why we wrote *Collaborating with Parents for Early School Success: The Achieving–Behaving–Caring Program.*

HOW TO USE PART II OF THIS BOOK

We have written the seven chapters of Part II, *For Parent Liaisons,* with you in mind. (We also encourage administrators to read Part II.) Each chapter begins with a set of steps for your guidance, and ends with one or more appendices containing materials that you can copy and use with your parent–teacher teams. Throughout each chapter you will see tips, scripts, and stories to use on the job (see Figure PII.2 for the icons that identify these elements).

After you have had some training, you will be ready to begin working with parents. Chapter 6 will help you reach out to parents whose children have been offered a place in the ABC Program. With your knowledge of the community, you will know the best ways to reach each family. Throughout this book, we use the word *parents* to mean the adults who are most responsible for caring for a child. While other family members may be sharing the child's life, we think that it is best to bring the one or two adults who are most important to that child into a close working relationship with the child's classroom teacher.

The steps in Chapter 7 will help you to lay the groundwork for solid relationships with the parent, the teacher, and the school administrator. If your ABC Program will be using parent and teacher questionnaires to evaluate the program, your supervisor will explain them to you, and tell you your role in getting them completed. This chapter lists the materials that you might want to have on hand for each PTAR meeting, and provides helpful hints to make the meetings much different from a typical parent–teacher conference.

Chapter 8 starts the PTAR process by telling the child's story, guided by a set of questions called Making Action Plans (MAPs). You will learn how to establish the ground rules, take notes that respect the wisdom of both parent and teacher, and move the PTAR team toward agreeing on mutual goals for the child.

The Action Research Cycle begins in Chapter 9, with parents and teachers deciding how to collect information (data) on the child. This chapter will give you guidance in creating agendas for each meeting, keeping the team focused on their mutual goals, and thinking about many ways to collect data. To bring the PTAR process to life, this chapter begins the stories of two children,

Tips and **Helpful Hints** are based on the experiences of many Parent Liaisons and our research team. You may develop a list of your own as you go along.

Scripts give you an idea of what to say at various points while starting a Parent–Teacher Action Research (say P-T-A-R) team.

Stories will give you examples to use in talking with parents and teachers. They might also give you ideas about working with your own PTAR teams.

FIGURE PII.2. Icons for identifying tips and helpful hints, scripts, and stories.

Bethany and Gray, giving examples of the way each of their teams learned to meet the children's needs.

Chapter 10 moves around the Action Research Cycle, with the parents and teacher sharing their reflections on what they noticed about the child since the previous meeting. You will find some questions that encourage reflection, and a way to help the team describe the child's behavior productively, rather than characterizing it or labeling the child. This chapter also helps the team develop a practical theory about what the behavior means to the child.

In Chapter 11, you will learn about brainstorming ideas, developing an action plan, and continuing to collect data as the team moves through the Action Research Cycle. If parents need extra support to carry out their part of the action plan, this chapter suggests some places where you might help them find that support.

Finally, Chapter 12 addresses some of the issues that you might encounter with your PTAR teams. After finishing the stories of Bethany and Gray, this chapter uses short vignettes about other children to illustrate ways to keep your teams moving in the right direction. Helpful hints for dealing with things that might go awry are threaded through the short stories. This chapter ends with suggestions on supporting children and families during transitions from grade to grade or school to school, and ways to bring closure to the PTAR process at the end of 2 years, or when the child no longer needs the extra support of a PTAR team. Use this book as a guide for your important work with parents and teachers in the ABC Program.

6

Enlisting Parent Participation in ABC

```
┌─────────────────────────────────────────────────────────────┐
│                          Steps                                 │
│  ─────────────────────────────────────────────────────────── │
│  1.  Send introductory letter to parents.                      │
│  2.  Phone parent to set date and time for invitational meeting.│
│  3.  Send follow-up letter to parents who do not respond.      │
│  4.  Conduct invitational meeting with parent.                 │
│  5.  Obtain signed consent form from parent.                   │
│  6.  End the meeting by setting up the next meeting date.      │
│  7.  Send welcome letter to parents.                           │
│  8.  Begin a Family Contact Sheet for your records.            │
└─────────────────────────────────────────────────────────────┘
```

After you have had some training, your first responsibility as Parent Liaison is to enlist the participation of parents whose children may benefit from the ABC Program. The steps given in this chapter are guidelines, not a formula that you must follow. Use your own wisdom to reach parents and invite them to become part of ABC in ways that are respectful and effective in your community.

STEP 1. SEND INTRODUCTORY LETTER TO PARENTS

The way children and families are chosen as possible participants in ABC will vary from one agency and school to the next. Some ABC Programs will have a standard screening process for selecting participants. Others may use more informal selection procedures, such as having preschool or elementary teachers suggest children who may benefit from the program. School guidance counselors, social workers, and other student support team members may also refer children for the program. Sometimes, a staff member from a community agency may contact school staff about a child and family as possible participants. Parents may learn about ABC from school newsletters, and ask if their children can participate.

Once a child is considered as a potential participant in ABC, your supervisor or a designated school staff member will provide you with a list of names, addresses, and phone numbers of families to contact. Begin with the first family on your list. Send a short note to the parent(s) to introduce yourself as Parent Liaison. Appendix 6.1 gives an example letter. You do not have to provide details about ABC in this letter. Instead, simply say that you will be in touch with the parent to make an appointment to talk in person about the program.

If you have not yet met the parent, use the parent's first and last name in the salutation of the letter. If two parents are in the home, address the letter to both. Be sure to check whether the child's mother and father have the same or different last names. Sign the letter with your own first and last name, and add the name of your community agency or school where you are employed. (Later, after you have met face-to-face with the parent and teacher, you may all agree to use only first names.)

TIP: You can make your own version of the Sample Introductory Letter, or you can copy the introductory letter from Appendix 6.1 as a form and fill in names for the parent, child, child's school, and your community agency or school.

STEP 2. PHONE PARENT TO SET DATE AND TIME FOR INVITATIONAL MEETING

Within a week after sending your introductory letter, contact the parent to make an appointment to talk in person about ABC. Use your own style to follow the sample script shown in Appendix 6.2. You will probably want to use the parent's first and last name when you first speak with him/her. If you already know the parent, you can judge whether to use just the first name in the phone call.

Keep the phone call brief and focused on choosing a date and time for a meeting. Be ready for some initial questions, but explain that you would like to save the details of the program for when you meet face to face. Ask the parent for a time when you can meet with him/her to describe the program. You might tell a little about yourself and how you became involved in the ABC Program. Do not go into too many details about yourself, however; keep the focus on the program.

Ask the parent to suggest a convenient place to meet. If the parent does not name a place to meet, you can suggest a neutral public area, such as the mall, a local library, or a community agency. If you suggest a place that might put a financial burden on the parent, such as a restaurant, say that you would like to buy him/her a cup of coffee! Make sure that both you and the parent know the directions to the meeting place.

Be sure to check whether the parent has any transportation problems for coming to meet with you. Your supervisor can tell you whether you have a budget for the costs of taxis or other transportation services. Ask your supervisor whether you should offer to drive the parent from home or work to a convenient location for the meeting.

You can also offer to go the parent's home or to the home of a relative for your invitational meeting, if you (and the parent) feel comfortable about doing so. However, some parents may feel uncomfortable about having someone whom they do not know visit them in their home. *You should not visit a home if you are concerned about your own safety.* For example, you may feel unsafe meeting in homes in very remote locations or in dangerous neighborhoods. If you have concerns about your safety, arrange transportation for the parent to a different, more public setting.

If you suggest meeting at the school, the parent may think that you are a member of the school staff. As Parent Liaison, you need to establish a neutral role for yourself, not a role that is closely aligned with the school, even if you are employed by the school. However, some parents may suggest meeting at the child's school because that is the most convenient place for them. If you and the parent decide to meet at the school, you will need to check with the school principal to find a private place to meet.

Gentle persistence is the key for making first contacts with parents. Sometimes it will take several attempts for your initial breakthrough. Some families may not have a phone or answering machine, so you may have to keep trying to contact parents. Some families may not have permanent homes, but instead may be living with relatives or in temporary quarters, such as a motel or shelter. Some parents may need more than one phone call before they can be sure that you care about them and their child.

 TIP: If you are having trouble reaching a parent by phone, try calling at different times of the day. If you leave a message, give the parent a few days to call you back before calling again.

If the family has no phone, ask a member of the school staff how to best contact the parent. Some families may have preferred methods of contact, such as phoning a neighbor or relative, or meeting the parent at school when they pick up a child. Do not phone a parent at work unless the parent has given permission for such phone calls to the school or agency. You may need to ask a school staff member to check with a parent to get permission for you to call the parent's work phone number.

During your first phone contact, you may learn that some parents are reluctant to participate in the ABC Program because they had poor experiences at school when they were children. Parents may also fear that ABC will be a negative experience for their child or that the school will label their child as a problem child. To address such fears, reassure parents that ABC is a program that focuses on positive things for children and respects their parents' wisdom. Then ask again if you can meet personally with them to describe the program in more detail.

If problems arise about the appointment date, or if a parent misses a scheduled meeting, be sympathetic and reschedule the meeting. Don't scold. Instead, reassure the parent that you are still eager to get together to describe the program. You might praise the parent for interest and effort, saying "Thank you for calling me to reschedule our meeting. I am pleased that you are interested in hearing about the ABC Program."

STEP 3. SEND FOLLOW-UP LETTER TO PARENTS
WHO DO NOT RESPOND

Discuss with your supervisor how often you should try to contact parents who do not respond to your letter or phone calls. We recommend that you try phoning at least three times at different times of the day. If the family has no phone or does not respond to your calls, try sending postcards or notes home from school with the child. Write your own phone number on the postcard or note and ask the parent to call you. Suggest good times to reach you. If your supervisor agrees, you may tell a parent to call you "collect" if the call would otherwise cost the parents a toll charge.

 TIP: Writing or typing your own personal follow-up letter or postcard may do the trick in sparking a parent's interest in the program. If you do not feel comfortable writing your own letter, or do not have the time, you can use the sample follow-up letter in Appendix 6.3.

If you get no response after these efforts, check with the child's teacher to see if family circumstances might have prevented a parent from responding. If no known circumstances are found, send a friendly follow-up letter again asking the parent to call you. You can also include a stamped, self-addressed postcard for the parent to mail back to show interest in the program. Appendices 6.3 and 6.4 show a sample follow-up letter and return postcard.

STEP 4. CONDUCT INVITATIONAL MEETING WITH PARENT

For many parents, the invitational meeting may be the first time they have met you in person. It is usually wise to dress in a casual and informal style. You want parents to see you as a supportive peer—another parent—not as a member of the school staff. Overdressing may intimidate some families, especially families with low income or families in rural communities. For example, in a rural community, jeans and a nice T-shirt or sweater may be most appropriate. On the other hand, dress that is too informal may seem disrespectful to some parents. Use your own judgment on what is appropriate for your community and the family you will be meeting. A good guideline is to wear what people in the community would wear to visit a neighbor.

 TIP: If you are meeting in the family's home, be prepared to meet the family pets. If you have fears or allergies to pets, it is OK to ask parents politely to keep the pets away. Also, if the parent smokes, feel free to explain that you are sensitive to smoke.

With a smile, handshake, and good eye contact, introduce yourself as the Parent Liaison for the ABC Program. Early in your conversation, offer a sincere compliment specific to that parent. If you are at the parent's home, say something about the flowers in the yard, the setting or view at the house, a pet or baby, or something nice about the room. If you are not meeting the parent at home, be prepared to offer a comment about something you have in common, or a compliment on the parent's choice of meeting place. Parents can never hear too many compliments, as long as they are heartfelt and appropriate.

 TIP: If you are meeting at a school, be sure to check in at the central office or some other specific location before going elsewhere in the building. You may also have to sign in and out, and you may be required to wear nametags for identification. Be sure to follow the school's required check-in procedures each time you enter the building.

Goals for the invitational meeting with parents are in Appendix 6.5. You can copy this outline to use as a guide for the meeting. Don't be shy about looking at your outline during the meeting, commenting that you do not want to forget anything important.

The first goal of the invitational meeting is to begin building trust and to put the parent at ease while talking with you. Begin the conversation by briefly reviewing who you are and why you are there. For example, you can say, "As I mentioned on the phone, I am the Parent Liaison for the ABC Program. Thank you for agreeing to let me tell you about this program. I love my job as Parent Liaison because I have seen such good results for children when parents and teachers make the time to work together."

You can then share something about your own children in school or your experiences as a parent. Sharing something about yourself can help to make a connection with parents. However, since you are there to learn about the family, keep stories about yourself brief. To turn the discussion toward the family, ask the parent to tell you something about the child. Keep the focus positive, such as asking, "What does [child] do best? What does [child] like to do for fun?" Your next goal is to provide information about the ABC Program. Begin by talking briefly about the positive results from research on the ABC model, as outlined in the list below.

 POSITIVE RESULTS FROM RESEARCH ON THE ABC PROGRAM

The ABC Program we are using was developed and tested through research at the University of Vermont. After 2 years in a similar program:

- Both parents and teachers reported that children improved in cooperation and self-control.
- Both parents and teachers reported that children had fewer problems, such as breaking rules.
- Teachers also reported that shy children became more outgoing.
- Classroom observers noted improvements in children's school behavior.

Then describe the features of the ABC Program, as outlined in Appendix 6.6. You can copy this outline to use in your meeting with parents. State that the program is intended to cover 2 years. Explain that during these 2 years, the child's teacher will teach social skills to all children in the class. Children will learn skills such as cooperation, sharing, making and keeping friends, and asking for help when they need it. The teacher will send materials home so that the parent will know which specific skill the class is working on.

Explain that the parent(s) and the child's teacher will meet first to develop mutual goals for the child. They then meet regularly as a team throughout the year and will decide together how often to meet and where. Most teams choose to meet for about an hour or an hour and a half once a month. Some may want to meet more often, especially in the beginning of the program.

Tell the parent that, as Parent Liaison, you will arrange the meeting times and places. Your role is to guide the team through a collaborative action research process, not to run the meetings. In the meetings, parents and teachers will work together as *equal partners* to develop their goals for the child. You may also want to summarize the ground rules for parent–teacher meetings, as discussed in Chapter 8. Emphasize that a key ground rule is that parents speak first.

Explain that between meetings, both the parents and teacher will gather information about the child; eventually they will make action plans to meet their mutual goals for the child. Your role as Parent Liaison is to support the parent in this process. Try not to go into too much detail about the team process in this invitational meeting. Assure the parent that the details of this process will become clearer as you work together. However, be sure to answer questions that the parent may have about the program. If you don't know the answer, say that you will find out, and subsequently call the parent with the answer. Be sure to write the question on paper before you move on with the rest of the meeting.

STEP 5. OBTAIN SIGNED CONSENT FORM FROM PARENT

When you feel that you have given the parent sufficient information about the ABC Program, ask, "Do you think you would like your child to be part of ABC?" If the parent wants to join the program, or is willing to consider joining the program, review the Parent Consent Form. Appendix 6.7 shows a sample Parent Consent Form. Your agency or school may have its own version of the Parent Consent Form. Your supervisor will give you copies of all forms to take to the invitational meeting.

Read through the consent form with each parent. Begin by emphasizing that participation is voluntary. State that parents may withdraw from the program anytime. If your ABC Program uses a formal evaluation process, the second paragraph of the Parent Consent Form will state that the parent will complete some questionnaires to help evaluate the program. The second paragraph also describes timing for meetings and the 2-year typical length of the program.

The third paragraph describes your role as Parent Liaison and guarantees of confidentiality. This is a very important section of the Parent Consent Form. Make sure that the parent understands that, as Parent Liaison, you may share information about the family with your supervisor.

 TIP: Be sure to review your agency's or school's version of the Parent Consent Form with your supervisor before the invitational meeting with parents. Bring a copy of the Parent Consent Form to the invitational meeting.

Assure the parent that you will not share personal information about the family at meetings with the teacher, unless the parent has given you prior permission. However, under certain circumstances, you may be required by law to break confidentiality. These circumstances, as listed below, are in the third paragraph of the Parent Consent Form:

1. Information subpoenaed (demanded) by a court of law.
2. Suspected cases of child abuse under state law.
3. Information that individuals intend to harm themselves or others.

Note that the fourth paragraph of the form states that the child's name, the parent's name, or the family's name will not be used in any reports about the program.

If you are meeting with only one parent, be sure to allow an opportunity for that parent to review the consent form with the other parent if he/she wishes to. You can ask if the parent needs time to discuss the program with another person. Parents who have shared custody of their children may choose to discuss the consent form with the child's other parent. Some parents who have trouble reading may want to have someone else review the consent form and other written materials you leave with them.

 TIP: If you leave the Parent Consent Form for the parent to sign later, also leave a stamped, self-addressed envelope for the parent to return the form to you.

After reviewing the Parent Consent Form, again ask the parent if he/she wants to join the program. If the parent agrees, then obtain the parent's signature on the form. Tell the parent that you will make a copy of the signed consent form and mail it to him/her within a couple of weeks. Also tell the parent that you will take the original form back to your supervisor to be kept in a confidential file.

 TIP: As indicated in Step 5, parents may also be asked to complete the first questionnaires for program evaluation. If the parent wants to do this on another day, then set up a time and place for this meeting before you leave. Schedule this second meeting with the parent after the invitational meeting and before the first parent–teacher meeting. See Chapter 7 for further instructions.

During your training, you will learn what your school system or community agency will do to evaluate whether the ABC Program works in your community. Ideally, the evaluation plan should include structured questionnaires that parents and teachers complete at the beginning and end of each year. Completing the questionnaires should take about an hour. Because of time constraints, scheduling a second meeting with the parent to complete the questionnaires is usually better. Chapter 7 provides instructions for completing questionnaires with parents. Finally, tell parents that you would like to sit down and talk with them at the end of each year to learn more about how the program worked for them and their children.

 TIP: The evaluation questionnaires may raise additional questions from parents. Plan to be present while parents complete the questionnaires. *Do not leave the questionnaires for parents to complete on their own without carefully reviewing them and answering any questions parents may have.* (We will discuss questionnaires further in Chapter 7.)

STEP 6. END THE MEETING BY SETTING UP THE NEXT MEETING DATE

If the parent agrees to participate in the ABC Program and signs the Parent Consent Form, then ask about good times for the first parent–teacher meeting. Be sure to bring your own calendar so that you can choose times convenient for you and the parent. This would be a good time to ask the parent for information you will need to complete your Family Contact Sheet (see Appendix 6.8). If you will be meeting to complete program evaluation questionnaires, arrange a time and place for that purpose. Try to avoid having to call the parent later for possible meeting dates.

Explain that the place for the parent–teacher meetings should be mutually agreeable and convenient for both parents and teachers. Choosing a neutral place where both parents and teachers will feel comfortable is best. For example, in community settings, teams may choose to meet in a private room of the town hall or library, an office conference room, the fire station, or a community agency. At school, teams may choose to meet in a library, cafeteria, or conference room. Ask the parent where he/she would prefer to meet. Any setting must have enough privacy that parents and teachers feel comfortable sharing sensitive or confidential information. In schools, you may want to avoid meeting in the teacher's classroom, or the principal's office, especially if the family has experienced discipline problems in the past.

Tell the parent that you will check the times and meeting place with the child's teacher and contact the parent later to confirm the arrangements. If you wish, you can give the parent your phone number in case he/she has any further questions or concerns. You can suggest the best times of the day to call you and also times when not to call. (Chapter 12 will give you additional ways to set your boundaries as the year goes on.)

If the parent declines the invitation to participate in the ABC Program, thank him/her for taking the time to talk with you. Give parents a phone number they can call if they change their minds about participating in the program. Let parents know that you are still available to answer any questions. Tell them there may be openings later in the year if they change their minds. When a parent decides not to participate in the ABC Program, move to the next family on your list of names and addresses and repeat Steps 1 to 6.

 TIP: If parents change their minds and ask to participate in ABC later in the year, contact your supervisor. Tell parents you will contact them after you check whether there are still openings in the program this year.

STEP 7. SEND WELCOME LETTER TO PARENTS

Within one week after your invitational meeting, send a brief welcome letter to parents who have agreed to participate in the ABC Program. You can make your own version of a welcome letter, or copy the sample welcome letter from Appendix 6.9 and fill in names for the parent, school, and child.

If you use the sample welcome letter, then add a brief note to make the letter more personal. For example, you can write, "I am looking forward to working with you," or "I am so happy to have you join our program," next to your signature on the letter. Continue to use first and last names in the welcome letter, unless you and the parent are now on a first-name basis. Include the name of the community agency or school where you are employed at the bottom of the welcome letter if it is not printed on the letterhead. You should also add your phone number and the best times when parents can reach you at the bottom of the letter. Enclose a copy of the signed Parent Consent Form with your welcome letter.

STEP 8. BEGIN A FAMILY CONTACT SHEET FOR YOUR RECORDS

Complete the information on a Family Contact Sheet (Appendix 6.8) for this child's family, noting the date, time, and type of contact (in this case, a meeting). If you have promised to get back to the parent with additional information, or need to speak with your supervisor about this family, note it in the Follow-Up column.

✓**Checklist of Materials You Might Need for Enrolling Families**

☐ Copies of Information for Parents from Appendix 6.6

☐ Copies of the local ABC Program brochure

☐ Stationery, postcards, envelopes, stamps

☐ A stamped, self-addressed #10 envelope

☐ The Parent Consent Form (Appendix 6.7)

☐ The Family Contact Sheet (Appendix 6.8)

☐ A notebook or pad of paper to note parents' questions

☐ Your own calendar

☐ Other

Sample Introductory Letter to Parents

[Date]

Dear [Mr./Mrs./Ms.]:

This year, _____ school is participating in the ABC Program, to make the first years of school a positive experience for all children. As part of the program, all students in your child's class will be learning social skills together, such as listening, showing consideration for others, and asking for help appropriately. In addition, some children will also have the opportunity to have an ABC parent–teacher team. There is an opening in the program for your child, _____ , and I would like a chance to talk with you about his/her participation.

As a Parent Liaison, I am also part of the ABC Program. If you decide to have your child participate, I will be working with you on the team meetings. I will contact you soon to explain the program in more detail and answer any questions you may have.

I am looking forward to meeting with you soon.

Sincerely,

_____

Parent Liaison

_____

Community agency or school

From Stephanie H. McConaughy, Pam Kay, Julie A. Welkowitz, Kim Hewitt, and Martha D. Fitzgerald (2008). Copyright by The Guilford Press. Permission to photocopy this appendix is granted to purchasers of this book for personal use only (see copyright page for details).

Sample Script for First Parent Phone Call

- *Introduce yourself as a Parent Liaison*

My name is [your first and last name].
Is this [parent's first and last name]? I am the Parent Liaison for the ABC Program. I recently sent you a letter about ABC, and promised to contact you.

- *The purpose of the program is to make the first years of school positive for all children.*
- *Tell a little about how or why you got involved in the ABC Program.*

I am a parent of [number] child(ren). As Parent Liaison, I work for [community agency, school, or other employer].

- *Schedule an appointment to meet with the parents about the program.*

I'd like to set up a time to meet with you and tell you a little more about the ABC Program, and how you and your child can participate in it.

- *Suggest a few different times that would work in your schedule.*

Would this Friday at 10:00 in the morning be OK or would you rather meet in the afternoon? Is there any other day that is better for you? I can also meet on [day]. I would like about an hour of your time.

- *If the parent seems hesitant, be sure to state that ABC is optional; families do not have to participate, but you would like a chance to tell him/her more.*
- *Determine a neutral place to meet.*

Where would be a convenient place for you to meet with me to talk about the program? (Suggest the local library, a mall, or a community agency.) I would also be happy to buy you a cup of coffee at [place].

- *If you feel safe in making a home visit:*

Would you like me to come to your house?

- *State the date that you have agreed to meet.*
- *Thank the parent for his/her time today.*
- *Give a phone number and best times when you can be contacted.*

I look forward to meeting you on [date]. If you need to reach me before then, my phone number is [phone number]. The best times to call me are [times].

From Stephanie H. McConaughy, Pam Kay, Julie A. Welkowitz, Kim Hewitt, and Martha D. Fitzgerald (2008). Copyright by The Guilford Press. Permission to photocopy this appendix is granted to purchasers of this book for personal use only (see copyright page for details).

Sample Follow-Up Letter to Parents
Who Have Not Responded to Initial Contacts

[Date]

Dear [Mr./Mrs./Ms.]:

As the Parent Liaison for the ABC Program at _____ school, I want to be sure that you have an opportunity to learn more about the program. There is an opening in the program for your child, _____, and I would like a chance to talk with you about participating. As part of the program, all students in your child's class are learning social skills together, such as listening, showing consideration for others, and asking for help appropriately. In addition, some children will also have the opportunity to have an ABC parent–teacher team, and that is why I have been trying to contact you.

I would appreciate your calling me so that I can tell you more about what the ABC Program offers to you and your child. My phone number is _____ and the best time to reach me is _____. If I am not at home when you call, please leave a phone number and a message telling me when would be the best time to get back to you.

If I do not hear from you by _____, I will call another family about the opening in the ABC Program. There may be space for you to join us later in the year, so please keep this letter as a reminder.

Hope to hear from you soon.

Sincerely yours,

_____

Parent Liaison

_____

Community agency or school

From Stephanie H. McConaughy, Pam Kay, Julie A. Welkowitz, Kim Hewitt, and Martha D. Fitzgerald (2008). Copyright by The Guilford Press. Permission to photocopy this appendix is granted to purchasers of this book for personal use only (see copyright page for details).

Sample Return Postcard for Parents
Who Have Not Responded to Initial Contacts

ABC PROGRAM

I am the Parent Liaison for the ABC Program, and would like to be sure that you have the information about the ABC Program offered at your child's school. Would you return this postcard to let me know whether I may send you information?

_____ Yes, I am interested in learning more about the ABC Program at this time.

_____ No, I am not interested at this time; please contact me later.

_____ No, thank you, I am not interested in hearing more.

_____

Name

_____

Address

_____

Best Way to Reach Me

_____

Best Times to Meet with Me

_____

Parent Liaison

_____

Community agency or school

From Stephanie H. McConaughy, Pam Kay, Julie A. Welkowitz, Kim Hewitt, and Martha D. Fitzgerald (2008). Copyright by The Guilford Press. Permission to photocopy this appendix is granted to purchasers of this book for personal use only (see copyright page for details).

Goals for Invitational Meeting with Parents

I. BUILDING TRUST

- Review who you are and why you are there.
- Ask questions about the child's positive qualities.
- Share something about your own child or experiences as a parent.

II. GIVING INFORMATION

- Talk about positive results of research on the ABC model.
- Explain what will happen in 2 years of the program.

III. GETTING PERMISSION

- Review the Parent Consent Form, highlighting important points.
- Ask if the parent wants to discuss the consent form with someone else.
- If parent agrees, obtain parent's signature on consent form.
- If parent chooses to discuss the consent form with someone else, leave a self-addressed, stamped envelope for parent to return the consent form to you. Give the parent a date when you would like to receive the consent form.
- Explain that you will make a copy of the signed consent form and mail the copy back to the parent.
- Tell the parent where the original consent form will be filed.

IV. CLOSURE

- If the parent says "yes" to the invitation to participate in the ABC Program:
  - Ask about good times and preferred place for the first parent–teacher meeting.
  - Tell the parent that you will check the times and place with the child's teacher and then confirm the meeting date and place.
  - Give the parent your phone number and suggest best times of the day to call you.
- If the parent says "no" to the invitation to participate in the ABC Program:
  - Thank the parent for the time talking with you.
  - Give the parent your phone number and the phone number of the agency or school to call in case he/she decides later to participate.

From Stephanie H. McConaughy, Pam Kay, Julie A. Welkowitz, Kim Hewitt, and Martha D. Fitzgerald (2008). Copyright by The Guilford Press. Permission to photocopy this appendix is granted to purchasers of this book for personal use only (see copyright page for details).

ABC Program: Information for Parents

- All children will learn social skills together in their classroom.

- You and your child's teacher will meet regularly to work toward mutual goals for your child.

- As Parent Liaison, I will schedule the meetings and attend each one to help them run smoothly.

- You and your child's teacher will gather information about the child and develop action plans to reach your mutual goals.

- For best results, the program should cover 2 years.

- You will fill out questionnaires to help evaluate the program (if required).

- You will meet with me [Parent Liaison] at the end of each year to give us your opinion on how ABC worked for you and your child, and how we can improve the program.

From Stephanie H. McConaughy, Pam Kay, Julie A. Welkowitz, Kim Hewitt, and Martha D. Fitzgerald (2008). Copyright by The Guilford Press. Permission to photocopy this appendix is granted to purchasers of this book for personal use only (see copyright page for details).

APPENDIX 6.7

Parent Consent Form

ACHIEVING–BEHAVING–CARING (ABC) PROGRAM

I, _____ , agree to have my child,

_____ , participate in the ABC

program, sponsored by _____ in cooperation with

_____ .

I understand that my child and I will participate in a program designed to promote social skills and positive school adjustment. I will be participating on a team with my child's teacher, supported by a Parent Liaison. Our team will work toward common goals for my child so that he/she will succeed in school. I understand that my participation is voluntary.

The time commitment will be about 1 hour a month for meetings with the teacher and the Parent Liaison during the school year, plus time to carry out action plans between meetings. The overall time that my child and I are involved with the program will be about 1 to 2 years, depending on how long it takes to achieve the team's goals for my child. I understand that I will be asked to complete questionnaires regarding my child's behavior and social skills at the start and end of each school year, to help evaluate the program.

I understand that the Parent Liaison will assist me in carrying out my responsibilities. The Parent Liaison will share information about my child and our family only in confidential supervision with _____ . No one else will have access to confidential information about my child and our family, without my permission, except under the following circumstances required by law:

1. Information subpoenaed (demanded) by a court of law;
2. Suspected cases of child abuse under state law;
3. Information that individuals intend to harm themselves or others.

My name, my child's name, and our family's name will not be used in any reports or public media about the program. I may withdraw from this program at any time without affecting our relationship with the school or the community agency. I have read and understand this consent form and agree to participate in the ABC Program.

_____   _____
Parent's Signature   Date

_____   _____
Parent's Address   ZIP Code

_____
Parent's Phone Number and Best Times to Be Reached

You will receive a copy of this signed consent form.

From Stephanie H. McConaughy, Pam Kay, Julie A. Welkowitz, Kim Hewitt, and Martha D. Fitzgerald (2008). Copyright by The Guilford Press. Permission to photocopy this appendix is granted to purchasers of this book for personal use only (see copyright page for details).

APPENDIX 6.8

Family Contact Sheet

ABC PROGRAM FAMILY CONTACT SHEET

Parents' Name(s): _____   Teacher's Name: _____

Child's Name: _____   Grade: _____

Child's Birthday: _____ Gender: _____   Referred by: _____

Address: _____   Phone: _____

Comments: _____

Date	Time	Type of Contact	Follow-Up

From Stephanie H. McConaughy, Pam Kay, Julie A. Welkowitz, Kim Hewitt, and Martha D. Fitzgerald (2008). Copyright by The Guilford Press. Permission to photocopy this appendix is granted to purchasers of this book for personal use only (see copyright page for details).

Sample Welcome Letter to Parents
Who Have Agreed to Participate

[Date]

Dear [Mr./Mrs./Ms.]:

Welcome to the ABC Program. I am delighted that you and your child will be joining us in the ABC Program. I look forward to working with you during this school year and next year.

As I explained during our visit, you and I will be meeting on a regular basis with your child's teacher to set mutual goals for your child. We will also be developing action plans for reaching our goals. You and your child's teacher will decide when and where to meet. Most teams choose to meet about once a month. I will be calling you in the next week to confirm the date for our first team meeting.

Enclosed with this letter is a copy of the form you signed giving permission for your child to participate in ABC. Please keep this copy for your own records. You will also receive copies of notes from each of our team meetings as we go along. If you have any questions, please feel free to call me.

Again, I am pleased to welcome you to our ABC Program.

_____

Parent Liaison

_____

Community agency or school

I can be reached at _____

Best times to call me _____

From Stephanie H. McConaughy, Pam Kay, Julie A. Welkowitz, Kim Hewitt, and Martha D. Fitzgerald (2008). Copyright by The Guilford Press. Permission to photocopy this appendix is granted to purchasers of this book for personal use only (see copyright page for details).

7

Getting Ready for PTAR Meetings

Steps
1. Introduce yourself to the principal and student support personnel.
2. Introduce yourself to the participating teacher.
3. Help parents prepare for first PTAR meeting.
4. Obtain parent evaluation questionnaires (when required).
5. Obtain teacher evaluation questionnaires (when required).
6. Confirm time and place for first PTAR meeting.
7. Assemble materials and prepare the room for PTAR meeting.

This chapter describes several steps that you can take between the time that you enlist parents to participate in ABC and your first PTAR meeting with parents and a teacher. Your program may require some of the steps; others are optional.

STEP 1. INTRODUCE YOURSELF TO THE PRINCIPAL AND STUDENT SUPPORT PERSONNEL

Before you became a Parent Liaison, the principal of the school agreed to adopt the ABC Program. However, you should not assume that every principal will know the details of the program. Some principals may choose to be very involved in ABC activities, while others may delegate the responsibility for the program to someone else. Whether they stay involved or they delegate, the principals of the schools where you will be working will want to know who you are. A brief face-to-face meeting with the principal is important to your future relationship with that school.

The school secretary or other front-office person is one of your best allies in making ABC work. You will want to learn his/her name immediately. Ask the school secretary to suggest the best way to introduce yourself to the principal. You may hear "Drop in anytime," but you will want to avoid the times when children are arriving or departing. Some secretaries will make an appointment for you, and others will suggest that you make a phone call directly to the principal to arrange a formal meeting. Some may ask the principal to talk with you on the spot! Carry an ABC brochure and the Information for Parents sheet (see Appendix 6.6) when you go to the school. If you do not have time for a formal meeting before the first PTAR meeting, be sure to phone the principal and offer to stop by to say "hello" on your way to the meeting.

Be prepared to answer any questions the principal may have about ABC. Questions most likely will concern your role in scheduling meetings between a child's parent and teacher and the location and timing of the meetings. You can explain that the parent and teacher will choose a mutually agreeable time and place for each meeting. Explain that most teams meet about once a month, but some teams may choose to meet more often, especially in the beginning of the program. You should also assure the principal that you or the child's teacher will check with him/her if the teacher will need any released time or classroom coverage during the meetings. Finally, ask the principal if teachers will earn professional development credit for participating in ABC.

Student support personnel can be great friends of the ABC Program in a school, and you will definitely want them to know who you are and what you are doing. Support personnel can include: school psychologist, guidance counselor, school social worker, special educator, behavior specialist, home–school coordinator, and school nurse. Ask the principal to introduce you, or to let student support personnel know that you will be dropping in to see them. Again, bring ABC brochures and the Information for Parents sheets to hand out. Assure them that you are aware of confidentiality issues, and do not share with them the names of the students and families who may become part of ABC. Suggest they discuss this with the principal, who will know the children's names.

STEP 2. INTRODUCE YOURSELF TO THE PARTICIPATING TEACHER

When you contact the school principal, ask about the best way to introduce yourself to the participating teacher. Some principals may want to introduce you to the teachers themselves. Other principals may suggest that you introduce yourself. If you are going to introduce yourself, ask the school secretary when a particular teacher might be available. Then contact the teacher to arrange a short appointment.

Usually, meeting on a one-to-one basis with each teacher is better than meeting with several teachers in a group. This allows you to answer each teacher's questions individually. Some teachers may be quite eager to participate in ABC, while others may not. Reluctant teachers may fear that the program will require more time and effort than they can afford, given their other responsibilities.

As one of our Parent Liaisons said, the best explanation is often the simplest: The ABC Program is extra time to focus on the needs of one child, and to share your compliments and concerns with the parents when they are most receptive. Another Parent Liaison called ABC "the gift we give the child." Teachers usually want to know:

- How often will they be meeting with parents?
- How are you going to get parents to come to the meetings?
- When and where will these meetings take place?
- What will we talk about at these meetings?

- Why will you, the Parent Liaison, be meeting with us? (What is your role?)
- What will happen at the first meeting?
- How much paperwork will we have to do?

You can reduce some of the teachers' concerns about meetings by explaining the process for PTAR meetings. Give the teacher a copy of the Ground Rules for PTAR Meetings in Appendix 8.2 and Making Action Plans (MAPs) in Appendices 8.3 and 8.4. Reassure teachers that the parents and teacher on each PTAR team will decide how often to meet and what action plans they will carry out for the child. Emphasize that your role will be to *facilitate* this process, not to direct what will happen in each meeting. You will be responsible for encouraging parents to attend and to participate, but you are *not* an advocate. Boost teachers' enthusiasm by telling some ABC success stories from this book. You might also want to bring a copy of the Information for Parents sheet (Appendix 6.6) so that teachers can see what you have told their student's parents. Let the teacher know that you will be doing brief introductions at the first meeting, and encourage the teacher to share some personal interest or hobby during the introductions.

If your ABC Program will be asking parents and teachers to complete questionnaires, refer to Step 5 in this chapter to answer teachers' questions about paperwork.

STEP 3. HELP PARENTS PREPARE FOR FIRST PTAR MEETING

The ABC Program emphasizes equal partnerships between parents and teachers. For many parents, working with teachers as equals will be a new, and perhaps intimidating, experience. Helping parents prepare for the first PTAR meeting is part of your role in supporting them. While you may have mentioned what will happen at the first PTAR meeting when you invited the parents to join ABC, a second meeting will give parents an opportunity to get to know you better. You will have the opportunity to learn more about the child and family.

Prepare parents for the first PTAR meeting by explaining its format in greater detail. To do this, you can give the parent a copy of Making Action Plans (MAPs) (Appendices 8.3. and 8.4). You can then describe the steps in the MAPs outline to explain how the team will talk about the child. (For more about MAPs, see Chapter 8.) For example, you might ask the parent to tell you one or two positive things about the child, and no more. The MAPs process is more effective when parents and teachers can hear each others' ideas; if you go too far into the questions with the parents ahead of time, they may not bring out those ideas in the meeting with the teacher. You might suggest that parents bring a photo of their child to the meeting.

Knowing the ground rules for PTAR meetings may reassure parents who are not comfortable talking with teachers. You can bring a copy of the Ground Rules for PTAR Meetings (Appendix 8.2) to leave with the parent. Even if you have already mentioned the ground rules in a previous meeting, repeating them may be helpful.

You can also use the second meeting to learn more about the family through casual conversation. Appendix 7.1 suggests questions to ask parents about the child's background. Be sure that you do not use this list to *quiz* the parents, so they don't feel that you have invaded their privacy. You may want to make a copy of this page for your notes about each family. It has space to write in the information that you learn.

Check with your supervisor about what kind of notes, if any, you should keep about the family. The agency may or may not permit you to keep notes, other than those you record at the PTAR meetings. If your supervisor wants you to keep field notes, think carefully whether you want to take notes during your meetings with parents, or write your notes after the meetings.

Taking notes while talking to parents may make the meeting seem too stiff and formal. If you want to take notes during the meeting, make sure that the parent sees everything you write. For example, you could jot down parents' comments while discussing the first one or two sections of the MAPs outline. Tell parents that you are taking notes just to be sure that you remember things. Also tell them that you will not share your field notes with anyone other than your supervisor. After the meeting, be sure to keep your field notes in a safe place where no one but you or your supervisor will see them.

STEP 4. OBTAIN PARENT EVALUATION QUESTIONNAIRES (WHEN REQUIRED)

Evaluation is important for measuring the success of the ABC Program. Continued funding usually depends on being able to prove that the program works. Some agencies or schools may choose to use structured questionnaires for evaluation, while other agencies may choose more informal ways to find out how well the program worked. When the agency or school uses evaluation questionnaires, your job includes helping parents to complete these forms. You may also be responsible for asking the child's teacher to complete questionnaires (see Step 5).

In the beginning of the program, parents should complete the questionnaires *within 1 month* of your invitational meeting, and *definitely before the first PTAR meeting* between the parent and teacher. Some agencies or schools may choose to use the same questionnaires at the beginning and end of each school year while a child is in the program. Other agencies or schools may ask for the questionnaires only at the beginning and end of the program. Your supervisor will have this information.

Tell parents that your agency or school will use the questionnaires to evaluate the success of the ABC Program. Some examples of questionnaires are the Child Behavior Checklist for Ages 6–18 (CBCL/6–18; Achenbach & Rescorla, 2001) and the Social Skills Rating System (SSRS; Gresham & Elliott, 1990). These questionnaires look at changes in the child's social competencies and skills as well as changes in behavior. The Family Empowerment Scale—School Version (FES-S; adapted from Koren, DeChillo, & Friesen, 1992) can also be used to collect parents' impressions of their own efforts to obtain support for their child in schools. (Note: You may copy only the Family Empowerment Scale—School Version in Appendix 7.2 for distribution; your ABC Program must purchase other measures from the copyright holders. Chapter 5 describes evaluation questionnaires in more detail.)

Parents will need about an hour to complete questionnaires. Assure them that all of the information they provide will be confidential, and will not be shared with anyone except the ABC Program staff. Emphasize that you will not share any of the individual children's information with school staff, unless parents grant you specific permission to do so. Explain that the ABC Program staff will use information from the questionnaires to evaluate the success of the program. No child's name or family's name will be used in any reports about the program.

Try to be present when parents complete the questionnaires. *Do not leave the questionnaires for parents to mail back to you later.* Some parents may want to complete them on their own without your help, sealing them into an envelope that you can return to the ABC office unopened. If they want to complete questionnaires on their own on another day, then choose a date when you will return to pick them up. Ask parents to look over the questionnaires to make sure they answered all questions.

Other parents may prefer to have you read the questions to them. Generally, the questionnaires require fifth-grade reading skills. Be sensitive to literacy or to physical challenges that may make it difficult for some parents to complete the questionnaires on their own. You may write parents' answers on the questionnaires for them if they prefer.

Appendix 7.3 shows standard instructions for the Child Behavior Checklist for Ages 6–18 or Child Behavior Checklist for Ages 1½–5, the Social Skills Rating System—Parent Version, and the Family Empowerment Scale—School Version. Your agency will develop similar instructions for other questionnaires. Be ready to answer any questions parents may have. Explaining the meaning of words or questions to parents is fine. However, be careful not to influence how parents answer the questions. If you are not sure how to answer a question, tell the parent that you want to ask your supervisor that question and you will call back later with an answer.

After parents have completed all of the questionnaires, collect them and thank parents for taking the time to answer them. Remind parents that the information will be kept confidential. Be sure to have parents complete questionnaires *before* the first PTAR meeting.

TIP: Notify your supervisor immediately if you have concerns about harm to the child. For example, notify your supervisor any time you see on the Child Behavior Checklist for Ages 6–18 that a parent has circled a "1" or a "2" for item 18: *Deliberately harms self or attempts suicide* and/ or item 91: *Talks about killing self.* Your supervisor will advise you on what to do next whenever you have concerns about parents' answers on the questionnaires.

STEP 5. OBTAIN TEACHER EVALUATION QUESTIONNAIRES (WHEN REQUIRED)

After you have obtained parental consent for a child to participate in the program, the child's teacher should also complete evaluation questionnaires. In the beginning of the program, teachers should complete the questionnaires *within at least 1 month* from the time the parent completed questionnaires. *Ideally, both parents and teachers should complete the questionnaires before their first PTAR meeting.* Some ABC Programs may choose to obtain the evaluation questionnaires from teachers at the beginning and end of each school year. Others may ask for teacher questionnaires only at the beginning and end of the program.

You do not have to be present while teachers complete evaluation questionnaires, as suggested for parents. The forms can be mailed to teachers from the ABC Program office, or you may deliver them. If you deliver them, you have the opportunity to answer any questions the teacher may have. Appendix 7.4 shows standard instructions for the Teacher's Report Form (for ages 6–18), the Caregiver–Teacher Report Form (for ages 1½–5), and the Social Skills Rating System—Teacher Version. (You can copy the instructions for these questionnaires to give to teachers. Your program may develop similar instructions for other questionnaires.) The agency or school coordinator should provide stamped, self-addressed envelopes for teachers and give them a deadline for returning the questionnaires.

TIP: If you know that a teacher has not completed evaluation questionnaires before the first PTAR meeting, ask him/her to do so as soon as possible after the meeting. Provide the teacher with a stamped, self-addressed envelope for returning the questionnaires.

STEP 6. CONFIRM TIME AND PLACE FOR FIRST PTAR MEETING

Parents and teachers need to find a mutually agreeable date and time for the first PTAR meeting. You need to locate a neutral place that is convenient for both parents and teachers, and make the necessary arrangements. Once you have both the time and place settled, you can either call or send a short note to parents and teacher to confirm. If you call, try to speak directly to the parents and teachers. If you have to leave a message, ask them to call you back to show that they got your message. You can also send a postcard 1 week before the meeting and call again with a reminder, 2 days before the meeting.

STEP 7. ASSEMBLE MATERIALS AND PREPARE THE ROOM FOR PTAR MEETING

Before each PTAR meeting, assemble the materials that you will need to conduct the meeting. You will feel more confident in your role as Parent Liaison if you plan ahead and are well prepared. The box below lists materials for meetings.

You will need writing materials for every meeting. For initial meetings, you might want to use a flip chart and easel, a roll of shelf paper, or a stand-up table chart to record comments by parents and teachers during MAPs. You can also use a notepad or NCR (no carbon required) paper for recording notes to distribute after the meeting has ended. Select writing materials that suit your own style. If you have them in your budget, you might bring three-hole binders for parents and teachers to use during the meetings and to use later to record their observations about the child.

The appendices at the end of Chapter 8 contain copies of materials that you can give as handouts at the initial PTAR meeting. These include Ground Rules for PTAR Meetings (Appendix 8.2) and Making Action Plans (MAPs)—Boy (Appendix 8.3) or Girl (Appendix 8.4). Be sure to make copies of these materials before your first PTAR meeting. If you have binders to give the parent and teacher, punch three holes in all materials to make insertion easier. You might also make a large copy of the Parent–Teacher Action Research Cycle (Appendix 8.1) to use as you describe the action research process.

MATERIALS FOR PTAR MEETINGS

- Writing materials:
  - Markers in several colors and one or two highlighters
  - Easel with flip chart, roll of shelf paper, or stand-up table chart
  - Notepads or no-carbon-required (NCR) paper
  - Three-ring binders for parents and teachers (optional)
- Handouts (three-hole punched)
  - Ground Rules for PTAR meetings (Appendix 8.2)
  - Making Action Plans (MAPs)—Boy or Girl (Appendices 8.3 and 8.4)
- Large copy of Parent–Teacher Action Research Cycle (Appendix 8.1)
- Tissues
- Tape recorder (optional)
- Beverages and light snacks (optional)

Bring a box of tissues to each meeting. Sometimes people have colds. Sometimes people cry. You will feel better if you are prepared for these possibilities in advance.

A tape recorder is optional. If you are thinking about using one, check with your supervisor to find out whether you are permitted to use an audio recorder. If you choose to use a tape recorder, then be sure to ask the parent and teacher whether this would be agreeable to them *before the meeting*. If others attend the meeting, make sure that all participants have agreed to have the meeting tape recorded. Be sure to state that, at any time, you can turn off the tape recorder at anyone's request, and that the material on the tape will be kept confidential.

Audio recording has several advantages: it makes notetaking easier during the meeting; it allows you to keep the discussion moving while taking notes; and it provides a complete record of the discussion that you can use to write more extensive notes later. Tape recording also has some disadvantages: it can be intimidating for some people and stifle discussion; it can make the meeting seem too formal; and tapes of confidential conversations require special storage and handling.

The Helpful Hints list below outlines other things to consider in getting ready for PTAR meetings. These are ways you can make PTAR meetings comfortable for everyone.

 HELPFUL HINTS FOR MAKING PTAR MEETINGS COMFORTABLE

- Encourage the PTAR team to choose a neutral place for the meeting.
- Verify that the parent has transportation.
- Make sure the seating arrangement puts everyone at an equal height, and allows parents and teacher to face one another.
- Arrange childcare for younger children who accompany parents to meetings.
- Provide tissues, water or other beverages, and/or snacks.

As discussed in Chapter 6, you should encourage the PTAR team to choose a neutral place for their meeting. The place should be mutually agreeable and convenient for both parents and teachers. Possible meeting places in community settings include a private room in the town hall or library, a bank conference room, the fire station, or a family center. At school, PTAR teams may choose to meet in an office, gym, library, or cafeteria. Meeting in the teacher's own classroom may not feel like a neutral place to parents. Be sure that the meeting place has enough privacy that parents and teachers will feel comfortable when sharing confidential information. In schools, you might want to avoid meeting in the principal's office, especially if the child has experienced discipline problems.

Give everyone a comfortable, adult-size chair. Make sure that everyone is sitting at the same physical level, and that parents and teachers can see each other easily. Sitting at a table will make it easier to take notes during the meeting. A round table is good because it makes the seating arrangement equal for everyone. If you use a rectangular table, avoid having either the parent or the teacher sitting at the head of the table.

Some parents may need to bring their younger children to the PTAR meeting. You might want to ask parents about this possibility ahead of time. If you can, arrange for childcare or babysitting by an older child during the meeting. The teacher could probably suggest the names of older students who would babysit. Bringing toys or other materials to occupy younger children during meetings is also helpful. Check with your supervisor on how to pay for any costs of childcare or babysitting.

Beverages and light snacks can be lifesavers for parents and teachers who have to make special efforts to get to meetings on busy days. At a minimum, you might want to provide water or other liquids (e.g., fruit juices, soft drinks, coffee), especially for meetings than might go beyond an hour, or those that occur at the end of a workday. If the budget allows, fruit or baked goods occasionally make a nice surprise.

Background on the Child and Family

- Who lives in the child's house?

- What are the names and ages of the child's siblings, if any?

- Where are the parents employed? What is their work schedule?

- How long has the family lived in this community?

- How long has the family lived at their current address?

- What does the child do during the summer?

- What activities does the child participate in besides school during the school year?

- With what organizations does the family have regular contact (e.g., community groups, recreational groups, house of worship)?

- What are the special strengths of the family?

- What do the parents say about the child's behavior, social skills, or temperament?

From Stephanie H. McConaughy, Pam Kay, Julie A. Welkowitz, Kim Hewitt, and Martha D. Fitzgerald (2008). Copyright by The Guilford Press. Permission to photocopy this appendix is granted to purchasers of this book for personal use only (see copyright page for details).

Family Empowerment Scale—School Version

Date: _____   Parent Name: _____   Student Name: _____

Here are a number of statements that describe several areas of a parent's or caregiver's life: your family, your child's school, and your community. The statements include many different activities that parents might do.

For each statement, circle the number that best describes how the statement applies to you. For questions that do not apply to you, answer "Never."

Even if other people may be involved in caring for and making decisions about your child, answer the questions by thinking of your own situation. Feel free to write any additional comments at the end.

ABOUT YOUR FAMILY...	NEVER	SELDOM	SOME-TIMES	OFTEN	VERY OFTEN
1. When problems arise with my child, I handle them pretty well.	1	2	3	4	5
2. I feel confident in my ability to help my child grow and develop.	1	2	3	4	5
3. I know what to do when problems arise with my child.	1	2	3	4	5
4. I feel my family life is under control.	1	2	3	4	5
5. I am able to get information to help me better understand my child.	1	2	3	4	5
6. I believe I can solve problems with my family when they happen.	1	2	3	4	5
7. When I need help with problems in my family, I am able to ask for help from others.	1	2	3	4	5
8. I make efforts to learn new ways to help my child grow and develop.	1	2	3	4	5
9. When dealing with my child, I focus on the good things as well as the problems.	1	2	3	4	5
10. When faced with a problem involving my child, I decide what to do and then do it.	1	2	3	4	5
11. I have a good understanding of my child's behavior.	1	2	3	4	5
12. I feel I am a good parent/caregiver.	1	2	3	4	5

(continued)

Adapted from Koren, DeChillo, and Friesen (1992). Copyright by the Regional Research Institute, Portland State University. Reprinted with permission in Stephanie H. McConaughy, Pam Kay, Julie A. Welkowitz, Kim Hewitt, and Martha D. Fitzgerald (2008). Copyright by The Guilford Press. Permission to photocopy this appendix is granted to purchasers of this book for personal use only (see copyright page for details).

ABOUT YOUR CHILD'S SERVICES...	NEVER	SELDOM	SOME-TIMES	OFTEN	VERY OFTEN
13. I feel that I have a right to approve all school services my child receives.	1	2	3	4	5
14. I know the steps to take when I am concerned my child is receiving poor school services.	1	2	3	4	5
15. I make sure that professionals understand my opinions about what school services my child needs.	1	2	3	4	5
16. I am able to make good decisions about what school services my child needs.	1	2	3	4	5
17. I am able to work with agencies and professionals to decide what school services my child needs.	1	2	3	4	5
18. I make sure I stay in regular contact with professionals who are providing school services to my child.	1	2	3	4	5
19. My opinion is just as important as professionals' opinions when deciding what school services my child needs.	1	2	3	4	5
20. I tell professionals what I think about school services being provided to my child.	1	2	3	4	5
21. I know what school services my child needs.	1	2	3	4	5
22. When necessary, I take the initiative in looking for school services for my child and family.	1	2	3	4	5
23. I have a good understanding of the school system that my child is involved in.	1	2	3	4	5
24. Professionals should ask me what school services I want for my child.	1	2	3	4	5

Comments:

Instructions to Parents
for Completing These Evaluation Questionnaires

CHILD BEHAVIOR CHECKLIST FOR AGES 6–18
OR CHILD BEHAVIOR CHECKLIST FOR AGES 1½–5

The Child Behavior Checklist (blue form) is a standard form that is often used to obtain parents' views of their child's strengths and problems. This form is used for many different kinds of children of different ages. Try to answer all of the questions as best you can, even if some questions do not apply to your child.

For the Child Behavior Checklist for Ages 6–18: Think about how things have been for your child *now or within the past 6 months.* For the questions on pages 3 and 4, if the item is not true of your child as far as you know, then mark a "0." If the item is somewhat or sometimes true of your child, then mark a "1." If the item is very true or often true of your child, then mark a "2."

For the Child Behavior Checklist for Ages 1½–5: Think about how things have been for your child *now or within the past 2 months.* If the item is not true of your child as far as you know, then mark a "0." If the item is somewhat or sometimes true of your child, then mark a "1." If the item is very true or often true of your child, then mark a "2."

SOCIAL SKILLS RATING SYSTEM—PARENT VERSION

The Social Skills Rating System is often used to obtain parents' views of their child's social skills. Again, try to answer all of the questions as best you can. Think about how things have been for your child *now or within the past 6 months.* If the item never occurs, then mark a "0." If the item sometimes occurs, then mark a "1." If the item occurs very often, then mark a "2."

FAMILY EMPOWERMENT SCALE—SCHOOL VERSION

The Family Empowerment Scale—School Version measures your impressions of your ability to obtain school services for your child. You should score each item 1 to 5 for how it applies to you now. For example, if the item is *never* or *not at all true* of you, mark a "1." If the item is *very often true* of you, mark a "5."

From Stephanie H. McConaughy, Pam Kay, Julie A. Welkowitz, Kim Hewitt, and Martha D. Fitzgerald (2008). Copyright by The Guilford Press. Permission to photocopy this appendix is granted to purchasers of this book for personal use only (see copyright page for details).

Instructions to Teachers
for Completing These Evaluation Questionnaires

TEACHER'S REPORT FORM (FOR AGES 6–18)

The Teacher's Report Form (green form) is a standard form that is often used to obtain teachers' views of a student's strengths and problems. This form is used for many different kinds of children of different ages. Try to answer all of the questions as best you can, even if some questions do not apply to this particular student.

On page 1, for Section V, check the box for "Yes" if the student has ever been referred for Early Essential Education, Speech and Language services, special education, or other forms of special help in school, and then briefly indicate what type of service or help. For Section VII, the questions about performance in academic subjects may not be applicable for children who have just started kindergarten. In this case, you can simply mark "NA" in that box to indicate the questions are not applicable. However, you can list standard kindergarten activities, such as calendar, counting, and circle time, as academic subjects in Section VII and rate those activities for the student. In Section VIII, rate the student's performance compared to typical students of the same age. For Sections IX and X, it is not necessary to provide the information requested unless you care to do so and it does not require too much time.

Try to answer all of the items listed on pages 3 and 4, even if some seem inappropriate for this particular student's age. All items may not seem applicable to this student because the form was developed for many different types of children over a wide age span. Think about whether each of the items is applicable to this particular student *now or within the past 2 months.* If the item is not true of the student as far as you know, then mark a "0." If the item is somewhat or sometimes true of the student, then mark a "1." If the item is very true or often true of the student, then mark a "2."

CAREGIVER-TEACHER REPORT FORM (FOR AGES 1½–5)

On page 1, for Section VI, check the box for "Yes" if the student has ever been referred for Early Essential Education, Speech and Language services, special education, or other forms of special help in school, and then briefly indicate what type of service or help.

Try to answer all of the items listed on the bottom half of pages 1 and 2, even if some seem inappropriate for this particular student's age. All items may not seem applicable to this student because the form was developed for many different types of children ages 1½–5. Think about whether each of the items is applicable to this particular student *now or within the past 2 months.* If the item is not true of the student as far as you know, then mark a "0." If the item is somewhat or sometimes true of the student, then mark a "1." If the item is very true or often true of the student, then mark a "2."

(continued)

From Stephanie H. McConaughy, Pam Kay, Julie A. Welkowitz, Kim Hewitt, and Martha D. Fitzgerald (2008). Copyright by The Guilford Press. Permission to photocopy this appendix is granted to purchasers of this book for personal use only (see copyright page for details).

SOCIAL SKILLS RATING SYSTEM—TEACHER VERSION

The Social Skills Rating System is often used to obtain teachers' views of a student's social skills. Again, try to answer all of the questions as best you can. Think about how things have been for this student *now or within the past 6 months.* If the item never occurs, then mark a "0." If the item sometimes occurs, then mark a "1." If the item occurs very often, then mark a "2."

We appreciate your time in answering all of these questions. You will be asked to complete the same forms again at the end of the ABC Program for this student. This information will help in evaluating the success of the program. All information on the forms will be kept in a confidential file. No names of students, families, or teachers will be used in reports about the program.

8

The First PTAR Meeting(s)

Reaching Mutual Goals

Steps

1. Make introductions.
2. Give an overview of ABC and PTAR.
3. Focus on the child.
4. Establish ground rules and describe MAPs.
5. Follow MAPs outline to discuss the child.
6. Agree on mutual goals for child.
7. Summarize meeting.
8. Set date for next meeting.
9. Distribute meeting notes.

The Parent–Teacher Action Research (PTAR) meetings are the cornerstones of the ABC Progam. In these meetings, parents and teachers work together as equal partners to achieve mutual goals for the child. The first PTAR meetings for each parent–teacher team are key to setting the stage for this partnership. As Parent Liaison, you act as a guide for the collaborative process. Although you are not running the meetings, you do need to keep things on track and make sure the team follows the ground rules. (You will find more on the ground rules later in this chapter.)

You will soon find your own style in following the steps outlined for the PTAR initial meetings. These steps may take only one meeting for some teams and two meetings for others. (Any more than two meetings, and your process may stop. Parents and teachers will be eager to make changes for the child, and will not want to wait several months to get going.) The number of meetings each team needs will depend on how much time people can spend at a meeting. Sticking to the time agreed upon for each meeting is important. If you run overtime, team members may be reluctant to meet again.

As you walk into the meeting room, remember your thoughts about the setting: Where should parents and teachers sit so that they face one another? Are all the chairs the same height? (If only one chair is different, take it yourself!) Is there enough heat, or moving air? Where should the easel be placed so that everyone can see it? Do what you can to make the space comfortable and private for the meeting.

STEP 1. MAKE INTRODUCTIONS

Although you will have already met the parent(s) and teacher before the first PTAR meeting, start the meeting with introductions. Begin by taking about 2 minutes to tell a little bit about yourself and how you became involved in the ABC Progam. Use your own style. Keep your introduction casual and brief. In this way, you can model introductions for the parent and teacher. Initial introductions are a way for each of the PTAR participants to get to know each other and begin building trust. The script below shows a sample introduction by a Parent Liaison.

HOW ONE PARENT LIAISON INTRODUCED HERSELF

Hi, I'm Nancy and I live in Maple Grove, Vermont. I have three children. One is off to college now. One is a sophomore in high school. My youngest is in eighth grade and has a learning disability in reading and written language. She is in special education and receives instruction in the Resource Room for an hour each day. Her teachers also make special accommodations for her, like giving her shorter reading and writing assignments and not penalizing her for spelling errors. (She has her own style of spelling—which even she thinks is pretty funny at times. But we all understand what she means.) I've been very active in my children's education throughout the years. I am also active in Parent-to-Parent, which is a support group for parents of children with special needs. I learned about ABC and the Parent Liaison position through our Parent-Child Center. I wish I had had a program like this when my kids were young. It is a great way to get results for kids—focusing on each child's unique talents and needs. I'm very excited to be working with you both.

After introducing yourself as Parent Liaison, invite the parent to introduce himself/herself. If the parent is uncomfortable with speaking, you might want to ask some leading questions such as "How many children do you have?" Then you could say something positive that you already know about the parent's talents. (For example, you might say "Did you know that [parent] does beautiful crocheting? I saw some of her work when we met.") Remember that even these initial introductions may be difficult for some parents, especially those who have had school problems as children.

Then invite the teacher to introduce herself/himself. By asking the parent to go first, you are demonstrating the ground rule that parents talk first in PTAR team meetings. Usually PTAR meetings will involve only the Parent Liaison, one or both parents, and one teacher. If, however, there are any other participants, you should also invite them to introduce themselves in the same way. Notice whether people use their first name (e.g., Juan, Lucille) or formal name (e.g., Mr.

Alvarez, Mrs. Jones) when introducing themselves. If there are discrepancies between parents' and teachers' use of first versus formal names, ask which name they prefer. You will probably want to encourage the same level of name formality for both parents and teachers. After introductions, explain that you will be taking notes, and will give them copies. Finally, ask about time limits for the meeting, and state the time at which you will stop.

STEP 2. GIVE AN OVERVIEW OF ABC AND PTAR

Though you explained ABC when you met with the parent and teacher, you will still want to give a simple overview of the program and the PTAR process. Parents and teachers will be reassured to hear that you describe the purpose and the general format for meetings consistently. This is also a good time to ask if there are any questions. You should feel comfortable in saying "I don't know, but I will write that down and get back to you with the answer." You can use the general script that follows, but feel free to adapt it to your own style.

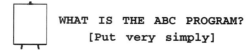

WHAT IS THE ABC PROGRAM?
[Put very simply]

```
ABC stands for Achieving-Behaving-Caring.

Our partners are [your employer] and [school].

ABC gives us extra time to focus on [child].

ABC makes the connection between home and school visible.

The social skills curriculum that [teacher] is using in the classroom
is [title of social skills program].

We will be meeting regularly, once a month all year, unless you decide
to meet more often.

At the end of this meeting I will ask you to set some dates for the
next meetings.

To start today, I'd like to summarize the PTAR process that we will
be using.

Do you have any questions before I continue?
```

Give the parent and the teacher copies of the Parent–Teacher Action Research Cycle in Appendix 8.1, and use it to describe the components of PTAR. You might want to make a larger copy of the Action Research Cycle to display during future meetings. As always, feel free to adapt the general script shown below to your own style. Try not to let too many questions derail the process. Explain that you want to turn the focus to the child as soon as possible, and defer some questions.

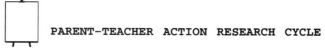

PARENT-TEACHER ACTION RESEARCH CYCLE

```
This diagram is a picture of the Parent-Teacher Action Research Cycle
that we will use to guide our thinking about [child].
P-T-A-R is the abbreviation we use for this approach to collaboration.
```

This process is different from regular parent-teacher conferences, and other types of meetings, like PTA meetings, or special education meetings to talk about individualized education programs (IEPs).

PT = PARENTS and TEACHERS

The P-T part of PTAR is a partnership between parents and teachers. You are the people who are nurturing [child]. You are the ones who have the most knowledge about [child]. Parents have wisdom from being part of this child's life and raising [him/her]. Teachers have wisdom from their training and their experience teaching many different children.

This is your team. You are equal partners in this process. No one else may attend your meeting unless you all agree to invite that person. The PTAR structure has ground rules to make certain that everyone offers valuable information, that everyone's contributions are heard by the whole team, and recorded faithfully in your own words.

A = ACTION

Action will come from setting mutual goals for [child] and helping [child] achieve those goals at home and at school.

R = RESEARCH

Your research involves observing [child] at home, at school, and other places where [he/she] may spend time. The information that you gather about [child] will guide your team in understanding [child], and learning how to make changes that will make school successful for [him/her].

Your information gathering can happen in many different ways. You will choose the process that fits [child]. Others, such as your school psychologist, school guidance counselor, or other teachers, may also become part of the research process, if you both want to have them participate.

You are the action researchers in the PTAR Cycle. I am here to be your guide through this process. It is up to you how you want to do it. Together, as equal partners, you will decide:

- How often you want to meet and for how long.
- Where you want to meet.
- What you want to do between meetings.
- Whether you want to invite others to the meetings.

This is a tested model. It works!

All of this will become clearer as we get into the Action Research Cycle. What are your biggest questions now about ABC or PTAR?

STEP 3. FOCUS ON THE CHILD

After giving an overview of PTAR, shift the focus to the child. If the parent brings the photo you asked for when you first met, display the photo where all can see it. One creative Parent Liaison traced the child's silhouette on shelf paper during a home visit, and used that as the chart paper for the initial meeting. Use the general script shown below as appropriate for a girl or a boy, or express the important points in your own words.

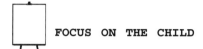 **FOCUS ON THE CHILD**

```
We want to get to know [child]. This child is very important to us;
[he/she] has gifts to give to the world. In order to give us those
gifts, [child] needs to know:

1. [He/she] is a member of the community.
2. How to use [his/her] power within the community.

[Child] has lessons to teach us:

1. [His/her] parents and teacher will learn what works best for [him/
   her].
2. What works for [him/her] may work well for other children.

[Child] has lessons to learn from us:

1. [He/she] is an important part of the home-school community.
2. The adults in that community will work together to help [him/her]
   learn.
```

STEP 4. ESTABLISH GROUND RULES AND DESCRIBE MAPs

After focusing on the child, discuss the ground rules for PTAR meetings, and ask the parent and teacher if there are any other rules they would like to add. These ground rules help to underline the differences between the ABC Progam and most traditional parent–teacher meetings. The list of hints shown below will help make your PTAR meetings succesful.

 HELPFUL HINTS FOR MAKING PTAR MEETINGS SUCCESSFUL

- Remember the ground rules and follow them.
- Bring a copy of the ground rules to display at the meetings.
- Listen to each person and acknowledge what was said.
- Look people in the eyes when they talk.
- Write each person's comments in their *exact* words—be brief, but do not paraphrase.
- Provide lots of positive, sincere feedback and praise.
- Acknowledge feelings without disapproval.

- Acknowledge that it is OK to disagree—there are no rights or wrongs.
- Adopt a system to identify mutual ideas and goals.
- Keep the discussion rolling—don't let one person go off on a tangent for too long.
- Acknowledge time constraints and keep to the agreed-upon meeting time.

Starting in this chapter we will use two stories, one about Bethany and one about Gray (not their real names) as examples of the PTAR process. The stories begin by describing how Bethany's and Gray's PTAR teams used MAPs.

 TIP: Give copies of Ground Rules for PTAR Meetings from Appendix 8.2 to each team member. At future meetings, you might display the ground rules as a reminder. Simply fold the page in the middle to form a tent that you can place where both parent and teacher can read the rules.

STEP 5. FOLLOW MAPs OUTLINE TO DISCUSS THE CHILD

The script shown below will help you to introduce MAPs to your PTAR team.

INTRODUCING MAPs

```
Today we will begin to learn from one another what our mutual goals
are for [child]. We'll use a process known as Making Action Plans,
which we abbreviate as MAPs. We will describe [child] and tell [his/
her] story, talk about your dreams and concerns, and say what we think
we need to know in order to help [him/her] reach our mutual goals
this year.

Later we will talk about:

1. How we will collect information (gather data) about [him/her].
2. How and when we will share that information with one another.
```

Even if you have already given each team member copies of Making Action Plans (MAPs) before the meeting, bring extra copies and distribute them (see Appendices 8.3 and 8.4). Choose the format that is appropriate for the child you are discussing, boy or girl; there is no real difference between them, but you may find it easier not to stumble over the pronouns. Using the script shown below, explain that the MAPs handout will guide your discussion of the child.

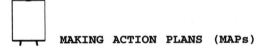

MAKING ACTION PLANS (MAPs)

WHO IS [THIS CHILD]?

```
What are [his/her] gifts? What does [he/she] do well?
What does [he/she] like? What does [he/she] dislike?
Who are [his/her] friends?
```

TELL US A LITTLE BIT ABOUT [CHILD's] STORY:

Where was [he/she] born? What town(s) has [he/she] lived in?
What special events does [he/she] remember?
What challenges has [he/she] faced?

WHAT ARE YOUR DREAMS FOR [THIS CHILD]?

What do you hope for in [his/her] life?
What would you like to see [him/her] learn this year?

WHAT ARE YOUR FEARS OR CONCERNS FOR [CHILD]?

What do you NOT want to see happen in [his/her] life?
What is standing in the way of [his/her] learning this year?

IS THERE ANYTHING ELSE WE SHOULD KNOW ABOUT [CHILD]?

Begin with the section *Who is this child?* by asking the *parent* to describe the child's gifts or talents and what he/she does well. Then ask the *teacher* to describe the child's gifts. Follow the MAPs outline to encourage the parent and teacher to elaborate on the child's story, tell their dreams for the child, and their concerns for the child. You may want to coach the parent by reminding him/her of your earlier conversation. Be sure not to reveal any concerns that the parent (or the teacher) may have shared with you in private.

As you progress through MAPs, write each person's comments where everyone can see them, on a flip chart or on paper in the middle of the table. You can shorten the comments, but be sure to use the parent's and teacher's *exact* words. Do not paraphrase or restate comments in your words. Recording the speaker's exact words shows that you value that person's thoughts. This may be a new experience for the parent who had difficulty in school.

 TIP: Record parents' and teachers' comments under headings that are similar to the MAPs outline (e.g., gifts, likes, dislikes, dreams, fears, etc.). This will help to keep the conversation on track and focused on the child.

Avoid criticizing any comments or sounding disapproving of what a parent or teacher might report. When someone makes a negative comment about the child, ask the speaker if he/she can restate the comment in a more positive way. See A New Perspective on Labels in Appendix 8.5 for positive words (*new encouraging labels*) that you can substitute for negative words (*old negative labels*).

Throughout the MAPs discussion, use a system for marking areas on the child's MAPs where there is agreement between the parent and teacher. You might use color-coding, underlining, or drawing boxes around words where parents and teachers agree. Marking areas of agreement will help foster communication and respect for one another's ideas and move the PTAR team toward developing mutual goals for the child.

BETHANY'S STORY: The PTAR Team Uses MAPs to Learn about Bethany

Bethany, a 6-year-old girl
Her teacher, Marietta
Bethany's mother, Anna, and father, Raymond
Parent Liaison, Nancy

Bethany would come home every day from first grade in tears. She did not like school or her teacher and did not feel good about herself or her abilities. Her teacher, Marietta, was worried about Bethany because she was behind other children in language arts and math. Bethany's highly educated and professional parents were thinking of sending her to a private school, but they really liked her first-grade teacher and preferred to have Bethany go to school in their hometown. Bethany's parents and teacher decided to try the ABC Progam to see if they could make her first-grade year more successful. Bethany's PTAR team included her mother and father, Anna and Raymond, her teacher, Marietta, and the Parent Liaison, Nancy.

At their first meeting, the PTAR team followed the MAPs process to learn more about Bethany. The Parent Liaison asked Anna to put a photo of Bethany on the table as she introduced her to the team. Nancy used a flip chart to record the parents' and teacher's comments during MAPs, underlining their areas of agreement. At the end of the meeting, she wrote the comments on NCR paper so that all of the team members had copies to take with them. Here are some examples of comments from the MAPs discussion of Bethany. The underlining indicates areas where Marietta agreed with Anna and Raymond.

BETHANY'S GIFTS:

Mom and dad—<u>love of language</u>, kind, generous, loves animals, <u>ability to stick with things</u>
Teacher—<u>high verbal skills</u>, good memory, interested in everything, questions things to get to the root of it, <u>creative</u>, plays well

LIKES:

Mom and dad—animals, <u>creating things/art projects</u>, jumping on trampoline, playing with dolls, <u>doing things with her family</u>
Teacher—<u>doing projects and making things</u>, <u>her family</u>, playing on the slide, being active outside at recess

DOES WELL:

Mom and dad—<u>talking</u>, entertaining herself, directing other people on what to do, singing, <u>creating things</u>
Teacher—<u>talking</u>, auditory memory, <u>creating things</u>

DISLIKES:

Mom and dad—people raising their voices, major changes in her life, team sports, <u>not being able to do work as well as other children</u>
Teacher—not having full explanation of things, having things marked wrong on her papers, reading out loud in class

DREAMS:

Mom and dad—happiness, good self-esteem, have good friends, courage to follow her dreams
Teacher—take risks, love of learning

WHAT SHE WOULD LEARN THIS YEAR:

Mom and dad—basic reading and writing, some math, learn how to learn, learn how to stand up for herself
Teacher—accept and build on her strengths, enjoy learning, accept and challenge herself in weak areas, initiate conversation in small groups, stick up for her thoughts and ideas

FEARS:

Mom and dad—creativity squelched, get scared and stop trying, not assert herself, feel bad about herself/low self-esteem
Teacher—shut down and stop learning, not try new things, not keep up to grade level in basics (reading, writing, math)

WHAT IS STANDING IN THE WAY OF HER LEARNING:

Mom and dad—poor fine and gross motor coordination and planning, afraid to try new things, kids told her she is slow, very sensitive
Teacher—doesn't believe in herself

ALSO NEED TO KNOW:

Mom and dad—her cognitive ability
Teacher—strategies to help her, how far to push her

GRAY'S STORY: The PTAR Team Uses MAPs to Learn about Gray

Gray, a 6-year-old boy
His first-grade teacher, Sarah
Gray's mother, Carla, and father, Edward
Parent Liaison, Judy

In kindergarten, Gray worked hard at first, but after about a month, he began refusing to do what the teacher asked. He complained of being bored and sometimes scribbled on his papers. Gray also had trouble getting along with other children. When his classmates reacted negatively to his verbal demands and controlling behavior, he sulked and sucked his thumb.

Gray's first-grade teacher echoed the concerns of his kindergarten teacher. She worried about Gray's "intensity" and "intrusiveness" and his lack of interest in learning. She was considering retaining him in first grade because of his social immaturity. The greatest concern of Gray's mother, Carla, was that Gray would "be pegged as the bad kid in class" and as an adult "he might be isolated or unable to work closely with others in a job situation."

To address their concerns about Gray, his first-grade teacher and his mother (who was also a teacher in another school) agreed to form a PTAR team through the ABC Program. With their agreement, the Parent Liaison, Judy, arranged to use a small room off the school library for the first two PTAR meetings.

The PTAR team followed the MAPs outline to share their views of Gray. Judy asked Carla to show a photo of Gray to introduce him. Judy used a stand-up table chart to record his mother's and teacher's comments during MAPs. She color-coded areas of agreement with a yellow highlighter (underlined here). At the end of the meeting, the teacher helped the Parent Liaison make copies of the notes on the school copy machine. Here are some examples of comments from the MAPs discussion of Gray:

GRAY'S GIFTS:

Mom—friendly, loving, sensitive, artistic, likes hugs and kisses, good at sports
Teacher—adds to discussion, good fine/gross motor skills, artistic

LIKES:

Mom—bedtime stories, drawing, writing, being with friends, sweets, pizza
Teacher—listening to stories, being a leader, telling his ideas to the class

DOES WELL:

Mom—sports, drawing, riding his bike, making bed, being outside
Teacher—sports, drawing and art projects, expressing his own ideas

DISLIKES:

Mom—certain foods (peas, carrots, salads), being told what to do, sharing toys, doing homework
Teacher—doing his work folder, waiting his turn, someone invading his space, being a follower

DREAMS:

Mom—to be happy, to make good choices, to finish high school and make good choices afterward, to get a good job, to be carefree, to not be thought of as "bad kid in class," to have friends
Teacher—to feel in control and be less intrusive/intense, to progress academically, to take responsibility (first steps), to get along with peers, to have more empathy

WHAT HE WOULD LEARN THIS YEAR:

Mom—basic skills in reading and math, how to get along better with other kids
Teacher—learn to give and take suggestions from others, learn to follow directions, learn to be more tolerant of others

FEARS:

Mom—being pegged as the "bad" child, may be isolated as an adult, won't be able to work closely with others in a job, will not pass first grade
Teacher—will develop serious social problems, will not learn basic skills to go to second grade, will be labeled as a "behavior problem" student

WHAT IS STANDING IN THE WAY OF HIS LEARNING:

  Mom—<u>lack of friends</u>, no interest in sharing, won't listen
  Teacher—<u>lack of empathy for others</u>, putting his needs first, low motivation for learning

ALSO NEED TO KNOW:

  Mom—what works best with him
  Teacher—how he behaves at home, what motivates him

STEP 6. AGREE ON MUTUAL GOALS FOR CHILD

Looking back at the child's story, encourage the parent and teacher to state their goals for the child. Goals can take many different forms and refer to any aspect of the child's functioning. Some goals may apply to academic achievement (e.g., Erin will come up to her age group in reading or math; Zachary will feel more confident in reading tasks).

Goals may also refer to children's emotions, behaviors, or social relations (e.g., Bethany will have higher self-esteem; Gray will take suggestions from peers; Maria can open up more and be more sociable; José will share materials; Shawn will control his temper and behavior in school; Bennie will make some friends).

Other goals may refer to more general aspects of children's lives at home or at school (e.g., Cara will make transitions more quickly, quietly, and happily; D'André can keep himself occupied; Juan will become more independent at home). As you lead the discussion of goals, ask questions, such as the following, to help the parent and teacher describe general goals more precisely.

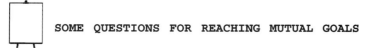

SOME QUESTIONS FOR REACHING MUTUAL GOALS

```
What would you like [child] to learn this year?
What would you like to see [child] doing by the end of this year?
Can you tell me more about what you mean by [goal]?
How would you know that [he/she] was reaching [goal]?
What would [goal] look like?
What would [goal] look like at home?
What would [goal] look like at school?
```

You might state some specific goals differently for home and school. For example, a mutual goal for Mai Lee might be "Mai Lee will feel comfortable interacting with other children." At school, a more specific goal might be, "Mai Lee would talk to other children and join them at recess." At home, a more specific goal might be, "Mai Lee would invite a child in the neighborhood to play." A mutual goal for Josiah might be, "Josiah will keep his hands to himself." At school, a more specific goal might be, "Josiah will make a transition from one activity to another without poking someone." At home, a more specific goal for Josiah might be, "Josiah will come to the dinner table without pushing or shoving his brother."

As the team begins to identify mutual goals for the child, record the goals in a place where everyone can see them. Remember again to write the goals in the parent's and teacher's own words. You can ask the team how they want to state the goal. Do not interpret the goals or restate them in your words.

Encourage the team to identify at least one mutual goal. Sometimes, the parents and teacher are clearly too far apart in their perspectives on the child to reach agreement on even one goal. Should that happen, you might ask them to set one goal for home and another for school. As they help each other work toward those goals, PTAR teams will usually find areas of mutual agreement. Then you can suggest that they set a new, mutual goal.

Some teams may generate many goals for a child. When this happens, ask the team to select two or three goals to work on at any one time. Ask the team which goals they feel are *most important* to focus on now. You can also ask the team which goals they think would be easiest to address first and which ones they can save for later. Focusing on too many goals at once can become overwhelming and discouraging, especially when the team moves to the data collection phase of PTAR. You can explain that the action research process works best when teams focus on a few goals at any one time.

When the team is satisfied with their mutual goals, write the goals on the spaces provided on the MAPs handouts. Give copies to the parents and teacher, and be sure to keep one for yourself.

 TIP: Ask your supervisor if the budget will cover the cost of a three-ring binder for each parent and teacher. Experienced Parent Liaisons found it worthwhile to punch holes in their handouts before distributing them. Give the binder out at this meeting with the MAPs pages already in it.

The next parts of Bethany's story and Gray's story show how two PTAR teams agreed on their mutual goals after their MAPs discussion of each child. You will notice that Bethany's team agreed to an extra meeting that first month to complete their work.

 BETHANY'S STORY: The PTAR Team Agrees on Mutual Goals

Bethany's PTAR team (both of her parents and her teacher) met twice in 2 weeks to go through the MAPs process and develop their mutual goals. Through the MAPs discussion, the PTAR team learned that Bethany was a creative child with good language skills, a good listening memory, and the courage to stick with and solve problems. Bethany was challenged by tasks that required muscle coordination, as well as activities that involved a series of steps because she had trouble planning ahead. Bethany's parents wanted her to feel more confident in reading, writing, and math.

After more discussion, the team decided that improving Bethany's self-esteem was the most important goal to focus on first. They felt that improving her self-esteem would likely lead to more confidence in reading, writing, and math. They also felt that helping Bethany with academic and motor skills would add to improving her self-esteem. The PTAR team members agreed on the following mutual goals for Bethany:

1. Will have higher self-esteem.
2. Will feel confident in the areas of reading, writing, and math.
3. Will improve motor skills.

GRAY'S STORY:
The PTAR Team Agrees on Mutual Goals

At the end of their MAPs discussion, Gray's PTAR team agreed that a major barrier to his success in school and in life was his lack of understanding of others. They decided that their most important mutual goal for Gray was that he learn to be more empathetic. They worded this general goal as, "To see the other guy's side." The team also agreed on two other goals that were more specific, but related to their general goal. They agreed that Gray needed to become more tolerant of other children's ideas and learn to give and take suggestions and directions from both peers and adults. Gray's PTAR team outlined their three mutual goals as follows:

1. To see the other guy's side.
2. To take suggestions from peers.
3. To "give and take."

STEP 7. SUMMARIZE MEETING

To bring each meeting to a close, summarize what was discussed during the meeting. At the end of this meeting, you might state briefly what the parent and teacher identified in the child's MAPs process. When the team has agreed to a set of mutual goals, restate these at the end of the meeting. You might mention that these goals will guide their work together throughout the year.

STEP 8. SET DATE FOR NEXT MEETING

As a final step, ask the parent and teacher to select a date and place for the next meeting. Setting the date for the next meeting before the team adjourns helps to keep the momentum for the PTAR process. It is also efficient and helps to avoid confusion later. Make sure that the date and place are agreeable for both the parent and the teacher, and any other persons who may have been asked to join the team. Some teams may choose to meet only once a month, while others may want to meet more frequently. Write the date and place for the next meeting at the end of the meeting notes.

 TIP: Ask teams if they want to set their meeting dates ahead for the whole year. You may find it easier to reschedule one or two meetings rather than spend time at the end of each meeting to find the next date.

STEP 9. DISTRIBUTE MEETING NOTES

Distribute meeting notes to all team members, either at the end of the meeting, or by mail, as soon as possible. If you used a flip chart to record comments, then you will probably need to copy the comments onto a smaller piece of paper. If you need to make photocopies of the notes, try to do so before everyone leaves. (You will probably also need permission and perhaps a code number to use a copying machine.) If you plan to type your notes at home before distributing them, you will find that easiest if done within 48 hours of the meeting.

TIP: Using NCR (no carbon required) paper for recording comments will make it easy to distribute the meeting notes as the team adjourns.

There are advantages to having parents and teachers carry away a set of notes from the meeting. This means that you either need to use NCR paper or be able to make multiple copies on the spot. On the other hand, sending the notes out by mail a few days after the meeting provides a timely reminder to parents and teachers that they have tasks to accomplish between meetings.

✓Checklist of Materials You Might Need for This Meeting

☐ Copies of the Parent–Teacher Action Research Cycle (Appendix 8.1)

☐ Extra copies of Making Action Plans (MAPs) (for either boy or girl) (Appendices 8.3 and 8.4)

☐ Copies of Ground Rules for PTAR Meetings (Appendix 8.2) and A New Perspective on Labels (Appendix 8.5)

☐ Three-ring binders for parent and teacher (if available)

☐ Chart pad, markers, and highlighter

☐ NCR paper (if available) and a pen

☐ Box of tissues

☐ Your own calendar

☐ Cold water and cups (or other refreshments)

☐ Other:

Parent–Teacher Action Research Cycle

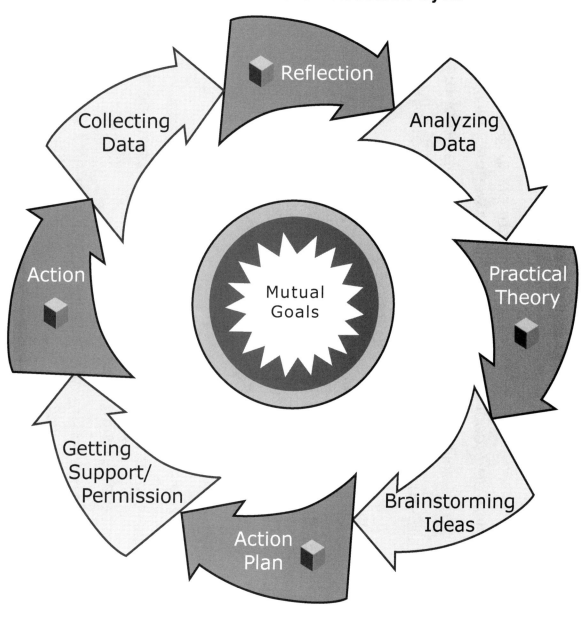

From Stephanie H. McConaughy, Pam Kay, Julie A. Welkowitz, Kim Hewitt, and Martha D. Fitzgerald (2008). Copyright by The Guilford Press. Permission to photocopy this appendix is granted to purchasers of this book for personal use only (see copyright page for details).

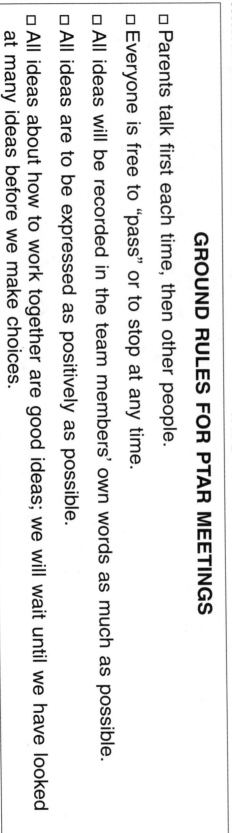

GROUND RULES FOR PTAR MEETINGS

☐ Parents talk first each time, then other people.

☐ Everyone is free to "pass" or to stop at any time.

☐ All ideas will be recorded in the team members' own words as much as possible.

☐ All ideas are to be expressed as positively as possible.

☐ All ideas about how to work together are good ideas; we will wait until we have looked at many ideas before we make choices.

-------- Fold Here --------

GROUND RULES FOR PTAR MEETINGS

☐ Parents talk first each time, then other people.

☐ Everyone is free to "pass" or to stop at any time.

☐ All ideas will be recorded in the team members' own words as much as possible.

☐ All ideas are to be expressed as positively as possible.

☐ All ideas about how to work together are good ideas; we will wait until we have looked at many ideas before we make choices.

From Stephanie H. McConaughy, Pam Kay, Julie A. Welkowitz, Kim Hewitt, and Martha D. Fitzgerald (2008). Copyright by The Guilford Press. Permission to photocopy this appendix is granted to purchasers of this book for personal use only (see copyright page for details).

Ground Rules for PTAR Meetings

APPENDIX 8.2

Making Action Plans (MAPs) for Boys

WHO IS THIS CHILD?

What are his gifts? What does he do well?
What does he like? What does he dislike?
Who are his friends?

TELL US A LITTLE BIT ABOUT THIS CHILD'S STORY

Where was he born? What town(s) has he lived in?
What special events does he remember?
What challenges has he faced?

WHAT ARE YOUR DREAMS FOR THIS CHILD?

What do you hope for in his life?
What would you like to see him learn this year?

WHAT ARE YOUR FEARS OR CONCERNS FOR THIS CHILD?

What do you NOT want to see happen in his life?
What is standing in the way of his learning this year?

IS THERE ANYTHING ELSE WE SHOULD KNOW ABOUT THIS CHILD?

OUR MUTUAL GOALS AS A PTAR TEAM

1. _____

_____

2. _____

_____

3. _____

_____

(continued)

From Stephanie H. McConaughy, Pam Kay, Julie A. Welkowitz, Kim Hewitt, and Martha D. Fitzgerald (2008). Copyright by The Guilford Press. Permission to photocopy this appendix is granted to purchasers of this book for personal use only (see copyright page for details).

WHAT WILL BE OUR CLUES THAT HE IS ACHIEVING THESE GOALS?

WHAT DO WE NEED TO KNOW TO HELP HIM ACHIEVE THESE GOALS?

HOW WILL WE COLLECT INFORMATION ABOUT HIS PROGRESS?

HOW WILL WE SHARE THAT INFORMATION WITH EACH OTHER?

Making Action Plans (MAPs) for Girls

WHO IS THIS CHILD?

What are her gifts? What does she do well?
What does she like? What does she dislike?
Who are her friends?

TELL US A LITTLE BIT ABOUT THIS CHILD'S STORY

Where was she born? What town(s) has she lived in?
What special events does she remember?
What challenges has she faced?

WHAT ARE YOUR DREAMS FOR THIS CHILD?

What do you hope for in her life?
What would you like to see her learn this year?

WHAT ARE YOUR FEARS OR CONCERNS FOR THIS CHILD?

What do you NOT want to see happen in her life?
What is standing in the way of her learning this year?

IS THERE ANYTHING ELSE WE SHOULD KNOW ABOUT THIS CHILD?

OUR MUTUAL GOALS AS A PTAR TEAM

1. _____

2. _____

3. _____

(continued)

From Stephanie H. McConaughy, Pam Kay, Julie A. Welkowitz, Kim Hewitt, and Martha D. Fitzgerald (2008). Copyright by The Guilford Press. Permission to photocopy this appendix is granted to purchasers of this book for personal use only (see copyright page for details).

WHAT WILL BE OUR CLUES THAT SHE IS ACHIEVING THESE GOALS?

WHAT DO WE NEED TO KNOW TO HELP HER ACHIEVE THESE GOALS?

HOW WILL WE COLLECT INFORMATION ABOUT HER PROGRESS?

HOW WILL WE SHARE THAT INFORMATION WITH EACH OTHER?

APPENDIX 8.5

A New Perspective on Labels

Old Negative Labels

Demanding	Moody	Defiant
Stubborn	Bossy	Wild
Selfish	Headstrong	Manipulative
Impatient	Fearful	Destructive
Picky	Whiny	Spacey

New Encouraging Labels

Conscientious	Flexible	Discriminating
Assertive	Curious	Energetic
Tenacious	Engaging	Sensitive
Observant	Cautious	Whimsical
Meticulous	Thoughtful	Perceptive

(Add some of your own)

From Stephanie H. McConaughy, Pam Kay, Julie A. Welkowitz, Kim Hewitt, and Martha D. Fitzgerald (2008). Copyright by The Guilford Press. Permission to photocopy this appendix is granted to purchasers of this book for personal use only (see copyright page for details).

9

The Action Research Cycle

Collecting Data

Steps
1. Create an agenda.
2. Summarize previous meeting and restate mutual goals.
3. Discuss collecting data in the Action Research Cycle.
4. Identify clues for reaching mutual goals.
5. Select methods for collecting data.
6. Discuss how parents and teachers will share data.
7. Summarize meeting.
8. Set date for next meeting and distribute meeting notes.

Now that you and the Parent–Teacher Action Research (PTAR) team have completed the MAPs process and set mutual goals for the child, Chapters 9, 10, and 11 guide you through the Action Research Cycle. Each chapter describes a separate meeting, covering one or more points of the Cycle. However, action research can play itself out in various ways with different teams. Some teams will progress right through the cycle, addressing each point in orderly succession. Other teams may move back and forth in the cycle, depending on what they learn about the child and themselves in the process. Some will stick with the mutual goals they first set, and others will want to go back and change their goals. Be sure to allow teams to go at their own pace in their own way.

As Parent Liaison, you can move back and forth between Chapters 9–11, following the pattern of each particular PTAR team. At first, you will want to progress around the cycle, becoming familiar with each point and helping parents and teachers understand it. You may want to tell your teams that you are learning along with them. After facilitating a few teams, you will be able to sense when to circle back to a particular point, and when to keep the team moving ahead. This chapter will help you get your teams started at the point marked with an arrow on the Action Research Cycle: *Collecting Data*.

STEP 1. CREATE AN AGENDA

Before each meeting begins, create an agenda for all to follow during the meeting. For this meeting, the agenda should focus on reviewing the PTAR team's mutual goals for the child and deciding how parents and teachers will collect data. Appendix 9.1 shows an example of an appropriate agenda for a PTAR meeting where parents and teachers decide how they will collect data. (We assume here that the PTAR team has agreed on their mutual goals at a previous meeting. For some teams, discussion of mutual goals and initial data collection may occur in the same meeting.)

Once a team has agreed to a set of mutual goals, you should always list the goals at the top of the agenda. On the sample agenda, under item 2, you can list the action research steps that the team will use during this meeting. Under item 3, you can ask if there are other issues that the team wants to discuss. You can use the sample agenda or create your own version. Give a copy of the agenda to each person attending or display the agenda on a chart for everyone to see.

STEP 2. SUMMARIZE PREVIOUS MEETING
AND RESTATE MUTUAL GOALS

Begin with a brief summary of the previous meeting (5–10 minutes). Use your copy of Making Action Plans (MAPs) from the previous meeting. You can also display a chart or diagram that the team developed during the initial MAPs discussion. Refer to your previous coding system (e.g., color-coding or underlining) to highlight areas where parents and teacher agreed. Be sure to summarize the positive qualities that the team identified for the child. You can also mention negative qualities or problems, but try to state these in a positive way whenever possible (refer to New Perspective on Labels in Appendix 8.5). Be sure to summarize comments from both the child's parents and teacher.

At the end of your summary, restate the mutual goals that the team identified for the child. Ask, "Are these goals stated accurately?" "Would you like to start with one goal, or work on all of them?" Be careful not to get slowed down by a lengthy discussion of the goals, or debates over the exact words to use. Remind the team that they may make changes to their goals later, and move on to deciding how to collect data.

 TIP: Keep the team moving forward into the Action Research Cycle. Don't let this meeting become bogged down by debates over the exact wording of the goals.

STEP 3. DISCUSS COLLECTING DATA
IN THE ACTION RESEARCH CYCLE

Explain to the team that the first step in the Parent–Teacher Action Research Cycle involves collecting data about the child. This means gathering information about the child's behavior before the team develops an action plan. For most teams, "data" is a good term to use because of its neutral connotation, and its connection to the action research that the team is doing. *Data* implies information that accurately describes what the child is doing, but does not characterize or label the child (see Table 9.1 for examples). For some parents and teachers, you might find that the term

TABLE 9.1. How Do You Know Data When You See It?

Data	Not data
Oct. 10: Gray came into the room smiling, said "Hi" to John, and hung up his coat.	Wednesday: Gray started the day in a better mood today. He seems to like John.
May 11: Bethany spent 15 minutes at the reading table, and asked to take a book home.	Friday: Bethany is now reading for pleasure.

data seems intimidating, too impersonal, or too psychological. With these teams, you can substitute terms like *facts* or *information*.

At this meeting you will want to display a copy of the Parent–Teacher Action Research Cycle from Appendix 8.1 for everyone to see. Explain that their mutual goals are at the center of the Action Research Cycle and collecting data is the beginning of the process (see Figure 9.1). Sometimes the process of collecting data will lead to redefining the team's mutual goals. Sometimes additional clues or observable indicators for goals emerge from the initial data collection. Collecting data can also help to clarify what the parent or the teacher means by a goal, that is, what actual behaviors would reflect achieving the goal.

Remind the parent and teacher that *they are the researchers* and *they are the experts who know the child best*. Using terms like "researchers" or "experts" can be a very effective way to describe the roles of team members. Parents are experts from living with and raising their child. Teachers are experts from their education and from interacting with this child and many other children of the same age. When parents view themselves as researchers, they recognize that they have important knowledge to contribute to the PTAR process, and often get more involved in

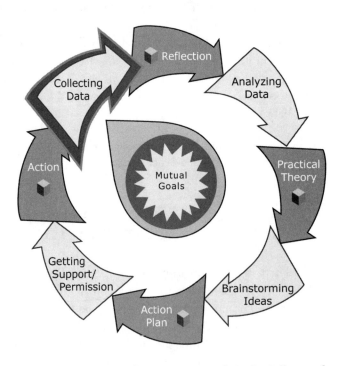

FIGURE 9.1. Parent–Teacher Action Research Cycle: Collecting data.

their child's education. When parents feel truly equal to teachers as members of the team, this fosters a sense of empowerment. As researchers, teachers can contribute important information from their perspective on the child in the classroom, their knowledge of the child's abilities, and their experience with other children. Teachers also may find action research empowering. In today's schools, some classroom teachers may feel de-skilled by the many specialists available to help with children's learning problems; doing action research can restore teachers' confidence, and helps them make useful changes in their practices.

 TIP: Be sensitive to differences in cultural background, educational level, resources, and language of the different members of the team. A good rule of thumb is to use language that you know the parent will understand.

STEP 4. IDENTIFY CLUES FOR REACHING MUTUAL GOALS

After discussing where collecting data fits into the Action Research Cycle, ask the PTAR team to identify clues for reaching their mutual goals. *Clues* are observable behaviors that show that the child is moving toward a goal.

To identify clues, ask the parent and teacher which specific behaviors or other aspects of the child's functioning would be different when the child has reached the goal. To start this discussion, you can ask the first two questions listed on page 2 of the MAPs outline (see Appendices 8.3 and 8.4): "What will be our clues that [child] is achieving these goals? What do we need to know to help him/her achieve these goals?" The script below shows examples of additional questions you might ask to help the team identify clues for mutual goals.

 IDENTIFYING CLUES FOR MUTUAL GOALS

```
What do you think is most important for [child] to learn this year?
What would be your clues at the end of the year that [child] is
    [goal]?
What would [goal] look like?
How will we know that [child] is reaching this goal?
What will be our clues?
What behavior would you be noticing at home? At school?
What would you see? What would you hear?
What would [child] be doing?
What would [child] be doing differently than [he/she] is doing today?
```

Encourage the team to think of specific behaviors that have a discreet beginning and end. Also encourage parents and teachers to think of behaviors that they can observe at home and at school. Some clues may be the same in both settings and some may be different. The clues that PTAR teams chose for Bethany and Gray are good examples. See Bethany's Story and Gray's Story at the end of this chapter.

The team's observations of clues for their mutual goals will become the *data* that they collect in the Action Research Cycle. Some teams may also decide to record observations of problem behaviors that get in the way of reaching mutual goals. As the discussion proceeds, record the examples that the parent and teacher identify as clues for each goal. As before, write these notes where everyone can see them (e.g., on a flip chart or on the MAPs outline).

STEP 5. SELECT METHODS FOR COLLECTING DATA

To help teams develop their data collection methods, start by asking, "How will we collect information about [his/her] progress?" (See the third question on page 2 of the MAPs outline.) Data collection can take many different forms. Encourage parents and teachers to choose methods that might work best for them. Try to keep the methods simple and easy to use within the daily routines of home and school. The script below lists some specific questions you might ask to help parents and teachers choose data collection methods.

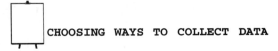

CHOOSING WAYS TO COLLECT DATA

```
What is the easiest way for you to make a record of what you notice?
What is the easiest way to keep track of your data/information?
What can I do to help you with data collection?
```

One way to make data collection easier is to limit it to certain periods of the day or to pick a time each day to record observations. Parents and teachers can also pick a particular time of day that is of special concern. For example, Gray's teacher decided to record her observations during transition periods at school because this was when Gray had the most trouble getting along with peers. Putting data collection materials in a place where they are easy to see is also helpful. For example, at home, a parent might choose to keep a notebook next to the phone or post a chart on the refrigerator. Teachers could keep a notebook in a special spot on their desks or carry a pad of Post-It Notes.

PTAR team members should agree on the frequency of their observations. Encourage parents and teachers to record their observations *every day*. While daily observations are best for giving a detailed picture of the child's behavior over time, they may seem like an impossible task to overloaded parents and teachers. (Besides, *daily* to a teacher means five times a week, where parents usually have 7 days to record!) One approach is to start the data collection process with an agreement for three or four observations per week, preferably with parents and teachers observing on the same day of the week. Remind parents and teachers that good days should be noted as well as difficult days. Later in the Action Research Cycle, the team will want to make daily observations in order to see changes in the child's behavior, and the process will not seem as overwhelming as it does at first. Arturo's story is an example of how daily observations led his PTAR team to an important discovery about his patterns of inattention and restlessness at school.

ARTURO'S STORY

Arturo's mother and classroom teacher were puzzled by his occasional spells of inattention and excessive activity in the classroom. When they collected data on every weekday for 1 month, they suddenly found a clue. Arturo had asthma, which sometimes required that he use a nebulizer when he first got up in the morning. He did not need to use an inhaler or any other medication at school, so neither the teacher nor the school nurse were aware of his asthma. However, when the team compared the notes taken daily by the mother and teacher, they saw that Arturo had used the nebulizer on each of the days when the teacher noted his restlessness and inattention. They agreed that mom would call to let the teacher know when he had used the nebulizer. She also would call Arturo's doctor to see if there were any side effects from using the nebulizer. The teacher stood closer to Arturo on those days to help him focus his attention.

Data collection methods can be the same or different at home and at school. For example, Bethany's mother and teacher each recorded their daily observations in a notebook. Gray's mother used a journal to keep notes of her observations about his daily life apart from school. During transition periods in the school day, Gray's teacher recorded instances of his specific behaviors in a notebook.

Another child's mother had a set of questions that she asked him each day after school. She recorded the child's answers on a worksheet to share at her PTAR team meeting each month. This is one way that teams can involve the children in the data collection process. Another method is when a teacher asks the child to record checks on a chart listing specific behaviors. If the child is directly involved in data collection, keeping the focus on positive behaviors is important. The list below shows different data collection methods that PTAR teams might use.

 HELPFUL HINTS FOR COLLECTING DATA

PARENTS CAN:

- Use journals or notebooks to record descriptive or anecdotal information.
- Use a tape recorder to dictate observations.
- Record the child's answers to a set of questions.
- Use checklists to record observations of specific behaviors.
- Keep a computer log or diary.

TEACHERS CAN:

- Use journals or notebooks to record descriptive or anecdotal information.
- Use time logs to record daily observations.
- Jot down observations on Post-It Notes.
- Use checklists, charts, or graphs to record observations of specific behaviors.
- Send daily or weekly feedback notes home to parents.
- Keep a computer log or diary.

Besides recording their observations of specific behaviors, parents and teachers should also note special circumstances at home or at school that can affect the child's mood and behavior. Examples of special conditions at home might include illness of the child or a family member, arguments between parent and child, fights with siblings or friends, visits from relatives or friends, time spent in a different household, rejection by a friend, or the child experiencing disappointment (e.g., the child was the only girl in the class not invited to someone's birthday party). Examples of special circumstances at school could include holidays or big events such as field trips, having a substitute teacher, the child missing a favorite activity, the child getting into a fight on the playground, the child being disciplined by a teacher or the principal, or the child forgetting or not finishing homework.

Special circumstances can also include positive events in the child's life. If the data collection method involves a checklist, chart, or graph, then teams can add an open-ended section to record circumstances surrounding behavior. Knowing these circumstances will be important when the PTAR team analyzes their data and begins to develop their practical theory about the child. The questions below show the three important elements to capture when collecting data. See Chapter 10 for more details.

The A-B-Cs of Data Collection

A. What was happening before this behavior occurred?

The Antecedent

B. Exactly what was the behavior? (Describe, don't analyze or label.)

The Behavior

C. What was the consequence of this behavior? (Then what happened?)

The Consequences

STEP 6. DISCUSS HOW PARENTS AND TEACHERS WILL SHARE DATA

The final step in the data collection process is deciding how parents and teachers will share the data or information that they collect about the child. You can move the team to this step by asking "How will you share that information with each other?" (See the last question on page 2 of the MAPs outline.)

Once the team has begun the Action Research Cycle, sharing data will become a routine part of the agenda. Sharing data can be done in many different ways, as long as the process is mutually agreeable, simple, and not technical. Some teams may choose to simply read or summarize the notes they recorded between meetings. Other teams may decide to review the information in a notebook, journal, or log that goes back and forth between the parent and the teacher. Parents may bring the answers that their child gave to a daily set of questions.

As parents and teachers share their data, communication improves. They come closer in their expectations and understanding of the demands of home and school environments and how the child responds to those environments. This sharing of information helps to build and solidify mutual respect and trust between parents and teachers.

STEP 7. SUMMARIZE MEETING

To bring the meeting to a close, summarize what was discussed in the meeting. Start by restating the PTAR team's mutual goals for the child. Then describe how the parent and teacher will collect data about the child. Encourage team members to record their observations on a daily basis and to pick a time that is easiest to do this. Arrange a time when you will contact parents between meetings. Assure them that you will help them adjust their data collection method if it is not working well for them.

STEP 8. SET DATE FOR NEXT MEETING AND DISTRIBUTE MEETING NOTES

At the end of the meeting, ask the parent and teacher to select a date and place for the next meeting. As before, make sure that the date is agreeable to both the parent and the teacher. Be sure to allow ample time for data collection. Then distribute your meeting notes to all team members (or mail the notes soon after the meeting). Make a note on your own calendar to call each team member 2 days before the next meeting.

BETHANY'S STORY: The PTAR Team Begins Collecting Data

In their second PTAR meeting, Bethany's PTAR team listed three mutual goals for her:

1. Will have higher self-esteem.
2. Will feel confident in the areas of reading, writing, and math.
3. Will improve motor skills.

The team discussed what they would need to know to determine whether Bethany was reaching their goals. They identified several clues that they would look for at school and at home:

Clues at school:
- Bethany would show the teacher her work.
- Bethany would help other kids with their work.
- Bethany would hand in her work on time.
- Bethany would play a ball game at recess.

Clues at home:
- Bethany would invite a friend over to the house.
- Bethany would show her schoolwork to Mom and Dad.
- Bethany would draw a happy picture of herself.
- Bethany would complete her homework.

To collect their data, Bethany's mother and teacher each used a notebook to record observations of her behavior each day. They planned to collect data for 2 weeks and then meet again to share their observations.

GRAY'S STORY: The PTAR Team Begins Collecting Data

In their second meeting, Gray's PTAR team agreed on the following three mutual goals:

1. To see the other guy's side.
2. To take suggestions from peers.
3. To "give and take."

The team decided to focus on helping Gray to see the other guy's side, although they realized that all three goals were closely related. They then identified the following clues that would show that Gray was moving toward their mutual goals.

Clues at school:
- Gray would wait his turn to talk.
- Gray would be quiet (and listen) when another child or the teacher talked.
- Gray would share materials with another child.
- Gray would make a transition to another activity without getting into a fight.
- Gray would make at least one friend at school.

Clues at home:
- Gray would play a board game and follow the rules.
- Gray would invite a child over to his house and the child would come.
- Gray would be invited to another child's house or to a party.

To collect her data, Gray's mother recorded notes in a journal each day. Gray's teacher used a notebook to record instances of specific behaviors that occurred during transition periods of each school day. In addition to recording clues that Gray was moving toward their mutual goals, Gray's mother and teacher also noted observations of his problem behaviors that got in the way of their goals.

✓Checklist of Materials You Might Need for This Meeting

☐ Copies of agenda for this meeting

☐ Parent–Teacher Action Research Cycle (Appendix 8.1)

☐ Notes from MAPs done for this child

☐ Copies of Ground Rules for PTAR Meetings (Appendix 8.2) and A New Perspective on Labels (Appendix 8.5)

☐ Chart pad and markers

☐ NCR paper and pens

☐ Box of tissues

☐ Your own calendar

☐ Other:

Sample Agenda for PTAR Meeting

ABC PARENT–TEACHER ACTION RESEARCH TEAM MEETING

Today's Date: _____

Child's Name: _____

PTAR Team: _____

Our Goals: _____

_____

_____

Agenda:

1. Summary of previous meeting and mutual goals:

2. Action research step for today:

3. Is there anything else to discuss?

4. Summary of today's meeting:

5. Plan for action between meetings:

6. Time and date for next meeting:

From Stephanie H. McConaughy, Pam Kay, Julie A. Welkowitz, Kim Hewitt, and Martha D. Fitzgerald (2008). Copyright by The Guilford Press. Permission to photocopy this appendix is granted to purchasers of this book for personal use only (see copyright page for details).

10

The Action Research Cycle

Reflection, Analyzing Data, and Practical Theory

Steps
1. Create an agenda.
2. Summarize previous meeting and restate mutual goals.
3. Encourage parents and teachers to share their data.
4. Begin reflection on the data.
5. Begin analyzing the data.
6. Develop a practical theory.
7. Summarize meeting.
8. Set date for next meeting and distribute meeting notes.

Since the PTAR team members have collected their initial data, this chapter guides you through the next three steps of the Action Research Cycle: *Reflection, Analyzing Data,* and developing a *Practical Theory.* As was done in Chapter 9, this chapter describes one meeting in which a PTAR team might address these phases of action research. However, you and your PTAR teams can move through these phases in any number of meetings, depending on the pace and pattern of each particular team.

STEP 1. CREATE AN AGENDA

Create a written agenda to follow during the meeting. From here on, try to use a similar agenda format for each PTAR meeting so that team members know what to expect. This will help to keep the team focused on their mutual goals for the child and on following the steps of the Action

Research Cycle. You can use a copy of the general agenda in Appendix 9.1 or your own version, but try to keep the format consistent across the year.

The top of the agenda should always list the team's mutual goals for the child. Under item 2 write in the action research steps for the meeting: sharing data, reflection, analyzing data, and developing a practical theory.

Leave space under item 3, *Is there anything else to discuss?*, to write in any other issues that the team wants to discuss. Give a copy of the agenda to each person attending or display the agenda on a chart for everyone to see. The purpose of item 3 is to allow time for parents and teachers to bring up any immediate concerns they may have. These may range from something as mundane as exchanging a permission slip for a field trip to something as significant as impending parental separation. You will need to use your judgment about the time that the team needs to address their mutual concerns. A question that may help here is "Do you need more time to talk about this now?" Remember that your goal is to continue with the Action Research Cycle, and keep the focus on the child.

STEP 2. SUMMARIZE PREVIOUS MEETING AND RESTATE MUTUAL GOALS

Remember to begin each meeting by summarizing briefly what happened in the previous meeting. Always include in your summary a reminder of the team's mutual goals for the child. You may also find it helpful to display a copy of the Ground Rules for PTAR Meetings (see Appendix 8.2) on a table or shelf where everyone can see them during the meeting.

STEP 3. ENCOURAGE PARENTS AND TEACHERS TO SHARE THEIR DATA

Follow the ground rule, *Parents talk first*, by inviting the parents to share the data (observations about the child) they have collected since the last meeting. Some parents may be reluctant or shy about sharing their observations, particularly if they are not used to speaking at meetings with teachers. This will change gradually as parents see that the teacher values their thoughts and ideas, as do you, their Parent Liaison. After parents share their observations, invite the teacher to share his/her data on the child. To encourage a parent (or a teacher) to share data, you can ask questions like those listed in the script below.

QUESTIONS FOR SHARING DATA

```
Would you like to share some of your data (log) about [child]?
What did you observe about [child]?
What did you write in your notebook/journal about [child]?
What have you noticed about [child] at [home/school]?
Tell me about a day when [goal].
```

```
Tell me about what happened when [child] came [home yesterday/this
  week/was in school yesterday/this week].
Tell me what [child] did [yesterday/this week].
Can you give me some more detail? What behaviors did you notice?
What did you see? What did you hear? What was [he/she] doing?
```

Sometimes only one member of the PTAR team may bring data to share. When this happens, do not scold the other person. Instead, assume that the person observed something, but did not write it down. Stay focused on the team's goals for the child and ask some more general questions, like "What have you noticed about . . . ?" or "Tell us about a day when. . . . "

Write parents' and teachers' information (data) where everyone can see them, as you did for the MAPs discussions in previous meetings. Again, be sure to follow the ground rules by recording parents' and teachers' comments in their own words as much as possible. You can also use the same system you used during MAPs to show areas where team members agree on their observations (e.g., underlining or color-coding words that indicate areas of agreement).

Encourage the team to state observations in positive terms whenever possible. If parents and teachers use negative language to describe the child, remind them of the ground rule, *All ideas are to be expressed as positively as possible.* You can then ask, "How can we say that in a positive way?" Sometimes you may need to model the process by rephrasing the statement yourself. When you do, be sure to ask the original speaker if he/she agrees with your positive rephrasing. Does it capture the original meaning? For example, when Gray's teacher reported that "He constantly interrupts other people's conversations," the Parent Liaison rephrased the statement by saying, "Can we say Gray likes to start all conversations himself?" This brought chuckles from Gray's teacher and his mother, but got the point across about positive statements.

 TIP: Keeping things positive can be challenging and requires good creative thinking. A New Perspective on Labels in Appendix 8.5 has a list of "new encouraging labels" that you can substitute for "old negative labels." You can bring a copy of this list to the meeting to help yourself and the team think of positive words to use in the data-sharing process.

STEP 4. BEGIN REFLECTION ON THE DATA

While parents and teachers are collecting their data, they have the opportunity to reflect on what they have observed (see Figure 10.1). Most of the time, parents and teachers will be reflecting on their data by themselves, outside of team meetings. Reflections can be part of their notetaking during data collection. Appendix 10.1 shows examples of questions that parents and teachers can ask themselves about specific behaviors they have observed about the child. You may want to make copies of this form to give to the parents and teacher for the notebooks they started in the first PTAR meeting.

During reflection, parents and teachers think about what impact the child's behavior may have on their own behavior or feelings. They can also think about what they might be doing to encourage or maintain the child's behavior. As one Parent Liaison commented, "Reflection is tricky. It is hard becoming aware of your own 'behaviors,' especially in a group. Empathize with both parent and teacher!"

Although the Action Research Cycle shows reflection in one place in the diagram, reflection

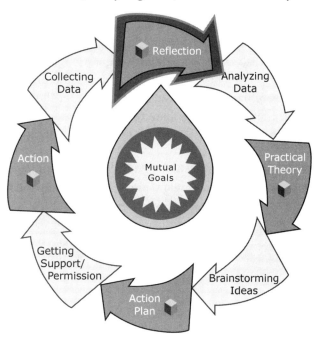

FIGURE 10.1. Parent–Teacher Action Research Cycle: Reflection.

can take place throughout the entire cycle. Often, PTAR team members will move back and forth between collecting data, reflecting on their data, and analyzing their data. More reflection can also occur as the team brainstorms ideas and develops their action plans.

As they reflect on their data, parents and teachers begin to understand how their own value systems and personal experiences influence the way they perceive the child and interact with the child. In this way, reflection can move parents and teachers to a better understanding of themselves and their relationships with the child. For example, a parent might realize that certain ways of disciplining the child (e.g., scolding, yelling) leads to temper tantrums and arguments. A teacher of the same child might realize that telling the child that he/she must do something *now* (e.g., complete math worksheets) leads to power struggles. Both the parent and teacher might also notice that the same child responds much better when he/she can choose between two acceptable activities (e.g., either work on math or spelling; either help set the table or feed the dog).

Parents and teachers might also notice that a child has more difficulty behaving appropriately during certain times or activities (e.g., circle discussions at school, dinnertime at home), in contrast to other times when the child behaves more appropriately (e.g., during art projects at school, playing with Legos at home). Such reflections are an important part of the Action Research Cycle because they can move parents and teachers toward changes in their own behavior that can improve their interactions with the child.

When parents and teachers come together in the PTAR meeting, they may decide whether they want to share some or all of their reflections. Some reflections may be too personal or sensitive to share. Be sure that the parents know that it is fine not to share. Sharing reflections requires a high level of trust between parents and teachers. Such self-disclosure may not occur until later in the school year, or may never occur. On the other hand, self-disclosure can be infectious; teams made some of the best parent–teacher connections during the ABC Program when a teacher spoke of her own experiences as a parent, relating them to the issues at hand.

As Parent Liaison, you can ask some of the reflection questions during the meeting. However, monitoring the sharing and reflection process is also important. You can judge whether encouraging a parent or teacher to share particular reflections is helpful for the team process. You should also respect team members' decisions *not* to share their reflections. This might be a time to put down your marker, and move away from writing on the chart pad. You can ask "Should I write this down?"

When parents and teachers share their reflections, be cautious about not letting the PTAR meeting become a therapy session or a dumping session. Instead, keep the focus on the child and the team's mutual goals for the child. You will sense when a parent or teacher goes off on a tangent or crosses boundaries for sharing personal information. When it feels as if this might be happening, you can bring the team back on target by restating the mutual goals and asking, "How does [issue] affect our goals for [child]?"

STEP 5. BEGIN ANALYZING THE DATA

The next step in the Action Research Cycle involves analyzing data (see Figure 10.2). (The data are parents' and teachers' observations about the child.) This step, unlike *reflection*, is best done in team meetings. On the following page are some questions that you can ask parents and teachers during data analysis.

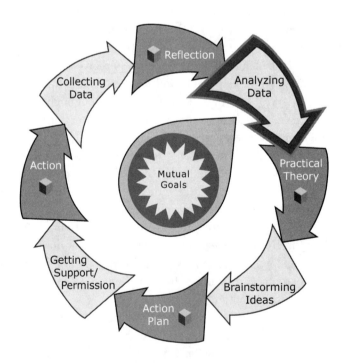

FIGURE 10.2. Parent–Teacher Action Research Cycle: Analyzing data.

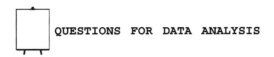 **QUESTIONS FOR DATA ANALYSIS**

Behavior:

What exactly did [child] do? (Describe the behavior without adding
   judgments or reactions.)
How many times?
How long?
How intense?

What is this behavior all about?

Under what circumstances did this behavior occur?
When did you notice that?
Have you noticed that [at home/at school]?

Before the behavior (Antecedent):

What happened just before this behavior occurred?
What time of day was it?
Who else was there?
What did you expect [child] to be doing?

After the behavior (Consequence):

What happened after the behavior occurred?
What did you do?
What did the other people do? How did they react?
Then what happened?
What did [child] do? How did [he/she] react?

To begin data analysis, it is usually good to focus first on the particular behavior that the parent or teacher observed. You can start this discussion by asking the parent or teacher, "What
exactly did [child] do?" Encourage the parent or teacher to describe the child's behavior in
observable terms, not to simply label or characterize it. For example, if a parent or teacher reports
that the child acted "inappropriately," ask that person "What does inappropriate look like to you?"
or "What did [child] *do* inappropriately?" Examples of specific descriptions might be "He threw a
temper tantrum—yelled and screamed," "She punched a kid in the stomach," or "He was joking
and poking the kid sitting next to him."

Ask about the time of day when the behavior occurred and who was present. It is also good to
ask what the parent or teacher expected the child to be doing. You can then ask parents and teachers to elaborate on the frequency, intensity, and duration of a particular behavior. You can do this
by asking, "How often does [child] do this in a typical day? How long does it usually last? On a
scale of 1 to 10, how intense or severe was this behavior?"

After a parent or a teacher has described a particular behavior in detail, encourage that person to think about the circumstances surrounding the child's behavior. For example, you can ask,
"What do you think this behavior does for [child]? Under what circumstances did this behavior

occur?" Then ask about the circumstances preceding the behavior: "What happened just before this particular behavior occurred?" (The technical term for whatever preceded the behavior is the *antecedent*.) Here a parent or teacher might describe particular events or actions by others that seemed to trigger the child's behavior (e.g., "I told him to turn off the TV," "Another kid pushed her on the playground," "We started to work on math problems").

Then ask about the circumstances or *consequences* following the behavior: "What happened after the behavior?" Here a parent or teacher may speak about his/her own actions or actions of others that were a reaction or consequence of the child's behavior (e.g., "I sent him to his room as a punishment," "The other child hit back and they got into a fight," "I scolded him about not paying attention"). This is the A–B–C (*antecedent, behavior, consequence*) sequence that we discussed in Chapter 9, when the team was first collecting data.

Be sure to ask if there were circumstances when the particular behavior did *not* occur. After their initial data analysis, the PTAR team might decide they want to collect more data to answer specific questions about their observations, or they might decide they are ready to move onto a practical theory about their data.

STEP 6. DEVELOP A PRACTICAL THEORY

When the PTAR team feels that they have gathered enough initial data on the child, they can begin to develop their practical theory about the child's behavior (see Figure 10.3). The *practical theory* is the team's best guess about why the child is behaving in a certain way. Examples of questions you can ask the PTAR team to help them think about practical theories follow.

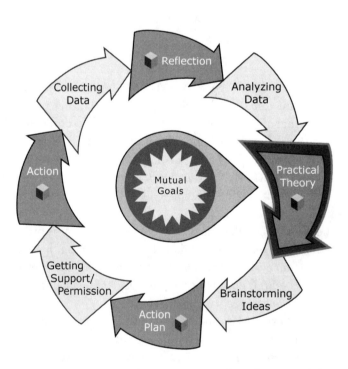

FIGURE 10.3. Parent–Teacher Action Research Cycle: Practical theory.

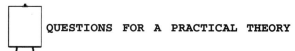

QUESTIONS FOR A PRACTICAL THEORY

What do you think is going on with [child]?

Why do you think [child] is behaving this way?

What does this mean to [child]?

What does this behavior do for [child]?

Why are we seeing this behavior now?

Why might this be happening [at home/at school]?

Why is this happening [at home/at school] and not [at school/at home]?

Could this be related to [specific factor/event]?

Are there any other [factors/events] that might be related to this behavior?

Are you seeing any patterns in this behavior?

To begin a discussion of practical theory, ask the parent and teacher, "What do you think is going on with [child]?" or "Why do you think [child] is behaving this way?" These questions lead the PTAR team to a *functional analysis* of the child's behavior. This means figuring out what function the behavior performs for the child. For example, clowning around in school could serve the function of getting attention from peers or the teacher (even if the attention is negative). Refusing to answer a question may also be attention-getting. Throwing a temper tantrum at home could serve the function of avoiding an undesirable activity (e.g., not doing math homework). Behaviors may also serve functions of self-regulation (e.g., drawing or doodling, or rocking back and forth to calm anxious feelings) or gaining control (e.g., interrupting a conversation to focus on what the child wants to talk about). If the parents or teachers are not familiar with the educational or psychological concept that behavior serves a purpose, you may want to talk with them between meetings, or give them explanatory written materials, as discussed later in this chapter.

The example below shows how you can record a team's practical theory, and offers some cautions to keep in mind when the PTAR team begins to develop its practical theory.

ONE WAY TO STATE A PRACTICAL THEORY

We think that [child] is _____

_____ (describe behavior) because

[he/she] _____ (informed guess).

CAUTIONS FOR DEVELOPING PRACTICAL THEORIES

- Avoid coming to conclusions too soon.
- Avoid making value judgments about the child's behavior.
- Avoid language that places blame.

The first caution is: *Avoid coming to conclusions too soon.* You can suggest that all ideas are "hypotheses" and write them down as possible explanations for the child's behavior. The team may then decide that they want to collect more data to check out their hypotheses.

The second caution is: *Avoid making value judgments about the child's behavior.* Try to encourage team members to describe behaviors without labeling them as *good* or *bad, appropriate* or *inappropriate,* and *acceptable* or *unacceptable.* Instead, remind parents and teachers of their goals, and ask them to talk about behaviors they would like to see or not see. Ask what type of behavior would work best for the child in a particular situation.

The third caution is: *Avoid language that places blame.* This means discouraging parents and teachers from accusing each other or a third person of causing the child's behavior (e.g., "Jerome throws temper tantrums at home because you [the teacher] give him too much homework," "Sherry is inattentive in class because you [the parent] let her stay up too late on school nights," "His father tells him that he'll never learn to read"). Instead, keep the discussion focused on the behavior, its antecedents, and consequences without casting blame on a particular person.

At times, parents and teachers may disagree on their practical theories about a child's behavior. Forcing a consensus on all practical theories is not necessary. The team could decide that two different practical theories apply to the same behavior in different settings, such as home versus school, classroom versus recess, or mother versus father. In some cases, you can suggest that this is an area where the team agrees to disagree on the *function* of the behavior.

When recording notes on practical theory, you can again underline or color-code areas where the team agrees and use a different marking system for where the team disagrees. The team may then decide to collect more data to test which of the two practical theories applies best in a particular situation. It is also good to encourage the team to find a common ground, even when there are two different practical theories. For example, on one PTAR team, the teacher observed that Sherry often fell asleep during silent reading. Sherry's mother thought that she was inattentive in class because she had to stay up late each night doing too much homework. Sherry's teacher thought Sherry probably watched too much TV each night. The Parent Liaison recorded the two practical theories and then suggested that perhaps the team could agree that Sherry needs more sleep on school nights.

You can also encourage the PTAR team to think about the big picture when developing practical theories. This means thinking about other circumstances, besides immediate events, that might contribute to a child's behavior at home or at school. Examples are upcoming holidays, school field trips, special family events, a substitute teacher in class, visitors in the home, the anniversary of a traumatic incident, disappointments or losses for the child, or other events that may bring unhappiness, anxiety, or excitement.

As Parent Liaison, be careful not to push parents and teachers toward forming practical theories too soon. After analyzing and reflecting on their data, the PTAR team may decide that they need to collect more data to check out hunches or guesses about the child's behavior. For example, the parent asking the child a series of questions on a regular basis can open up a good dialogue about troubling issues or events, and thereby produce new insights (reflections) into the child's behavior.

If the PTAR team decides on more data collection, this means that they are returning to the beginning of the Action Research Cycle. *This is fine.* There are no rules about the direction of travel through the cycle. If they need more data, teams can go back to collecting data instead of moving to practical theory. In this case, you can continue to Steps 7 and 8 to adjourn this particular PTAR meeting.

Bethany's Story and Gray's Story at the end of this chapter are examples of how their PTAR teams proceeded through reflection, analyzing data, and developing a practical theory for each child. These vignettes are brief summaries of a much more fluid process, in which PTAR teams moved back and forth in the Action Research Cycle before they settled on a practical theory. As each team collected additional data, they later modified their practical theories and some of their mutual goals for the child.

When the PTAR team focuses on practical theory, this is the point in the Action Research Cycle when they may decide to call on outside expertise. As Parent Liaison, you should be prepared to offer information and materials that could be helpful for learning more about the child. These can include research-based publications, websites, brochures, and handouts from professional organizations. Appendix 10.2 lists national resources you can contact, and Appendix 10.3 leaves space for you to enter state and local resources. The National Association of School Psychologists (NASP) is a particularly good resource for handouts and reading materials on a wide variety of issues relevant for school-aged children, such as their book of handouts, *Helping Children at Home and School II: Handouts for Families and Educators* (Canter, Paige, Roth, Romero, & Carroll, 2004).

This is also the point at which the PTAR team may wish to invite other people to the next team meeting, such as school psychologists, guidance counselors, special educators, or other family members. The parent and teacher must agree on whom they want to invite to the meetings. When other people attend the PTAR meetings, your role is to keep the focus of discussion on the child and keep decisions in the hands of the parent and teacher. As Parent Liaison, you can remind the team that the parent and teacher are the action researchers, and that they are the ones who will develop the action plan for the child.

When the PTAR team decides that they have collected sufficient initial data and have developed their practical theory, they are ready to move on to brainstorming ideas for action and developing an action plan. Chapter 11 describes these steps in the Action Research Cycle.

STEP 7. SUMMARIZE MEETING

Bring the meeting to a close by summarizing the PTAR team's observations on the child and their practical theory. Restate the team's mutual goals for the child. If the team has decided to collect more data, summarize the data collection that parents and teachers will do before the next meeting.

STEP 8. SET DATE FOR NEXT MEETING
AND DISTRIBUTE MEETING NOTES

At the end of the meeting, set an agreeable date and place for the next meeting. Distribute meeting notes to all team members (or mail notes shortly after the meeting). Make a note on your calendar to contact the parent between meetings, and to remind both parent and teacher 2 days before the next meeting.

BETHANY'S STORY: The PTAR Team's Reflection, Data Analysis, and Practical Theory

Bethany's PTAR team met again after 2 weeks of collecting data. Bethany's mother, Anna, reported that Bethany came home at least two or three times a week crying and saying, "Other kids don't like me" or "Other kids think I'm dumb." She also observed that Bethany was reluctant to show her parents any of her schoolwork. One day, Anna said, Bethany showed her a drawing she had done at school. After Anna told her how much she liked the drawing, Bethany brightened up and let her mother put the drawing on the refrigerator. Bethany's teacher, Marietta, reported that Bethany was reluctant to try new things at school. For example, when the class started working with colored blocks to learn new addition and subtraction facts, Bethany gave up quickly, saying, "I can't do it." Then she started to cry when the teacher encouraged her to try. She also refused to read aloud in front of other children and would not let other children see what she wrote for a story assignment. Several times, Bethany tore up papers when she thought she had made mistakes. Anna added that Bethany enjoyed having stories read to her at bedtime, but she seldom tried to read any of the words herself.

As Anna and Marietta reflected on their data, they realized that Bethany had particular problems learning new things that required two or more steps. Marietta noted that Bethany seemed happier when she worked alone with a teacher's aide than she was when working with a group of children. Bethany also tried harder when she was praised for her efforts, even small efforts. From their reflections and data analysis, the PTAR team developed a practical theory that Bethany was performing poorly in academic areas because of her difficulty with multistep tasks and lack of self-confidence. The team guessed that Bethany's reading, writing, and math skills would improve if she could learn things one step at a time and became more willing to try new things. This practical theory led to the action plan for Bethany discussed in the next chapter.

GRAY'S STORY: The PTAR Team's Reflection, Data Analysis, and Practical Theory

Gray's PTAR team met again after 3 weeks of collecting data. Gray's mother, Carla, observed that he was "extremely persistent" in getting his own way. For example, when playing a board game with his older brother, Gray would change the rules when he was about to lose. He also yelled and screamed when his brother tried to make him help with a chore or when he was playing a game and she said it was time for bed. Carla said Gray desperately wanted other kids to come over to his house to play, but no one would come when he asked. She said that Gray often cried about having no friends of his own. Gray's teacher, Sarah, reported observations of many "negative" behaviors in school, especially when Gray had to change from one activity to another. Examples were shouting out questions when another child was talking, hiding his work folder at the beginning of a new lesson, grabbing materials during cooperative group projects, refusing to stop playing at the end of recess, pushing or hitting other children in the hallway, and kicking other children while lining up for lunch.

As Gray's team reflected on their data, Carla noted that she and her husband often had to depend on Gray's older brother, James, to baby-sit until they came home from work each day. She noticed that James bossed Gray around a lot and hit him "to make him mind." James also teased Gray until he got mad and cried. Sarah noticed that Gray behaved much better when he could work one on one with the teacher or when he was put in charge of an activity with only one other child. Gray's PTAR team developed several practical theories to explain his behavior. They guessed that Gray was probably mimicking his older brother when he hit or kicked other kids or grabbed things from other kids. They also guessed that Gray was unaware of how his negative behavior affected other people and that he did not know more socially accepted ways to get what he wanted. These reflections and further data analysis led to the action plan for Gray discussed in the next chapter.

✓Checklist of Materials You Might Need for This Meeting

☐ Copies of agenda for this meeting

☐ Parent–Teacher Action Research Cycle (Appendix 8.1)

☐ Notes from previous meeting

☐ The Ground Rules for PTAR Meetings (Appendix 8.2) and A New Perspective on Labels (Appendix 8.5)

☐ Copies of Questions to Encourage Reflection (Appendix 10.1)

☐ Examples of National Resources (Appendix 10.2)

☐ State and Local Resources (Appendix 10.3)

☐ Chart pad and markers

☐ NCR paper and pens

☐ Box of tissues

☐ Your own calendar

☐ Other:

APPENDIX 10.1

Questions to Encourage Reflection

Behavior

- How do I feel when this behavior happens?

- What would it mean to me to have this behavior change?

- When have I seen this behavior before?

- What do I do to contribute to this behavior?

- What is my role in maintaining this behavior?

From Stephanie H. McConaughy, Pam Kay, Julie A. Welkowitz, Kim Hewitt, and Martha D. Fitzgerald (2008). Copyright by The Guilford Press. Permission to photocopy this appendix is granted to purchasers of this book for personal use only (see copyright page for details).

National Resources

☐ **The Federation of Families for Children's Mental Health** is a parent-run organization concerned with all aspects of emotional and behavioral health. Their website also has links of interest to children and adults.

> Reach the Federation at:
>
> 9605 Medical Center Drive, Suite 280
> Rockville, MD 20850
> Phone: (240) 403-1901
> FAX: (240) 403-1909
> E-mail: ffcmh@ffcmh.org
> *www.ffcmh.org*

☐ **The National Association of School Psychologists (NASP)** is a particularly good resource for handouts and reading materials on a wide variety of issues relevant for school-aged children. Their book, *Helping Children at Home and School II: Handouts for Families and Educators,* is a very useful resource.

> Reach NASP at:
>
> 4340 East West Highway, Suite 402
> Bethesda, MD 20814
> Phone: (301) 657-0270
> Toll-Free: (866) 331-NASP
> *www.nasponline.org*

☐ **The National Information Center for Children and Youth with Disabilities (NICHCY)** provides information to parents, teachers, advocates, students, and the general public on issues related to disabilities. A child does not have to have an identified disability in order to get information from NICHCY. This free resource has links to specific organizations and agencies in your state, as well as those that have national offices. Its *Zigawhat!* link is directed to children, and answers questions about everything from ADD to LdKidzone.

> Reach NICHCY at:
>
> P.O. Box 1492
> Washington, DC 20013
> Toll-free: (800) 695-0285
> FAX: (202) 884-8441
> E-mail: *nichcy@aed.org*
> *www.nichcy.org*

☐ **Parent Information and Resource Centers (PIRCs)** are funded by the U.S. Department of Education. They bring parents, educators, and those who work with families a wealth of information about helping children get ready for school and succeed in school, from the early grades through high school.

> *www.ed.gov/programs/pirc*

From Stephanie H. McConaughy, Pam Kay, Julie A. Welkowitz, Kim Hewitt, and Martha D. Fitzgerald (2008). Copyright by The Guilford Press. Permission to photocopy this appendix is granted to purchasers of this book for personal use only (see copyright page for details).

State and Local Resources

	Address	Telephone

Library _____

Parent Center _____

School Psychologist _____

School Social Worker _____

School Guidance Counselor _____

Special Educators _____

Title I Coordinator _____

Parent Information Resource Center _____

Parent-Managed Organizations:

    Parent-to-Parent _____

    Federation of Families for Children's Mental Health_____

    Other _____

Community Mental Health Agency _____

From Stephanie H. McConaughy, Pam Kay, Julie A. Welkowitz, Kim Hewitt, and Martha D. Fitzgerald (2008). Copyright by The Guilford Press. Permission to photocopy this appendix is granted to purchasers of this book for personal use only (see copyright page for details).

11

The Action Research Cycle

Brainstorming Ideas, Action Plan, Getting Support and Permission

---

Steps

1. Create an agenda.
2. Summarize previous meeting, mutual goals, and the team's practical theory.
3. Brainstorm ideas for action.
4. Develop an action plan.
5. Discuss getting support and permission.
6. Discuss collecting data during the action plan.
7. Summarize meeting.
8. Set date for next meeting and distribute meeting notes.

Now that the PTAR team members have developed their practical theory about the child's behavior, this chapter guides you through the last three steps of the Action Research Cycle: *Brainstorming Ideas* for action, developing an *Action Plan*, and *Getting Support and Permission*. It also discusses how the team will continue to collect data while they carry out their action plan. This chapter describes one meeting for a PTAR team to address these last phases of action research. However, by now you are well aware that PTAR teams can move through the phases of action research in many different ways.

STEP 1. CREATE AN AGENDA

Begin the meeting by handing out a copy of the agenda to each team member or displaying the agenda for everyone to see. As indicated in previous chapters, you can use the general format for an agenda in Appendix 9.1, or create your own version of an agenda. Be sure to record the team's mutual goals at the top of the agenda. Under item 2 in the general agenda, list the particular steps of the Action Research Cycle that you will discuss in the meeting, as shown previously in Chapters 9 and 10. For this meeting, the action research steps are: brainstorming ideas for action, action plan, getting support and permission, and collecting data during the action plan. Under agenda item 3, you can add other issues that the team wants to discuss.

STEP 2. SUMMARIZE PREVIOUS MEETING, MUTUAL GOALS, AND THE TEAM'S PRACTICAL THEORY

Begin this meeting by restating the team's mutual goals for the child and briefly summarizing what happened in the previous meeting. Focus particularly on the team's practical theory about the child's behavior. Then ask the team to share additional data they have collected since the last meeting. After the parents and teacher analyze their new data, ask them if they want to make any changes in their practical theory.

STEP 3. BRAINSTORM IDEAS FOR ACTION

The team's practical theory serves as the basis for brainstorming ideas for their action plan (see Figure 11.1). Start this step by asking, "If your practical theory is right, what does [child] need to have happen differently at home and at school? *Brainstorming* involves thinking creatively about different approaches parents and teachers can take to reach their mutual goals for the child. You can begin by encouraging the team to think about the implications of their practical theory for

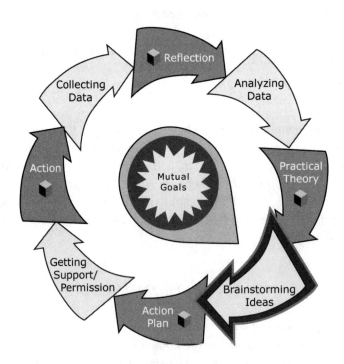

FIGURE 11.1. Parent–Teacher Action Research Cycle: Brainstorming ideas.

developing action plans. Then explain the Rules for Brainstorming shown in Appendix 11.1. You can copy these rules and give them to each team member or display them somewhere for all to see. This step can be fun, and shared laughter helps to build trust.

Explain that in brainstorming, all ideas are good ideas. The purpose of brainstorming is to generate many different ideas without judging any as good or bad, possible or impossible. Later the team will decide which ideas they want to use for their action plan. Tell the team you will record each speaker's ideas in his/her own words, just as you did earlier for the MAPs discussion. Encourage the team to piggyback on each other's ideas to generate new ideas. Stress that *put-downs* (e.g., "That will never work!") are against the rules because negative comments stifle creative thinking. Then ask the team to agree on a time limit for brainstorming. Usually 10 to 15 minutes is sufficient.

 TIP: Encourage PTAR teams to think about their practical theories when they brainstorm ideas for action. Also encourage teams to think about how they can build on the child's strengths and what each team member (parent and teacher) does well.

The Helpful Hints below outlines some ways that you can encourage PTAR teams to brainstorm ideas for action. Some teams may need prompting to think creatively. You might say that they are just "throwing ideas out on the table" or "trying them on for size." Tolerating silence is also an important feature of brainstorming to allow people time to think. When a parent or teacher does express an idea—any idea—praise that person for the suggestion, and write it down immediately. Once people start talking, one idea often leads to another. You can encourage this by asking a parent or teacher, "Can you piggyback on that idea?"

 HELPFUL HINTS: SOME WAYS TO ENCOURAGE BRAINSTORMING

- Encourage creative thinking: Hold up an ordinary item such as a paperclip, and ask them to name *all* the possible uses for it.
- Praise people for saying something.
- Encourage piggybacking on others' ideas.
- Keep your own comments brief.
- Allow silences for people to think.
- Try humor when things get tense or people are reluctant to talk.
- Remind the team to stick to the time limit for brainstorming.

To get parents and teachers talking more, keep your own comments or reactions brief. The best approach is to ask questions. The script below shows examples of the different kinds of questions you can ask to encourage parents and teachers to generate ideas and to elaborate on ideas. Record all brainstorming ideas in the speaker's own words, as you did during the MAPs process. Seeing the list of ideas grow can be very encouraging.

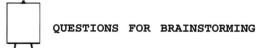 **QUESTIONS FOR BRAINSTORMING**

What can we do at home and at school to change this behavior?
If our theory is correct, what can we do to make things better for [child]?

What would work here? What worked for some other children?
What else might work? What could we do with a magic wand?
What has worked and what hasn't?
What is the most outrageous thing we could do?
Where can we go from here?
What are pieces of a plan that might work for [child]?
Can you remember a time when something really worked for [child]? What
  was it that worked?
Can you use what [child] is good at to help with this?
What are some things that could be done consistently at home and at
  school?
How can we make this fun for [child]?
How can we make this fun for you?
What needs to happen first?
What part of this will be hard? What part will be easy?
What support do you need to carry this out?
How can I help you with this plan?

Sometimes humor works well to ease tension and to encourage discussion during brainstorming. You can even suggest that team members try for fantastic or silly ideas. For example, after hearing about how Gray's brother bullied and teased him, the Parent Liaison suggested that maybe the team could send the brother to summer camp on the moon. This brought a laugh from everyone. The team then discussed practical ways that Gray could spend time away from his brother and more time alone with a parent.

 TIP: Sometimes parents or teachers might be reluctant to express an idea because they fear it might be rejected or sound ridiculous. You can break through reluctance when you suggest that "silly" ideas are welcome. Sometimes, silly ideas turn out to be not so silly, and lead to good ideas worth trying.

As suggested earlier, a good practice is to set a time limit for brainstorming. A time limit shows that the brainstorming process will not go on forever. This can be helpful for team members who are reluctant to consider new ideas. A time limit also discourages parents and teachers from jumping into action plans too quickly without considering a variety of options. If a team is still actively brainstorming when the time limit is up, ask them if they want to set a new time limit or go on to develop an action plan.

STEP 4. DEVELOP AN ACTION PLAN

After brainstorming ideas for action, the team members need to decide what they want to do in an action plan (see Figure 11.2). Ask them to think about how an action plan relates to their mutual goals for the child. Remind the team that they are testing their practical theory about the child's behavior. Then ask them how they think an action plan may help to change the child's behavior and meet the child's needs.

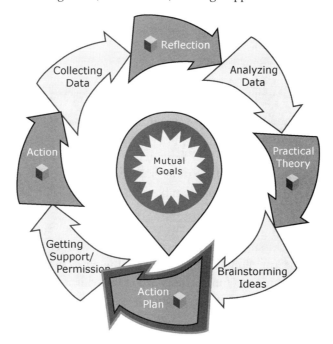

FIGURE 11.2. Parent–Teacher Action Research Cycle: Action plan.

Look at the list of brainstorming ideas. Ask the parents and teacher to *prioritize* the list, by giving each idea a number, with "1" as their top choice. Prioritizing leads to agreement on the action plan. You might ask the team which actions they think are more doable than others. Often, starting with simpler actions that are easy to carry out is best. This will give the team a sense of accomplishment from the beginning of their action plan. As the parents and teacher gain confidence and trust in each other, they may choose to try actions that require more effort and more cooperation.

The action plan itself should be simple. You may want to suggest that the team choose only two or three actions to carry out at any one time. If the team tries to do everything at once, they may just end up exhausted and discouraged.

The action plan should include actions for both the parent and teacher to carry out. This will ensure that the plan is a *team* effort. If all of the actions are to be carried out in just one setting, or by just one person, the plan may be unfair. A lopsided plan can create resentment and undermine cooperation if it seems that some team members are not doing their part. You also might want to steer away from plans that require a sequence of actions (i.e., first the parent will do something, then the teacher will do something, or vice versa). Plans that require a sequence can lead to stalemates as each person is waiting for the other to take the next step.

Once the team has chosen two or three actions, write each choice on the action plan. Ask the parents and teacher to decide who will be responsible for that action, when the action will happen, and how often or how long the action will occur. You can use a simple chart like the one shown in Appendix 11.2 to record *what, who,* and *when* for each action.

TIP: You can copy the ABC Action Plan from Appendix 11.2 or create different versions of action plans to use with each team.

If you use the ABC Action Plan, first record the team's mutual goals for the child. Then write each action in the boxes under *What*. Record each action in simple and doable terms, for example, *Teach the skills of joining a group; Assign recess buddies; Invite another boy to go to a game.* In the boxes under *Who*, write the name or role of the person who will carry out each action. You can use first names if parents and teachers have used them in team meetings or just write *teacher, mother, father,* or other family member. In the boxes under *When*, write the day and approximate time when they will carry out the actions, for example, *Tuesday and Thursday mornings; morning recess every day; next Saturday.*

You should tie the overall time frame for the action plan to the schedule of PTAR meetings. For example, you can suggest that the team try a particular action plan for the time between the current meeting and the next meeting. Often, teams will need to modify their plans as they go along. Some teams may choose to meet more frequently for a while (e.g., once a week for a month) to check on their progress. Keeping the time frame short will encourage frequent checkups and guard against setting expectations too high at first. But also choose a time period that is long enough to give the plan a chance to succeed. You can remind parents and teachers that children's behavior usually doesn't change overnight. It will probably take a while before they see changes. One month is usually a good time frame for trying most action plans.

Occasionally, a team member may seem hesitant or skeptical about the time frame or certain parts of the action plan. Ask that person to say more about his or her concern; you may find that the parent or teacher has offered to do more than is possible. In that case the team needs to go back to adjust the assignments they have taken on, or the times in which they will do their part. If the concerned person simply wants to fine-tune the plan, you can say, "I would suggest that you try this out for a couple of weeks (or a month) and see how it works. It doesn't have to be perfect."

Figures 11.3 and 11.4 show examples of action plans that PTAR teams developed for Bethany and Gray. As you can see, each plan states the team's mutual goals for the child, which were discussed earlier in Chapter 8. Chapters 9 and 10 described the steps in the Action Research Cycle that led up to the PTAR team's action plans for Bethany and Gray. In each case, the PTAR team moved back and forth in the Action Research Cycle. They started with collecting data, then shared and reflected on their data, and developed practical theories about the child's behavior. After arriving at some practical theories, the two teams brainstormed many different actions that they might take to achieve their mutual goals for the child. They then prioritized which actions to take first.

The action plans shown here for Bethany and Gray are early versions of each PTAR team's efforts. Each action plan also indicates who would obtain support or permission (Step 5), when needed, and what data the team would gather as it carried out the plan (Step 6). As time went on, each team modified its action plan, as needed. Sometimes the team changed or dropped a part of the plan when it was not working well. Later, each team added new action steps to address mutual goals that were not a focus of earlier plans. In Chapter 12, you will learn more about how these two PTAR teams worked to make the first 2 years of school more positive for Bethany and Gray. Chapter 12 also tells stories of how PTAR teams collaborated on behalf of several other children.

ABC ACTION PLAN

Today's Date: November 14, 2005

Child's Name: Bethany

PTAR Team: Anna (Mother), Marietta (Teacher), Nancy (Parent Liaison)

Our Goals: 1. Will have higher self-esteem

2. Will feel confident in areas of reading, writing, and math

3. Will improve motor skills

Action Plan:

What	Who	When
Give opportunities for leadership roles (e.g., speak first in class, hand out papers)	Marietta	Morning circle time, Language Arts, ongoing through day
Preteach new skills one at a time	Marietta	Language Arts, Math
Write a diary with Bethany about her day; emphasize positives	Anna or Raymond	Half-hour before bedtime

Support or Permission Needed:

None

Data Collection during Action Plan:

Marietta records successes in notebook at school. Anna records successes in notebook at home.

FIGURE 11.3. Bethany's action plan.

STEP 5. DISCUSS GETTING SUPPORT AND PERMISSION

Some action plans will be easy for parents and teachers to carry out on their own. Other action plans may be more difficult. As Parent Liaison, you need to be especially alert to the demands an action plan may place on the parent. Some parents may need extra support to carry out their part of the plan.

When a team is beginning an action plan, you might call both the parent and the teacher between meetings to check on how things are going. Sometimes a reminder or a friendly phone call asking, "How are you doing with [child's] new plan?" is all that they need. Ask parents and teachers when would be a good time for you to call to check in. Later, when the plan is up and running, you may not need to do these check-ins.

ABC ACTION PLAN

Today's Date: December 2, 2005

Child's Name: Gray

PTAR Team: Carla (Mother), Sarah (Teacher), Judy (Parent Liaison)

Our Goals: 1. To see the other guy's side

            2. To take suggestions from peers

            3. To "give and take"

Action Plan:

What	Who	When
One-on-one instruction in "partnering" (Ungame)	School guidance counselor	Once a week, Tuesday mornings
Structured board games at home (e.g., checkers)	Carla or Edward	Half-hour each night
Give leadership roles in school (e.g., handing out papers, lining up kids for lunch)	Sarah	At least once each morning and afternoon
Daily behavior chart with checks for: sharing materials; waiting his turn; listening to another person	Sarah	Three times for each school day: before morning recess; morning recess to lunch; after lunch (not lunch recess or specials)
Read points on behavior chart; give reward for meeting goal	Carla	Friday every week

Support or Permission Needed:

Sarah will check with guidance counselor to enroll Gray in weekly sessions using the "Ungame."

Data Collection during Action Plan:

Sarah will record checks for successes (and challenges) in notebook each day; give Gray's reward each Friday and record it in notebook.

FIGURE 11.4. Gray's action plan.

Use your own judgment about whether and when to call parents and/or teachers. You may want to set limits regarding phone contacts, such as saying you will check in once a week and talk for 10 minutes. When you do call, keep the conversation related to the team's mutual goals and action plan.

 TIP: Be careful not to move into the role of a social worker for the parent or consultant for the teacher. If a parent seems to need more support than you can provide between meetings, you should refer him/her to agencies or support services in the community. Reflect on your conversations with the parent; if you find yourself giving advice too often, or feel "in over your head," you probably are. Ask your supervisor to suggest a referral. The teacher has other professionals within the school who should be available for consultation.

You can learn more about resources and support services available through the Parent Information Resource Center (PIRC) and other community agencies, as well as through national organizations and Internet websites. You can also suggest books and other reading materials for parents and teachers. Sometimes it is good to have some reading materials on hand to distribute at PTAR meetings.

Appendix 10.2 contains addresses and phone numbers for national organizations that could be helpful resources for parents and teachers. You can add your own state and local resources to the form in Appendix 10.3 as you continue in your role as Parent Liaison. Additional books for recommended reading are listed at the end of the References section of this book.

Some action plans may require obtaining support or permission from someone who is not a member of the PTAR team, such as the school principal, school psychologist, or guidance counselor. For example, the team may need permission from the principal and guidance counselor to involve a child in a smaller social skills group at school. Or they may need permission to have the child help serve meals in the school cafeteria.

When support or permission is required, the action plan should specify who will obtain it and when this will be done. In the PTAR meeting, discuss whether the teacher will seek support or permission, or the parent, or both. Sometimes getting support for an unusual plan from a school administrator can be very effective if the parent and teacher ask together. As Parent Liaison, you can also play a role in obtaining support or permissions. Each situation will be different, even for two teams in the same school.

STEP 6. DISCUSS COLLECTING DATA DURING THE ACTION PLAN

While parents and teachers carry out their action plan, they also need to continue collecting data on the child. This data collection is essential to evaluate whether the plan is working and to assess the child's progress toward the team's mutual goals. Data collection should include observations by both parents and teachers. Be sure to include the data collection methods as part of the action plan.

The data should include clues or observable behaviors related to the team's mutual goals for the child, as discussed earlier in Chapter 9. You can ask the PTAR team, "How are we going to know that the plan is working? What data will we need?" The script below lists some additional questions you can ask to help the team decide what data to continue collecting during their action plan.

QUESTIONS FOR COLLECTING DATA DURING ACTION PLANS

```
How will we know whether [child] is reaching our goal?
What clues will we notice when we are moving toward our goals?
What behavior would you be noticing?
What would you see? What would you hear?
What would [child] be doing?
What would [child] be doing differently?
Does [child] behave differently with different people (e.g., mom, dad,
   teacher, friend)?
Does [child] behave differently during certain times of day or situa-
   tions?
```

The methods for collecting data can be similar to those discussed in Chapter 9, such as recording observations in notebooks or journals, dictating observations into a tape recorder, writing a child's answers to a set of questions, or noting observations on checklists. Some teams may decide to continue using the same data collection methods they used previously. Other teams may decide to change some of their data collection methods. The most important thing is to continue collecting observations that will help the team to figure out whether their plan is working or whether they have to make changes in the plan.

TIP: Don't get discouraged if an action plan doesn't work perfectly or parts of the plan don't work at all or "backfire." When this happens, the team can use the information to modify the plan or to develop a new plan. Sometimes the plan may simply need more time. Sometimes the team may need more data to develop a better plan.

STEP 7. SUMMARIZE MEETING

Bring the meeting to a close by summarizing the PTAR team's action plan and how they will collect data until the next meeting. Restate who will seek any support or permission that may be necessary to carry out the action plan.

TIP: Make sure that both the parent and teacher know exactly what they will do in the action plan. If a parent has trouble reading, use an alternative method to record the data for that child, such as tape-recording. You can also offer to check in with the parent and/or teacher before the next meeting to see how their action plan is going.

STEP 8. SET DATE FOR NEXT MEETING
AND DISTRIBUTE MEETING NOTES

At the end of the meeting, set a mutually agreeable date and place for the next meeting. Distribute meeting notes to all team members (or mail notes soon after the meeting). Be sure to include a copy of the action plan with the notes.

✓**Checklist of Materials You Might Need for This Meeting**

☐ Copies of agenda for this meeting

☐ Parent–Teacher Action Research Cycle (Appendix 8.1)

☐ Notes from previous meeting

☐ The Ground Rules for PTAR Meetings (Appendix 8.2)

☐ Rules for Brainstorming (Appendix 11.1)

☐ Copies of ABC Action Plan (Appendix 11.2) or your own version

☐ Chart pad and markers

☐ NCR paper and pens

☐ Box of tissues

☐ Your own calendar

☐ Other:

Rules for Brainstorming

- All ideas are good.

- All ideas will be recorded in the speaker's own words.

- Piggybacking on someone else's ideas is encouraged.

- No one may "put down" anyone else's idea.

- Stick to the time limit.

From Stephanie H. McConaughy, Pam Kay, Julie A. Welkowitz, Kim Hewitt, and Martha D. Fitzgerald (2008). Copyright by The Guilford Press. Permission to photocopy this appendix is granted to purchasers of this book for personal use only (see copyright page for details).

ABC Action Plan

ABC ACTION PLAN

Today's Date: _____

Child's Name: _____

PTAR Team: _____

Our Goals: 1. _____

2. _____

3. _____

Action Plan:

What	Who	When

Support or Permission Needed:

Data Collection during Action Plan:

From Stephanie H. McConaughy, Pam Kay, Julie A. Welkowitz, Kim Hewitt, and Martha D. Fitzgerald (2008). Copyright by The Guilford Press. Permission to photocopy this appendix is granted to purchasers of this book for personal use only (see copyright page for details).

12

Questions, Challenges, and Transitions

```
┌─────────────────────────────────────────────────────────────────┐
│            Questions to Be Addressed in This Chapter              │
│  ─────────────────────────────────────────────────────────────  │
│  • What records should I be keeping?                              │
│  • What should I be doing between PTAR meetings?                  │
│  • What should I do if there are conflicts between the parents and teacher? │
│  • What should I do when serious child or family problems come up? │
│  • Can a child's goals be academic as well as behavioral?         │
│  • When should other people attend the PTAR meeting?              │
│  • What happens when children move to another teacher or another school? │
│  • How do we end the PTAR process?                                │
└─────────────────────────────────────────────────────────────────┘
```

Now that you know how to use the Action Research Cycle to help guide parents and teachers in their work, you undoubtedly have questions like those above. This chapter will answer some of them, but many of your questions can only be answered in the context of your community and conversations with your supervisor and peers. The ABC Program does not use cookie-cutter methods to address the specific concerns presented by individual children and families, and neither can you.

Your role is to support parents and to guide PTAR teams as they figure out a child's needs and the right actions to take. It is not up to you to decide how to help the child; it is up to the parents and teachers. When you have information and resources to contribute to the discussion, you can offer suggestions, leaving both parents and teachers free to use your ideas or not.

We have been using the stories of Bethany and Gray to illustrate the Action Research Cycle. The conclusions to their stories illustrate how ABC worked for them and their families. Bethany's story illustrates how the ABC Program and subsequent special education services can work together on behalf of the child. Gray's story shows how the relationship between parents and teacher can be an uncomfortable one, with several disagreements. The PTAR process, however, allowed all parties to continue focusing on Gray's needs. You will also read about Gray's own contributions to the team meetings, and the value of consulting an outside expert when some of a child's issues require professional intervention. Short vignettes about other children in the ABC Program address some common issues faced by Parent Liaisons.

THE REST OF BETHANY'S STORY: Progress in First and Second Grades

Bethany is the 6-year-old girl whose story we followed in Chapters 8–11. Bethany's PTAR team consisted of her mother and father, Anna and Raymond, her teacher, Marietta, and Parent Liaison, Nancy. Because Raymond traveled a lot for business, he was not able to attend every PTAR meeting. However, he still participated by faxing his observations and comments about Bethany for the team to share. Bethany's PTAR team met twice to go through the MAPs process, which led to three mutual goals for Bethany: (1) Will have higher self-esteem; (2) Will feel confident in areas of reading, writing, and math; and (3) Will improve motor skills (see Chapter 8). They then discussed clues for their data collection phase of the action research cycle (see Chapter 9).

Bethany's parents and teacher spent 2 weeks recording daily observations of Bethany in notebooks. In their third PTAR meeting, analysis and reflection on their data led the team to a practical theory that Bethany was performing poorly in academic work because she had difficulty with multistep tasks and lacked confidence. They agreed to focus their efforts on their first goal of building Bethany's self-esteem. After some discussion, they all felt that improving self-esteem might carry over to their second and third goals of having Bethany gain more confidence in reading, writing, and math, and improving motor skills. They then developed the action plan described in Chapter 11.

Bethany's PTAR team continued to meet once a month. Each time, they started by sharing their observations and successes. Anna loved speaking first because it gave her more of a feeling of control over her daughter's education. Through their shared observations, Marietta and Anna learned that Bethany did better in her school work when the teacher "pre-taught" new skills and presented them one at a time. They agreed this was a good strategy to keep in their action plan. They also added rephrasing instructions and using role playing because these strategies seemed to help Bethany when she "got stuck" or didn't understand something. Midway through the year, the team also added small, structured homework assignments to their action plan to build Bethany's confidence in reading, writing, and math (goal 2).

As the first-grade year progressed, Anna reported that Bethany was now writing in her diary every night. Marietta reported that Bethany frequently checked her writing portfolio and said she was proud of her work. By February, Raymond reported that Bethany "was walking taller and handling herself more confidently." Anna was thrilled that Bethany was reading to her at home for the first time and felt good about it.

In addition to collecting data for the PTAR team meetings, Bethany's parents and teacher completed standardized rating scales at the beginning and end of each year. Scores on the rating scales showed how each child's social skills and behavioral and emotional problems compared to large, national samples (norms) of boys and girls in the same age range. Administrators used anonymous group data from these rating scales to evaluate the effectiveness of the ABC Program, as described in Chapter 5.

At the beginning of first grade, rating scale scores near the 90th percentile indicated that Bethany's parents and teacher were reporting more behavioral and emotional problems than were typical for girls her age. In particular, Bethany showed high levels of anxiety, unhappiness, and social withdrawal. Low scores on the rating scales also indicated that Bethany had fewer social skills than other children, particularly skills for cooperating and asserting herself. Bethany's teacher also rated her academic performance below grade level compared to other students in her class. At the end of first grade, Bethany's parents and teacher completed the same rating scales again. This time, Bethany's social skills were closer to normal for her age and she showed less anxiety and social withdrawal than she did at the beginning of first grade. Bethany's PTAR team decided that she should be promoted to second grade, but continue with Marietta as her teacher for the next year.

After 2 months in second grade, Marietta reported that Bethany was still struggling with reading and writing, even though she now seemed more confident about her learning. The PTAR team agreed to refer Bethany for a special education assessment. (When Bethany was in first grade, Anna and Raymond had refused to have her evaluated.) The test results revealed that Bethany had above average cognitive ability, with especially good verbal skills for listening, speaking, and understanding familiar ideas. However, Bethany took longer than most children her age to grasp new ideas and process information. In addition, her reading and writing skills were below average for her age and grade. Anna and Raymond were surprised by the large differences between Bethany's ability and achievement scores. The school multidisciplinary team recommended special education services for specific learning disabilities in reading and written language. Because it now seemed clear that Bethany's poor school performance was not just due to low self-esteem and lack of confidence, Anna and Raymond agreed to special education services.

The PTAR team continued to meet once a month throughout Bethany's second-grade year. At the end of the year, Marietta felt that Bethany continued to need specialized instruction for basic reading and writing skills, but now she was much more confident about her learning. Instead of complaining that she couldn't do new learning tasks, Bethany tried things on her own and knew when to ask for help. She also accepted leadership roles in class, such as handing out materials, contributing to group discussions, and asking other students if they needed help when she finished early. She enjoyed reading to other children and doing small group projects. At home, Bethany liked to do her homework and showed her work to her mother and father. In first grade, Bethany had been afraid to do any of these things. At the end her second-grade year, Bethany drew a large, colorful picture of herself smiling and holding a book, with a rainbow overhead. Marietta reported that hers was "the best self-portrait I had ever seen by a second grader." Anna was also proud to report that Bethany had gone on a vacation trip with a friend and asked to go to an overnight camping trip in the summer. Scores on parent and teacher rating scales corroborated these positive reports by showing normal social skills and no severe behavioral and emotional problems compared to other girls Bethany's age.

THE REST OF GRAY'S STORY: Progress in First and Second Grades

Gray is the 6-year-old boy whose story we followed in Chapters 8–11. Gray's PTAR team consisted of his mother, Carla, his teacher, Sarah, and Parent Liaison, Judy. After going through the MAPs process, the PTAR team concluded that a major barrier to Gray's success in school, and in life, was his lack of understanding of other people. They realized that seeing other people's points of view was difficult for many 6-year-olds, but they felt that more empathy would help Gray get along better with peers and adults. They also recognized that Gray desperately wanted to have friends, like other children do. With this in mind, the PTAR team agreed on three mutual goals for Gray in their second meeting: (1) To see the other guy's side; (2) To take suggestions from peers; and (3) To "give and take" (see Chapter 8).

Carla used a notebook to record daily observations of Gray's behavior at home. Sarah recorded instances of specific behavior problems as they occurred each day in school. When they shared their data in the third PTAR meeting, Sarah realized that her recordings created a very negative picture of

Gray. She agreed to begin noting positive behaviors as well as problems. Carla reported that Gray showed many more problems after he had been left home alone with his older brother, James. As we learned in Chapter 10, James often teased and hit Gray and bossed him around. Carla reported one incident when James locked Gray in a closet to punish him. The Parent Liaison, Judy, and Sarah suggested that this behavior was "bullying" because James was so much older and more powerful than Gray. Although this was hard for Carla to hear, she said she would talk with James about how he treated Gray and lay down limits about what he could or could not do. Judy agreed to follow up with phone calls to Carla to see how this worked out at home.

The PTAR team's reflection on their data led to practical theories that Gray's aggressive behavior might be mimicking his older brother and that he lacked positive social skills to get what he wanted (see Chapter 10). They designed the action plan described in Chapter 11, which included a behavior chart and reward system, weekly guidance sessions for learning "partnering" skills, and other efforts to help Gray develop empathy and more positive social interactions. The team also tried to help Gray cope with aggressive behavior from his brother at home.

Gray's PTAR team continued to meet once a month for the rest of his first-grade year. The team experienced several ups and downs in their collaborative efforts. At times, Carla questioned whether Sarah really liked Gray despite the teacher's positive assurances. Carla rejected Judy's suggestion for family counseling. However, midway through the year, Carla enrolled Gray in an after-school sports-and-crafts program to reduce the amount of time spent with his brother as baby-sitter. Sarah arranged additional opportunities at school for Gray to practice his partnering skills in helping activities with kindergarten children.

By the end of Gray's first-grade year, Carla reported several successful "give-and-take" behaviors in board games at home. She also said Gray was more cooperative in games with his brother and did not try to change the rules as he had earlier. Sarah noted more frequent positive behaviors, such as staying seated quietly on the rug during circle time, sharing materials with other children, raising his hand, and waiting his turn to speak. She also noted fewer incidents of whining about directions, arguing with other children about materials, and hitting or shoving in line. In the final 10 weeks of school, Sarah observed 27 successful and only 3 unsuccessful transitions to new activities. She reported that Gray also had a very successful school field trip.

As in Bethany's case, Gray's mother and teachers completed standardized rating scales at the beginning and end of his first- and second-grade years. At the beginning of first grade, high scores on the rating scales indicated that Gray was exhibiting severe behavioral and emotional problems compared to other boys his age. He showed particularly severe aggressive and rule-breaking behaviors with scores above the 97th percentile. Gray's first-grade teacher also reported more attention problems and fewer social skills than other children his age. By the end of first grade, the rating scales showed evidence of improvements in Gray's social skills and rule-breaking, but he continued to show more aggressive behavior than typical for boys his age.

The PTAR team decided to place Gray in a multi-age classroom for second grade to give him opportunities to learn leadership behaviors with younger children. The team met with Gray's new teacher, Dorothy, to share their observations and action plan. The same Parent Liaison, Judy, used the MAPs process to introduce Gray to Dorothy. This was also a way for the new PTAR team to re-evaluate the goals for Gray. Dorothy said her dreams were for Gray "to channel his energy in positive ways . . . to assume appropriate leadership roles . . . and to begin in-depth learning." Carla's dreams were for Gray "to be happy . . . to have a lower frustration level." Carla and Dorothy both feared that Gray might "lose friends because of his intensity."

In the second PTAR meeting, the team decided to involve Gray more directly in their action research process. Gray joined them in the third PTAR meeting, at which Judy asked him questions about himself:

Gray, what is important to you? "Working hard . . . being fair."

What are your dreams? "When I grow up, I'll be a scientist with magical powers and potions. I'll have a partner who'll be friendly."

What do you like? "I like math . . . working with clay . . . computers . . . when my teacher gives choices . . . friends who are friendly."

If you could have your wish, what would it be like at home? "My brother wouldn't tease me. When I get home from school, James would say, 'How was your day, Gray? What did you do today? What were your favorite things?' And I would answer him. Then I would ask James the same questions."

What would your mother and father do? "They would ask me the same questions. 'How was your day, Gray? What were your favorite things?' And I would answer them. And they wouldn't turn away."

Gray's responses helped the PTAR team realize how much he wanted a closer, more caring relationship with his older brother and parents. Gray's responses also revealed his desire for having friends and his growing interest in learning. The team used this information, along with their own observations, to revise their mutual goals to focus on leadership and learning, in addition to their original goals of improving Gray's empathy and social interactions. They retained a behavior chart and reward system along with special time with parents in their action plan and added weekly participation in a friendship group with the school guidance counselor. They also added special time in the school day for Gray to work on his own art and science projects and show them to his classmates. At home, Carla encouraged James to play board games with Gray to develop more positive interactions between the two brothers.

After 2 months in second grade, Judy suggested that Gray might need more intensive services to address his behavioral and emotional problems. Gray's parents again rejected family counseling, but they did agree to enlist the services of the school psychologist. The PTAR team and the school psychologist revised Gray's action plan to provide more consistency and a menu of reward options in his behavior plan. Gray's teacher added opportunities to practice specific social skills that Gray learned in class. With the parents' permission, the school psychologist began weekly cognitive behavioral therapy sessions with Gray.

By the end of second grade, scores on parent and teacher rating scales showed considerable declines in Gray's attention problems, rule-breaking and aggressive behaviors, and improvements in his social skills, compared to his scores at the beginning of first grade. The PTAR team found these results very encouraging. At the same time, the rating scales still showed some worrisome aggressive behavior. This argued for continued support in third grade to help Gray sustain the progress he had already made. The school psychologist planned to consult with Gray's new teacher and provide weekly "check-in" meetings with Gray next year. The new teacher agreed to form a PTAR team with Carla and Judy to help Gray in his transition to third grade.

WHAT RECORDS SHOULD I BE KEEPING?

At a minimum, you will want to maintain a contact sheet for each family such as the one in Chapter 6 (Appendix 6.8), noting the date, time, type of contact, and necessary follow-up actions. Your meeting agenda in Chapter 9 (Appendix 9.1) gives you a format for recording the content of each meeting. You can also make notes on that agenda to remind parents, the teacher, and yourself of your responsibilities between meetings. If you don't have a way to give the PTAR team copies of the notes at the end of the meeting, be sure to mail those notes to them as soon as you can. Before you begin keeping any other notes about your ABC families, check with your supervisor about your employer's guidelines for taking notes on confidential material, as we suggested in Chapter 7.

If your program and your time permit, you may want to write your own evaluation of each meeting. Think of this evaluation as doing your own action research! Appendix 12.1 gives you a very basic format to follow which allows you to reflect on the meeting process. These simple evaluation questions also can be used with the parents and teachers at any time, and are especially useful at the end of the year. For more depth in your own reflection, here are a few additional questions that you might ask yourself:

- What will this meeting mean for the child?
- What beliefs, attitudes, or assumptions were evident in this meeting?
- What patterns or themes are beginning to emerge?

WHAT SHOULD I BE DOING BETWEEN PTAR MEETINGS?

You have four main tasks between meetings of each PTAR team: (1) *supporting* the parents, (2) *reflecting* on the meeting process, (3) *following up* with any tasks you have promised to do, and (4) *preparing* for the next meeting. Cody's story, as told by his Parent Liaison, illustrates how these tasks fit into the PTAR process.

 CODY'S STORY as Told by His Parent Liaison

Cody lived with his parents and three older siblings, two of whom had many behavioral issues in school. His mother, Janette, often struggled in her relationships with school staff. A dropout in eighth grade, Janette had negative feelings about most of her own school experiences and worried about her children being treated fairly at school. Cody's trouble controlling his temper was especially challenging to his teachers. At times he would shut down and become completely uncommunicative, and other times he would explode and throw things in the classroom.

During the first year, our PTAR meetings were held outside the school in a meeting room at the town library. I felt it was important to have a neutral place to meet so that Janette could begin building a fresh relationship with the school staff. Evelyn, Cody's first-grade teacher, had also taught Janette's older children. She was nervous about working with Janette, who could be easily excitable and defensive. Our first meeting was a little tense, but we were all able to work through the MAPs process. Janette and Evelyn described Cody as a happy, loving child who was eager to help others. They both said he does not like being told "no," and often would have temper tantrums. Teacher and parent together set two goals to focus on for Cody: to be proud of himself and to become a better reader. They felt that these two goals would help to make Cody calmer and better able to deal with consequences in a controlled manner.

As the meetings progressed, I saw that Janette had a difficult time keeping data to share at our meetings. At our next team meeting, we developed a set of questions that Janette could ask Cody about his school day. I typed up the questions, using a large font to make them easier for her to read, and sent her 15 copies. (See the script below for Cody's questions.) With many telephone reminders from me, Janette proudly brought her worksheets to our next meeting. Janette said that her older son had wanted her to ask him the questions, too, so she did, but wrote the answers on a sheet of notebook paper. She said "Writing the answers down makes them more important." Even though Janette continued to have a hard time remembering to collect data for the meetings on a regular schedule, she always came with some data and a positive attitude. Gradually, Janette learned to express her feelings and thoughts with more tact than she had used in the past.

Janette and Evelyn focused on helping Cody be proud of himself. They felt that he would feel more pride in himself if he could learn to control his temper. Evelyn gave Janette suggestions on dealing with his temper at home. She suggested that Janette praise Cody when she found out he had a good day at school and also when she saw him working through a problem without using his fiery temper. I gave Janette some information from our local "Parent's Assistance Hotline" on how to deal with temper tantrums, and also gave her the toll-free number so she could speak to someone directly.

The other goal focused on Cody's reading skills. Evelyn gave Janette ideas about working on letter recognition and reading at home. One suggestion was to take turns reading easy books to one another line-by-line. I took Janette and Cody to the library to look for new books to read—books that were also easy for Janette. Appropriate books, with new stories, helped to increase Cody's interest in reading.

Toward the end of the first year of PTAR meetings, Janette made the comment, "I have the best communication with Evelyn of all the teachers that I have ever had to deal with at this school." She also said, "I have gotten more support from Evelyn because she knows me better." Evelyn said, "The meeting sets us at ease because I know the parent's expectations a little bit better."

Our second year of PTAR meetings also started outside the school. Anita, Cody's second-grade teacher, had also taught one of Cody's siblings, and initially there were negative feelings between Janette and Anita. But again, both were able to use the meetings to speak positively, and to work out some plans to continue to focus on the reading goal. Janette was able to take suggestions that Anita gave her to help work with Cody at home with his reading and journal writing. By midyear, we moved our meetings into the school and held them in Anita's classroom. Both Anita and Janette were comfortable with this decision.

Throughout the school year, Anita expressed concerns about Cody's academic progress. In the spring, she brought up the idea of retaining Cody in second grade. Anita was very nervous about how Janette would react to this, but to her surprise, Janette was in full agreement with retention. She could clearly see that Cody needed the extra year in the second grade. At the end of the year, Janette said she really liked Anita's ideas on ways to work with Cody at home, and she really liked having more contact with the teacher. Anita also liked the parent contact.

The collaboration and mutual respect of the PTAR process helped Cody's teams work together successfully. Janette was able to find a positive, nonthreatening way to communicate with both the first- and second-grade teachers. This, in turn, made her feel much more comfortable in the school setting. Janette slowly learned how to deal with Cody's temper tantrums more calmly, which helped him to remain emotionally calm and better able to accept the consequences for his own actions. By the end of Cody's second year in the ABC Program, everyone saw a marked change. Cody was much more cooperative, more able to control his temper, and began to show a willingness to learn.

QUESTIONS FOR CODY

(Please write down his answers, 2 or 3 times every week)

Today is _____ , _____ .
            (day)   **(date)**

```
What was the hardest work you did at school today?
(Finish by saying "I am very proud of you for doing such hard work.")
```

What was the easiest work today?

```
(Finish by saying "I am happy that [name of work] was easy for you
today.")
```

How did you help someone today?

```
(Say "I am proud of you for being such a good helper.")
```

Please show me some work that you brought home and tell me about it.

```
(Write down what he shows you and what he says about it.)
(Finish by saying "I am proud of you for being such a good student,
  Cody.")
```

Supporting the Parents

The Parent Liaison supported Janette between meetings by making data collection easier and by taking her and Cody to the public library to find books to read at home. The Parent Liaison also gave Janette parent-friendly written information on temper tantrums, and a number to call for help when she felt that the tantrums were getting out of her control. Janette welcomed the Parent Liaison's visits and phone calls, and was eager to learn how to better manage Cody's behavior. Not every parent will need or want your support in dealing with issues at home, nor would you have time to give every family such support. Some parents may be quite content to talk with you only at PTAR meetings.

Parents need to know that you are there to support them. However, your offers to help should be given carefully and strategically, with your own time and energy in mind. Set your boundaries very clearly from the beginning. Tell parents when they may call you and when they may not, and stick to your own rules. This is especially important if you are using your home telephone number as a contact point. Keep your conversations with parents on the topic, and focused on meeting the child's goals. If you sense that parents are asking for more support than you can give, say that you need to speak with your supervisor to find out where they can get that support from others. Remember, you are a source of helpful information, not a set of helping hands.

 TIP: If the parents talk about ongoing tensions with the teacher, don't get drawn into playing the blame game. Simply say "We need to put this issue on our next PTAR meeting agenda, and talk about how it affects reaching your goals for your child."

Reflecting on Your Notes from the Meeting

Janette's Parent Liaison reviewed her notes right after the second meeting of Cody's PTAR team, a meeting that she did not think had gone very well. The Parent Liaison realized that she felt uncomfortable because Evelyn and Janette didn't really talk with each other. All of their comments and questions were directed to her. She thought that the seating arrangement might have contributed to the lopsided conversation. Parent and teacher sat next to each other on one side of the table, and the Parent Liaison sat on the other side. She made a note to herself to sit at the head of the table before either of them arrived at the next meeting, and to have only two other chairs at the table, one on each side of her. This small modification in the room layout made it easier for parent and teacher to look at each other instead of at the Parent Liaison. This changed the conversation to an even give-and-take between them.

Following Up with Tasks That You Agreed to Do

Review the PTAR meeting notes, especially item 5, Plan for Action between Meetings, on the agenda to see what you agreed to do. Look at your follow-up notes on the Family Contact Sheet for additional reminders of follow-up actions. The rule of thumb here is never promise to do something without writing it down on the spot!

In the third PTAR meeting, Cody's PTAR team came up with questions for Janette to ask Cody as part of her data collection. The Parent Liaison then made a note to remind herself to put the questions on a one-page worksheet for Janette and Cody. While the Parent Liaison was typing, she came up with the idea of adding reminders to Janette to praise Cody after he answered each question. She called Janette to ask if that would be all right to add to her worksheet. Janette liked the idea, and then reminded the Parent Liaison that they had not set a date to visit the public library with Cody. She said that Cody was asking her every day when they would go. They scheduled the date on the spot and went to the library later that week.

Preparing for the Next Meeting

Because Janette's Parent Liaison was in contact with her each week between meetings, Janette did not need a postcard reminder of the date of the next meeting. However, Cody's teacher appreciated getting a postcard a few days in advance of the meeting, and a phone message the day before.

 TIP: Develop a reminder system for your PTAR teams that includes a way for parents and teachers to let you know if they need to change the scheduled meeting.

Besides sending postcard and telephone reminders for the next meeting, you should prepare by making sure that the usual meeting place is available, and that the space is reserved for the meeting. Janette's Parent Liaison, for example, checked with library personnel to be sure that the meeting room was not being used for another purpose that day. She also prepared the agenda, and made copies for each of them.

WHAT SHOULD I DO IF THERE ARE CONFLICTS BETWEEN THE PARENTS AND TEACHER?

Sara Lawrence-Lightfoot (2003) made the following statement in a chapter entitled "Natural Enemies," where she discussed the issues that often lead to conflict between parents and teachers:

> We must admit that conflict is endemic to parent–teacher dialogues, that it is not to be ignored or avoided. Rather, it is to be met with open eyes and open hearts, made visible and named, and worked with over time. (p. 73)

Some conflicts are inevitable because the parents must speak for the needs of their children as individuals, and teachers must keep the needs of all of their students as a class foremost in their minds. Other conflicts come from a buildup of frustrations on both sides when parent–teacher conferences become empty rituals, and seem meaningless. Lawrence-Lightfoot calls for more frequent, more honest and open conversations between parents and teachers, and a safe place where each can regroup, recover, and save face.

ABC's PTAR meetings are designed to be a safe place where conversations can be open and honest. They focus on one child's needs, provide contact at least monthly, and should be safe places for both parents and teachers. They may feel unsafe, however, when open and honest communication first begins, and conflicts arise. Old, unpleasant emotions may flood back into the minds of both parents and teachers, and their words or body language may unintentionally cause ill feelings.

Your job as a Parent Liaison is to accept, perhaps even welcome that conflict, and help to manage it productively. A PTAR meeting should not become a debate, and there should be no winners or losers. The Ground Rules (Appendix 8.2) and the Parent–Teacher Action Research Cycle (Appendix 8.1) can help you manage conflicts. The following script gives suggestions for entering the discussion when conflict arises.

 **QUESTIONS AND ANSWERS FOR MANAGING CONFLICT**

Excuse me, but I would like to be sure that I understand the issue. [Name of speaker], I think that you are saying [restate the issue]. Am I right?

If wrong, say

Thanks for correcting me. I now understand that [restate again].

Repeat until you really understand the issue.
There is a good chance that the other person will as well.

I'd like to use our ground rules, and try to say that as positively as possible. Could we say [reframe the issue from negative to positive]? Did I get that right?

Let's go back to the Action Research Cycle, and see if we can solve this problem. [Name of other person], it is your turn to talk about this issue now. How do you see it affecting our goals for [name of child]?

You may need to repeat the process of clarifying statements.

We have at least two choices right now. We could stop and gather more information about this problem, reflect on it, and come back next time to discuss it further. We could also leave our agenda for today and continue the discussion of this issue. Which would you rather do?

Remember, you can always agree to disagree.

With a strategy like the one suggested, you can achieve some distance from the original statement, and some of the heat will go out of the discussion. If the problem is not related to the PTAR team's goals for the child, ask the parent and teacher if they would like to continue discussing the issue, or go back to the original agenda. If they choose to keep the discussion going, remind them to follow the ground rules. Remember, they can also agree to disagree so that you can move on. This does not solve the problem, but treats it and the participants with respect.

WHAT SHOULD I DO WHEN SERIOUS CHILD OR FAMILY PROBLEMS COME UP?

Many of the children who participated in our initial ABC projects were living in stressed families. Rarely was the child's behavior the apparent cause of the stress, but parents often attributed the child's behavior to problems within the family. Although poverty and isolation were big stressors for many parents, separation, divorce, or other family crises affected many of the children. Some parents were depressed, fighting drug or alcohol addictions, or seriously ill. Other parents had little knowledge of child development, with no role models for their parenting. Social services had intervened in several of the families.

As a Parent Liaison, you may find some family issues difficult to understand and the values of some of the families may be at odds with your own. If you find such problems overwhelming, your supervisor is your best resource. Remember to keep your focus on the needs of the child and helping parents and teachers stay on the agenda in your PTAR meetings. The ABC Program is not designed to address parents' personal issues or family problems. Sam's story, written by his Parent Liaison, illustrates how one child was supported by his PTAR team through a series of life changes that might have thrown him off track.

SAM'S STORY as Told by His Parent Liaison

"Why is Sam in the ABC Program?" asked his first-grade teacher, Marlene. She knew that his attendance in kindergarten had been poor, but Sam certainly did not act out in class or have other behaviors that would cause her concern. Teachers often thought of ABC as suitable for students with externalizing problem behaviors—inappropriate or excessive actions directed at other children, adults, or classroom equipment. Sam's internalizing behaviors were more of a problem for him than for other children.

During the screening for the ABC Program, Sam's kindergarten teacher reported that Sam was often lost in his own thoughts, and that he complained about many aches and pains. Sam's mother, Zoe, worked 12-hour shifts, with an alternating pattern of days on and off, and commuted 1 hour each way to her job. It was sometimes difficult for her to find time to spend with her children. She kept Sam home from school on her days off to be with her and his lively younger sister. With tears in her eyes, Zoe told me later that she had a hard time "letting go" of Sam.

Planning PTAR meetings for Sam was a difficult task for me. Zoe's own unhappy childhood made her extremely uncomfortable coming to school, but our small town offered no other places for her and Sam's teacher to meet. We set dates for meetings, but Zoe would neither come nor call. Marlene was exasperated and ready to back out of the ABC Program entirely. I made many home visits and held long telephone conversations with Zoe, encouraging her to be more involved in her son's education. I tried to help Zoe understand and tolerate Marlene's sometimes brusque way of talking to parents. She finally agreed to come to a meeting, but only if I would give her a ride. Eventually she came on her own, but I held my breath until she arrived.

By April, we were holding regular PTAR meetings in the nurse's office, the most neutral territory that could be found in the school. Marlene and Zoe were able to talk politely to each other in the PTAR meeting, and to work together on an action plan to increase Sam's independence and school attendance. (I was delighted to see Marlene drop her intimidating teacher facade by sharing anecdotes from her own experience as a parent.) At the last meeting of the year, Zoe brought a rose for each member of the team, and said that the ABC Program had made a big difference for both her and her son. She and Marlene met with Sam's second-grade teacher, and Zoe asked what she could do over the summer to get him ready for the next school year.

Sam's second-grade year began so smoothly that neither Zoe nor his new teacher, Donna, felt the need to meet monthly. At the end of November, however, Sam suddenly missed many days of school. His teacher learned that Zoe had moved to an apartment closer to her job, leaving the children with their father, David. He was eager to continue to work with the ABC Program, and began calling me often to talk about helping the children adjust to their parents' separation. After a week of nightly calls, I suggested that he call the "Parents Assistance Hotline" when he needed to talk, and sent him a packet of materials on helping children deal with separation and divorce.

David began to use a regular home–school journal with Donna, who often included photos of Sam in the journal. Donna also arranged for Sam to meet with the school guidance counselor. At a March PTAR meeting, Donna noted that Sam had developed some nice friendships with other students, and David said that Sam had become very responsible about homework. David and Zoe were divorcing, but they talked often about the children, and were going to move close enough to each other to share custody. One day Sam felt confident enough to ask Donna if he could meet with the principal about moving to a new school.

In June, the PTAR team held a transition meeting at Sam's new school. Both parents attended, and talked easily with the new teacher and principal about their arrangements for caring for the children. They said that they planned to be closely involved with Sam's school, and asked the teacher to give both of them any information. The principal said that she wished all children who were entering a new school could have the benefit of a transition meeting like Sam's.

CAN A CHILD'S GOALS BE ACADEMIC AS WELL AS BEHAVIORAL?

ABC stands for Achieving–Behaving–Caring, which indicates that academic goals are as appropriate as behavioral goals. Although the ABC Program was developed to prevent emotional or behavioral problems from interfering with a child's success in school, many PTAR teams recognized that a lack of academic success was interfering with the child's social and emotional well-being. Like Samantha's mother in the next story, some parents also lacked confidence in their own academic skills, and felt incapable of helping their children succeed in school.

 ### SAMANTHA'S SUCCESS as Told by Her Parent Liaison

Samantha was referred to the ABC Program by her first-grade teacher because of her shyness and the teacher's concerns about her lack of reading skills. The teacher felt that the ABC Program would be a good way to address the concerns of the school staff and the parents early in the school year. As we began to meet monthly, I came to realize that Samantha's mother, Phyllis, had her own deep-seated fears for her daughter—fears born of her own school experience and inability to read. Our PTAR meetings worked two-fold: they served to set realistic academic goals at home and at school, and they helped to allay Phyllis's fears that her daughter would struggle and fail in school as she herself had.

Each month, our PTAR meetings provided me with very clear evidence of Samantha's accomplishments. So I was surprised in March when Phyllis said that she was very worried that her daughter was not making progress. I had forgotten how little Phyllis herself could read, and had assumed that she could see progress from our notes as well as I could. We sat down together, and I went over our meeting agendas, notes, and data collection. Samantha's teacher had kept charts of Samantha's progress in learning new reading words. We laid out the charts on a table, and I read our meeting notes aloud. Phyllis could see and hear that Samantha had indeed made good progress.

In our PTAR meetings, we were able to address issues of homework and television, with a nonjudgmental approach. Phyllis was open to ideas from the teacher on how to make after-school hours more productive by limiting the amount of time spent watching TV. The teacher limited the amount of work that she sent home and talked to Phyllis on the phone to explain the requirements of different assignments. At the end of our 2 years of working together, Samantha was working very well on her own, and becoming a confident student. She felt successful in school despite her initial struggles with reading, and now was even offering to read aloud to the class. Her teacher was pleased to report that Samantha had achieved second-grade reading skills. Phyllis thanked the teacher and me during our final meeting, and amazed us by asking how she could sign up for Adult Education so she could learn to read and keep up with her daughter.

WHEN SHOULD OTHER PEOPLE ATTEND THE PTAR MEETING?

Sometimes a team may want someone with special knowledge about one of the child's issues to meet with them regularly. Other teams may bring in a specialist when they are making their action plans, or ask for additional support in evaluating the child's needs. When parents are separated or divorced, they may want to ask the other parent to attend meetings. Your role as a Parent Liaison is to keep the meeting focused on the child, regardless of who is in attendance.

Because ABC is intended as a prevention program, the selection of children for the ABC Program often excludes children who are already eligible for other support services, such as special education or mental health services. Nonetheless, your PTAR teams should feel free to invite a special educator, the school psychologist, guidance counselor, or social worker, or even another teacher to attend a meeting as a consultant when appropriate. At the end of that meeting, be sure that all parties are clear whether the consultant should be asked to come to another meeting. Once a consultant enters the process, decision making can slip out of the hands of the parent and the classroom teacher and into the hands of the specialist. If this seems to be happening, make sure that this is a conscious team decision. If extra support is what the child really needs, then the PTAR team should probably refer the child to student support services, as Bethany's team did.

Before inviting an additional person to join in a PTAR team meeting, make sure that the parents and the teacher agree to the invitation. If one member of the PTAR team invites a new person to attend without consulting the others, the trust that you are helping them to build can be broken. Even if the child receives other support services from the school, has a community mental health counselor, or lives with grandparents, none of those helpers should attend a PTAR meeting without a specific invitation from the team.

If you meet at the school, you may walk into the meeting room and find that someone has decided to attend the PTAR meeting without a specific invitation from the team. If this happens, ask the team members if they invited that person. If no one did, then explain politely to the additional person that no one else should attend a PTAR meeting unless the invitation comes with the agreement of both parent and teacher, and with your prior knowledge. Manny's story illustrates some of the problems that can arise with uninvited guests.

MANNY'S STORY

Manny's mother, Estella, said that Manny's dad, Tomas, wouldn't allow her to sign Manny up for the ABC Program. Their Parent Liaison met Tomas in the grocery store, and asked him if he would be willing to give Estella permission to join the program. Tomas said that Estella would never come to a meeting with a teacher, but *he* wasn't afraid to go to the school. He admitted that Manny had a bad temper just like his own, and his temper was why he and Manny's mother couldn't live together. Tomas agreed to come to the PTAR meetings himself, and work with Manny's teacher on helping Manny control his temper. Maybe he could learn something that would make his weekends with Manny go more smoothly.

The first PTAR meeting with Tomas went well until Manny's teacher suggested that she would like to have Manny's mother come to the next meeting. Tomas refused to attend a meeting if Estella was coming. Estella told the Parent Liaison on the telephone that it was better for Manny to have Tomas at the PTAR meetings rather than her.

When the Parent Liaison walked into the room scheduled for their next meeting, however, she found that Manny's classroom teacher, the guidance counselor, the primary-level special educator, and Estella were all there. Before she could say anything, Tomas walked in, took one look at the group around the table, and stormed out of the school. The special educator took over the meeting, explaining that the staff wanted to meet with mom and dad together, and that the PTAR meetings were the only times that Tomas would come to the school. The Parent Liaison said that this was obviously not a meeting of Manny's PTAR team, so she should not be there, and excused herself.

When the Parent Liaison contacted Manny's teacher the next week, the teacher agreed to meet with Tomas in the future at the local coffee shop for an early breakfast, rather than at the school. She apologized to Tomas for the way that their previous meeting had been disrupted by others. After the Parent Liaison reviewed her notes from Manny's MAPs meeting, Tomas and the teacher set their goals for Manny, and began to work together again.

The one other person who might attend PTAR meetings is the child. Children may stay in the room during the meeting for lack of other child care, and parents and teachers sometimes invite the child to participate in the discussion. At the end of the first-grade year, many children are able to participate in their transition meetings, and some second graders will be able to attend more meetings. Children usually enjoy hearing their parents and teachers review the MAPs process, with its emphasis on the child's strengths. Occasionally children realize for the first time that they are doing something that worries their parents or teacher, and speak out with reasons for their behavior that no one would have known. Children may suggest solutions and take responsibility for their own behavior in a very mature fashion. Kyle's story illustrates how children can become involved in PTAR teams.

KYLE SPEAKS UP

Kyle was a first grader with challenges in his speaking skills when he began the ABC Program. He was often teased by the other children on the school bus about the way he talked, which made him so upset that he did not want to ride on the bus anymore. His mother, Renee, formed a PTAR team for Kyle with his classroom teacher, Sonya. They asked the speech pathologist to come to the team meetings whenever she could. All three adults scheduled times to work with Kyle on his word lists. The speech pathologist introduced new words to Kyle, Sonya reviewed last week's words with him, and Renee reviewed words from the week before.

In first grade, Kyle stayed in the same room as the adults during the after-school PTAR meetings, playing quietly with the computer or building with blocks. Although he did not interrupt the meetings or talk about them later with his mother, the team knew he was listening to every word. In second grade, Kyle would occasionally come up to the table to correct something that his mother, his teacher, or his speech pathologist had slightly wrong. Eventually he joined the team at the table for most of every meeting, reading or coloring, but always listening so he could speak up when he was ready. At the end of his 2 years in the ABC Program, Kyle participated fully in his transition meeting, telling his third-grade teacher what he needed her to know about him.

With the support of the three adults closest to him, Kyle became very aware of his own progress in speaking skills and was highly motivated to keep working. At the end of his first-grade year, Kyle volunteered to read an excerpt from his journal to the whole class, and spoke every word clearly. In evaluating their efforts at the end of the second-grade year, the speech pathologist wrote, "I have never seen a child with this type of articulation disorder make so much progress in such a short time." Renee wrote, "My son's gains have made him proud of himself and more confident in himself. I only wish that we had the ABC Program when my oldest son started school."

WHAT HAPPENS WHEN CHILDREN MOVE TO ANOTHER TEACHER OR ANOTHER SCHOOL?

Transitions can be difficult for young children, and this is especially true for children with emotional or behavioral issues. One of the purposes of the ABC Program is to create consistency and harmony between home and school so that the child feels comfortable and secure in each place. Moving to another classroom or another school disrupts that sense of security. With support from you, parents and teachers can plan transitions to minimize disruption.

Transitions from Grade to Grade

In some schools, children stay with the same teacher for 2 years, such as in multi-age classrooms, or teachers stay with a group of students for more than one grade (called *looping*), which reduces disruption when students advance to the next grade. Without these arrangements, the Parent Liaison can help in the transition from grade to grade. It is good to start planning for the next year 2 months before the end of the present school year. Enlist the child's current teacher as a guide for planning a successful transition, then find out if all of the teachers at the next grade level are willing to be part of the ABC Program. Also, learn the process and timeline for assigning students to next year's teachers. If the school permits parents to request a teacher for the next year, find out how those requests should be made, and help the parents request a teacher who is willing to be part of ABC. If the ABC Program will be new for the teachers in the next grade, speak to your supervisor about planning a meeting to introduce them to the program.

With the team's permission, invite next year's teacher to attend the last PTAR meeting for the year. If the class assignments are not made until after that last PTAR meeting, perhaps you can ask all possible teachers to meet with the team (again, with the team's permission). Some schools group their classrooms into grade-level teams, with an experienced teacher as the lead teacher. The lead teacher is often a good substitute for an assigned teacher, especially when there will be new teachers joining the school at the next grade level. Be sure that the parents are prepared for a meeting with more than one teacher, which can sometimes be intimidating.

The last PTAR meeting of the year is usually a celebration of the child's success. As Parent Liaison, you should be prepared to review (briefly) the action research process, the team's practical theory, and the action plan that the child's parents and current teacher implemented. You may want to revisit the MAPs process as part of this transition meeting. Both the child and the new teacher will hear about the positive changes that the child has made over the year, and the direction in which the parent and teacher believe the child is moving. While focusing on the positive, don't skip over the concerns that they may still have about the child.

As always, have an agenda, take good notes, and share those notes with all who participate in the meeting. If the team is meeting with the teacher who will definitely be working with the child next year, go ahead and set up a date for the first PTAR meeting in the new school year. You may need to change the meeting date after the summer break, but at least you will have a start on PTAR at the beginning of the new school year. If the child will be participating in an academic summer program, ask the parents to bring any end-of-program reports to the first PTAR meeting in the new school year.

 TIP: If your job extends through the summer months, try to call the parents with whom you are working at least once a month. Some parents may be moving, or making other major changes through the summer. Staying in touch will prevent having to track them down in the late summer.

Transition to a New School

Families may also move at any time during the year, and the school to which the child goes may or may not be part of the ABC Program. Depending on the location of the new school and the way that your ABC Program is administered, you may or may not be able to continue as Parent Liaison for that family at the new school. Under any circumstances, you can help make the transition as positive as possible for the child. At your next PTAR meeting, ask the parents and teacher what they would like to tell the teacher at the new school. Help them by providing copies of the MAPs discussion for that child, notes from the meetings, and possibly copies of any evaluation questionnaires that parents and teachers have completed. (Parents may need to sign a consent form giving the ABC Program permission to release documents to the new school. Always check with your supervisor before promising copies of anything to anyone.) If the new school does not have an ABC Program, give the parents a copy of the ABC brochure or other material that explains ABC, with a school or agency telephone number to call for more information about the program.

If the new school has an ABC Program, or is interested in continuing it for the child, you can participate in the transition. However, explain to the parents that *they* need to make the first contact with the new school about ABC. If your program allows, you may accompany the parent to the school to help explain ABC to school staff, and to ask for a teacher who is willing to continue the work. Successful transitions usually require many telephone calls before all the pieces are in place.

LaMonica's story below tells about a very complex transition. You may never be involved with a child whose issues require such careful support, but her story illustrates the way in which ABC could make a difference for children in foster or adoptive placements. Many elements of LaMonica's story apply in simpler transitions as well.

 ## LaMONICA'S MOVE

LaMonica started kindergarten at Boxwood Elementary in January, when she and her younger sister were moved into a foster home in the Boxwood school district. She had not been in preschool or kindergarten before, but had a few school-readiness skills. The girls had been living with their father for 3 years, and had been removed from his home for issues of neglect and abuse. Social services planned to return them to their mother as soon as she met certain requirements. LaMonica's kindergarten teacher referred her to the ABC Program to give her extra support during these transitions, with the hope of preventing serious behavior problems arising in first grade.

The Kings, foster parents for both girls, were eager to work closely with LaMonica's first-grade classroom teacher, Mrs. Abbott. They were concerned about some sexualized behaviors that they saw at home, and wanted to be sure that the school addressed these issues as well. However, Mrs. Abbott's data, collected both in class and at recess, did not show these behaviors. At her request, the school guidance counselor and the principal also observed LaMonica, without knowing about the Kings' specific concerns, and reported only that some of the first and second graders did not seem to know any playground games. Their only game was "catch and kiss," chasing each other around in little groups until the girls caught a boy, or vice versa. The guidance counselor noted that LaMonica was quite bossy with the other girls, and often ended up being excluded. Perhaps as a result, LaMonica was not a frequent player in the game, and often spent the whole recess on the swings. The Kings and Mrs. Abbott debated LaMonica's behavior with each other until their Parent Liaison asked if they could agree to disagree so that they could move on to addressing mutual goals for LaMonica.

At this point, LaMonica's birth mother, Mo'Nique, joined the team, and asked if her social worker could come to some of the PTAR meetings when they came up together to see the children. The social worker informed the team that the girls were due to move home with their mother in the summer, and would be attending school in a different school district. The team began to focus on LaMonica's readiness for second grade, and to plan for the transition.

Supported by her social worker, Mo'Nique contacted the principal in the new school, and asked if her daughter's teacher could do the ABC Program with her next year. She gave the principal the number for the ABC Program. At the principal's request, the Parent Liaison met with the primary-level team to explain how Parent–Teacher Action Research (PTAR) worked. She invited Mrs. Jackson, the teacher who volunteered to take part in ABC, to come to Boxwood to attend the last PTAR meeting of the year. Using staff development funds, Mrs. Jackson took a professional day and observed in Mrs. Abbott's classroom all day before the meeting. She explained her enthusiasm, saying "The opportunity to work with and really get to know the parents outside of a school setting does make a difference on how I interact with a child in the classroom. It is also important that they know me as a mother, grandmother, and a person . . . not just a 'scary' teacher."

A few weeks later, LaMonica and her sister stayed overnight with their birth mother and attended their new school for a day. Mrs. Jackson helped Mo'Nique register the girls for a summer day camp that focused on literacy, and they set the date for their first PTAR meeting in September.

The Parent Liaison enjoyed her work with LaMonica's new team. They kept the focus on building her academic skills, and filling in some of the remaining gaps in her early learning. She stopped being so bossy and quickly made friends in the new school. Mrs. Jackson reported that LaMonica gave her frequent family updates as Mo'Nique prepared to give birth to another child, but showed no jealousy and only pride when another sister was born. At the end of the second-grade year, LaMonica was on grade level in reading and close to grade level in math. The team invited the social worker to come to the final PTAR meeting to join the celebration. The social worker thanked the Parent Liaison and the ABC team for their help in making LaMonica's transition to home a success.

HOW DO WE END THE PTAR PROCESS?

In our research, children stayed in the ABC Program for 2 years, and that is the length of time that we would recommend for most teams. Our research showed that 2 years in the program produced better results than only 1 year (McConaughy, et al., 2000). However, some children's teams had accomplished their goals and were ready to disband before the 2-year period was up. Other PTAR teams chose to stop their monthly meetings once their goals were accomplished, but were ready to start again if needed. For some children, ABC should go on longer than 2 years. Your ABC Program's administrator will decide whether its resources can be stretched and its services extended to students beyond the first 2 years of school.

For the final meeting, you might consider:

- Inviting the child, as in Gray's and Kyle's cases.
- Inviting next year's teacher, whether or not ABC is ending for that child, as in Sam's and LaMonica's cases.
- Inviting last year's teacher to see the child's additional progress.
- Reviewing the child's accomplishments, as in all of our stories.
- Using the Evaluation Questions from Appendix 12.1 to help the whole team evaluate the PTAR process.

Our last Helpful Hint provides some maxims that Parent Liaisons followed in our ABC research. We hope that they will be helpful to you when you are puzzling over the right thing to do.

 HELPFUL HINTS: MAXIMS FOR ABC PARENT LIAISONS

- Respect the wisdom of parents and teachers.
- Listen more than you speak.
- See the whole child.
- Turn off your judgment and turn on your empathy.
- Keep the decisions in the hands of the parents and teachers.
- Remember that compromising is part of collaboration.
- Trust the process.

APPENDIX 12.1

Evaluation Questions for PTAR Meetings

1. What went well?

2. What could have gone better?

3. What would you do differently next time?

4. Were there any "turning points" or "critical events"?

5. What questions still need answers?

From Stephanie H. McConaughy, Pam Kay, Julie A. Welkowitz, Kim Hewitt, and Martha D. Fitzgerald (2008). Copyright by The Guilford Press. Permission to photocopy this appendix is granted to purchasers of this book for personal use only (see copyright page for details).

References and Recommended Reading

REFERENCES

Abidin, R. R., & Robinson, L. L. (2002). Stress, biases, or professionalism: What drives teachers' referral judgments of students with challenging behaviors? *Journal of Emotional and Behavioral Disorders, 10*(4), 204–212.

Achenbach, T. M. (1986). *Direct Observation Form.* Burlington, VT: University of Vermont Research Center for Children, Youth, and Families.

Achenbach, T. M. (1991a). *Manual for the Child Behavior Checklist/4–18 and 1991 profile.* Burlington, VT: University of Vermont, Department of Psychiatry.

Achenbach, T. M. (1991b). *Manual for the Teacher's Report Form and 1991 profile.* Burlington, VT: University of Vermont, Department of Psychiatry.

Achenbach, T. M., & Rescorla, L. A. (2001). *Manual for the ASEBA school-age forms and profiles.* Burlington, VT: University of Vermont Research Center for Children, Youth, and Families.

Alameda, T. (1996). R.A.I.N.makers: The consumer's voice. In K. Hooper-Briar & H. Lawson (Eds.), *Expanding partnerships for vulnerable children, youth, and families* (pp. 46–56). Washington, DC: Council on Social Work Education.

Alberg, J., Petry (Tashjian), C., & Eller, S. (1994). *The social skills planning guide.* Longmont, CO: Sopris West.

Algozzine, B., & Kay, P. J. (2002). *Preventing problem behaviors: A handbook of successful prevention strategies.* Thousand Oaks, CA: Corwin Press.

Bond, M., & Keys, C. (1993). Empowerment, diversity, and collaboration: Promoting synergy on community boards. *American Journal of Community Psychology, 21*(1), 37–57.

Caldarella, P., & Merrell, K. W. (1997). Common dimensions of social skills of children and adolescents: A taxonomy of positive behaviors. *School Psychology Review, 26,* 264–278.

Canada, G. (1995). *Fist stick knife gun: A personal history of violence in America.* Boston: Beacon Press.

Canter, A. S., Paige, L. Z., Roth, M. D., Romero, I., & Carroll, S. A. (2004). *Helping children at home and school II: Handouts for families and educators.* Bethesda, MD: National Association of School Psychologists.

Cartledge, G., & Kleefeld, J. (1991). *Taking part: Introducing social skills to children.* Circle Pines, MN: American Guidance Service.

Charney, R. S. (1992). *Teaching children to care: Management in the responsive classroom.* Greenfield, MA: Northeastern Foundation for Children.

Cheney, D. (1998). Using action research as a collaborative process to enhance educators' and families' knowledge and skills for youth with emotional or behavioral disorders. *Preventing School Failure, 42*(2), 88–93.

Cheney, D., & Osher, T. (1997). Collaborate with families. *Journal of Emotional and Behavioral Disorders, 54*(5), 36–44.

Christenson, S. L., & Sheridan, S. M. (2001). *Schools and families: Creating essential connections for learning.* New York: Guilford Press.

Cochran-Smith, M., & Lytle, S. L. (1993). *Inside/outside: Teacher research and knowledge.* New York: Teachers College Press.

Committee for Children. (1997). *Second step: A violence prevention curriculum.* Seattle, WA: Author.

Cross, K. P. (1981). *Adults as learners: Increasing participation and facilitating learning.* San Francisco: Jossey-Bass.

Delgado-Gaitan, C. (1991). Involving parents in the schools: A process of empowerment. *American Journal of Education, 100*(1), 20–46.

Dishion, T. J., McCord, J., & Poulin, F. (1999). When interventions harm: Peer groups and problem behavior. *American Psychologist, 54*(9), 755–764.

Dunst, C., Trivette, C., & Deal, A. (1988). *Enabling and empowering families: Principles and guidelines for practice.* Cambridge, MA: Brookline Books.

DuPaul, G., & Eckert, T. L. (1994). The effects of social skills curricula: Now you see them, now you don't. *School Psychology Quarterly, 9*, 113–132.

Epstein, M. H. (2004). *Behavioral and Emotional Rating Scale: A strength-based approach to assessment* (2nd ed.). Austin, TX: PRO-ED.

Fantuzzo, J., McWayne, C., Perry, M. A., & Childs, S. (2004). Multiple dimensions of family involvement and their relations to behavioral and learning competencies for urban and low-income children. *School Psychology Review, 33*(4), 467–480.

Feil, E. G., Walker, H. M., & Severson, H. H. (1995). The Early Screening Project for young children with behavior problems. *Journal of Emotional and Behavioral Disorders, 3*, 194–202.

Forest, M., & Pearpoint, J. C. D. (1992). Putting all kids on the MAP. *Educational Leadership, 50*, 26–31.

Frazier, J. (1999). Shared ownership: Parents as partners in education. In J. P. Comer, M. Ben-Avie, N. M. Haynes, & E. T. Joyner (Eds.), *Child by child: The Comer Process for change in education* (pp. 52–62). New York: Teachers College Press.

Garrity, C., Jens, K., Porter, W., Sager, N. W., & Short-Camilli, C. (2004). *Bully-proofing your school: A comprehensive approach for elementary schools* (3rd ed.). Longmont, CO: Sopris West.

Greenberg, M. T., Weissberg, R. P., O'Brien, M. U., Zins, J. E., Fredericks, L., Resnik, H., et al. (2003). Enhancing school-based prevention and youth development through coordinated social, emotional, and academic learning. *American Psychologist, 58*, 6–7, 466–474.

Gresham, F. M. (1981). Assessment of children's social skills. *Journal of School Psychology, 19*, 120–134.

Gresham, F. M. (1998). Social skills training: Should we raze, remodel, or rebuild? *Behavioral Disorders, 24*, 19–25.

Gresham, F. M., & Elliott, S. N. (1990). *Social Skills Rating System.* Circle Pines, MN: American Guidance Service.

Gresham, F. M., MacMillan, D. L., & Bocian, K. (1996). "Behavioral earthquakes": Low frequency, salient behavioral events that differentiate students at-risk for behavioral disorders. *Behavioral Disorders, 21*, 277–292.

Gresham, F. M., Sugai, G., & Horner, R. H. (2001). Interpreting outcomes of social skills training for students with high-incidence disabilities. *Exceptional Children, 67*(3), 331–344.

Harry, B. (1992). *Cultural diversity, families, and the special education system: Communication and empowerment.* New York: Teachers College Press.

Hawkins, J. D., Kosterman, R., Catalano, R. F., Hill, K. G., & Abbott, R. D. (2005). Promoting positive adult functioning through social development intervention in childhood: Long-term effects from the Seattle Social Development Project. *Archives of Pediatrics and Adolescent Medicine, 159*(1), 25–31.

Henderson, A. T., & Berla, N. (1994). *A new generation of evidence: The family is critical to student achievement.* Washington, DC: Center for Law and Education.

Henderson, A. T., & Mapp, K. L. (2002). *A new wave of evidence: The impact of school, family, and community connections on student achievement.* Austin, TX: National Center for Family and Community Connections with Schools, Southwest Educational Development Laboratory.

Ho, B. S. (2002). Application of participatory action research to family–school intervention. *School Psychology Review, 31*(1), 106–121.

Individuals with Disabilities Education Improvement Act (IDEA), Pub. L. No. 108-446, § 663, 118 Stat. 2785 (2004).

Irwin, J. W. (1996). *Empowering ourselves and transforming schools: Educators making a difference.* Albany, NY: State University of New York Press.

Jackson, N. F., Jackson, D. A., & Monroe, C. (1983). *Getting along with others: Teaching social effectiveness to children.* Champaign, IL: Research Press.

Jenson, W. R., Rhode, G., Evans, C., & Morgan, D. P. (2004). *The Tough Kid Principal's Briefcase.* Longmont, CO: Sopris West.

Kamps, D. (2002). Preventing problems by improving behavior. In R. Algozzine & P. Kay (Eds.), *Preventing problem behaviors: A handbook of successful prevention strategies* (pp. 11–36). Thousand Oaks, CA: Corwin Press.

Kamps, D., & Kay, P. J. (2002). Preventing problems through social skills instruction. In R. Algozzine & P. Kay (Eds.), *Preventing problem behaviors: A handbook of successful prevention strategies* (pp. 37–84). Thousand Oaks, CA: Corwin Press.

Kay, P. J., & Benway, C. (1998, April). *The essential role of parents as members of the research team in early intervention for children with emotional and behavioral issues.* Paper presented at *Building on Family Strengths,* the annual conference of the Research and Training Center on Family Support and Children's Mental Health, Portland, OR.

Kay, P. J., & Fitzgerald, M. (1997). Parents + Teachers + Action Research = Real Involvement. *Teaching Exceptional Children, 30,* 8–11.

Kazdin, A. (1995). Treatment of antisocial behavior in children: Current status and future directions. *Psychological Bulletin, 102,* 187–203.

Koren, P. E., DeChillo, N., & Friesen, B. J. (1992). Measuring empowerment in families whose children have emotional disabilities: A brief questionnaire. *Rehabilitation Psychology, 37,* 305–321.

Koroloff, N. M., Elliott, D. J., Koren, P. E., & Friesen, B. J. (1994). Connecting low-income families to mental health services: The role of the family associate. *Journal of Emotional and Behavioral Disorders, 4,* 240–246.

Kurcinka, M. S. (1991). *Raising your spirited child.* New York: HarperCollins.

Lawrence-Lightfoot, S. (2003). *The essential conversation: What parents and teachers can learn from each other.* New York and Toronto, Canada: Random House.

Lawson, H., & Briar-Lawson, K. (1997). *Connecting the dots: Progress toward the integration of school reform, school-linked services, parent involvement, and community schools.* Oxford, OH: The Danforth Foundation and the Institute for Educational Renewal at Miami University.

LeBuffe, P. A., & Naglieri, J. A. (1999). *Devereux Early Childhood Assessment.* Lewisville, NC: Kaplan.

Leff, S. S., & Lakin, R. (2005). Playground-based observational systems: A review and implications for practitioners and researchers. *School Psychology Review, 34,* 475–489.

Lodge, R. (1998). *California's healthy start: Strong families, strong communities for student success.* Davis, CA: Healthy Start Field Office, University of California, Davis.

Maeroff, G. I. (1988). *The empowerment of teachers: Overcoming the crisis of confidence.* New York: Teachers College Press.

McConaughy, S. H., & Achenbach, T. M. (2008). *Manual for the ASEBA Direct Observation Form.* Burlington, VT: University of Vermont Research Center for Children, Youth, and Families.

McConaughy, S. H., Kay, P. J., & Fitzgerald, M. (1998). Preventing SED through parent–teacher action research and social skills instruction: First-year outcomes. *Journal of Emotional and Behavioral Disorders, 6*(2), 81–93.

McConaughy, S. H., Kay, P. J., & Fitzgerald, M. (1999). The Achieving–Behaving–Caring Project for preventing ED: Two-year outcomes. *Journal of Emotional and Behavioral Disorders, 7*(4), 224–239.

McConaughy, S. H., Kay, P. J., & Fitzgerald, M. (2000). How long is long enough? Outcomes for a school-based prevention program. *Exceptional Children, 67*(1), 21–34.

McConaughy, S. H., & Leone, P. E. (2002). Measuring the success of prevention programs. In B. Algozzine & P. Kay (Eds.), *Preventing problem behaviors: A handbook of successful prevention strategies* (pp. 183–219). Thousand Oaks, CA: Corwin Press.

McGinnis, E., & Goldstein, A. P. (1997). *Skillstreaming the elementary school child: New strategies and perspectives for teaching prosocial skills.* Champaign, IL: Research Press.

Merrell, K. W. (2002). *School Social Behavior Scales—Second Edition.* Eugene, OR: Assessment-Intervention Resources.

Merrell, K. W., & Caldarella, P. (2001). *Home and Community Social Behavior Scales.* Eugene, OR: Assessment-Intervention Resources.

Moles, O. (1996). *Reaching all families: Creating family-friendly schools.* Washington, DC: Office of Educational Research and Improvement, U.S. Department of Education.

National Center on Secondary Education and Transition. (2004, August). NLTS2 Data Brief. Vol. 3, Issue 2 (National Longitudinal Transition Study). Retrieved April 28, 2005, from *www.ncset.org*

No Child Left Behind (NCLB) Act, 107 U.S.C., Pub. L. No. 107-279, § 3801 (2002).

Northeast Foundation for Children. (1998). *Responsive classroom.* Turners Falls, MA: Author.

Osher, D., Dwyer, K., & Jackson, S. (2004). *Safe, supportive, and successful schools step by step.* Longmont, CO: Sopris West.

Perrone, V. (1991). *A letter to teachers: Reflections on schooling and the art of teaching.* San Francisco: Jossey-Bass.

Quinn, M. M., Rutherford, R. B., & Leone, P. E. (2001, February). *Students with disabilities in correctional facilities.* Arlington, VA: Eric Clearinghouse on Disabilities and Gifted Education. Retrieved May 31, 2005, from *www.ericec.org/digests/e621*

Reynolds, C. R., & Kamphaus, R. W. (2004). *Behavior Assessment System for Children—Second Edition (BASC-2).* Circle Pines, MN: American Guidance Service.

Rhode, G., Jenson, W. R., & Reavis, H. K. (1992). *The tough kid book.* Longmont, CO: Sopris West.

Ruffalo, S. L., & Elliott, S. N. (1997). Teachers' and parents' ratings of children's social skills: A closer look at cross-informant agreements through an item analysis protocol. *School Psychology Review, 26,* 489–501.

Sheridan, S. M. (1995). *The Tough Kid Social Skills Book.* Longmont, CO: Sopris West.

Spande, G. E., & Thurlow, M. L. (1994). Matching state goals to a model of school completion outcomes and indicators (Technical Report No. 9). Minneapolis, MN: University of Minnesota, National Center on Educational Outcomes. Retrieved May 11, 2005, from *www.education.umn.edu/NCEO/OnlinePubs/Technical9*

Squires, J., Bricker, D., & Twombly, E. (2002). *Ages & Stages Questionnaires: Social–Emotional (ASQ:SE)*. Baltimore, MD: Brookes.

Sugai, G., Sprague, J. A., Horner, R. H., & Walker, H. M. (2000). Preventing school violence: The use of office discipline referrals to assess and monitor school-wide discipline interventions. *Journal of Emotional and Behavioral Disorders, 8*, 94–101.

Thompson, S. (1996). How action research can put parents and teachers on the same team. *Educational Horizons, 74*(2), 70–76.

U.S. Department of Education. (2002). *Twenty-fourth Annual Report to Congress on the Implementation of the Individuals with Disabilities Education Act.* Retrieved July 27, 2005, from *www.ed.gov/about/reports/annual/osep/2002/*

U.S. Department of Health and Human Services. (1999). *Mental health: A report of the Surgeon General.* Rockville, MD: U.S. Department of Health and Human Services, Substance Abuse and Mental Health Services Administration, Center for Mental Health Services, National Institutes of Health, National Institute of Mental Health.

Volpe, R. J., DiPerna, J. C., Hintze, J. M., & Shapiro, E. S. (2005). Observing students in classroom settings: A review of seven coding systems. *School Psychology Review, 34*, 454–474.

Walker, H., & Severson, H. (1990). *Systematic Screening for Behavior Disorders (SSBD).* Longmont, CO: Sopris West.

Walker, H. M., Severson, H. H., & Feil, E. G. (1995). *The Early Screening Project (ESP).* Eugene, OR: Oregon Research Institute.

Walker, H. M., Severson, H. H., & Todis, B. J. (1990). Systematic Screening for Behavioral Disorders (SSBD): Further validation, replication, and normative data. *Remedial and Special Education, 11*, 32–46.

Walker, H. M., Stiller, B., Golly, A., Kavanagh, K., Severson, H. H., & Feil, E. G. (1998). *First step to success: Helping young children overcome antisocial behavior.* Longmont, CO: Sopris West.

Ysseldyke, J., Krentz, J., Elliott, J., Thurlow, M. L., Erickson, R., & Moore, M. L. (1998). NCEO framework for educational accountability. Minneapolis, MN: University of Minnesota, National Center on Educational Outcomes. Retrieved February 11, 2005, from *www.education.umn.edu/NCEO/OnlinePubs/Framework/FrameworkText*

Zins, J., Weissberg, R., Wang, M., & Walberg, H. J. (Eds.). (2004). *Building academic success on social and emotional learning: What does the research say?* New York: Teachers College Press.

RECOMMENDED READING

Algozzine, B., & Kay, P. J. (2002). *Preventing problem behaviors: A handbook of successful prevention strategies.* Thousand Oaks, CA: Corwin Press.

Cochran-Smith, M., & Lytle, S. L. (1993). *Inside/outside: Teacher research and knowledge.* New York: Teachers College Press.

Irwin, J. W. (1996). *Empowering ourselves and transforming schools: Educators making a difference.* Albany, NY: State University of New York Press.

Kurcinka, M. S. (1991). *Raising your spirited child.* New York: HarperCollins.

Lawrence-Lightfoot, S. (2003). *The essential conversation: What parents and teachers can learn from each other.* New York and Toronto, Canada: Random House.

Shockley, B., Michalove, B., & Allen, J. B. (1995). *Engaging families: Connecting home and school literacy communities.* Portsmouth, NH: Heinemann.

Index

Page numbers followed by an *f* or *t* indicate figures or tables.

222